# IN SEARCH OF YOUR
# ASIAN ROOTS

## Genealogical Research
## on Chinese Surnames

尋根溯源
中國人的姓氏
趙賀筱岳編著

*by Sheau-yueh J. Chao*

## CLEARFIELD

Printed for
Clearfield Company, Inc. by
Genealogical Publishing Co., Inc.
Baltimore, Maryland
2000

International Standard Book Number: 0-8063-4946-8

*Made in the United States of America*

# Contents

# Introduction

The Chinese people possess one of the oldest and richest genealogical traditions in the world. Genealogical roots are found in ancient China as evidenced in the oracle bone inscriptions of the Shang (商, ca. 1700-1122 B.C.) Period. Following the Chou 周 conquest of the Shang 商 around 1122 B.C., genealogical history and tradition flourished and were preserved by the feudal government of the Chou 周 dynasty with the records of the generations of emperors, lords, and officials.

Genealogical records have always been cherished by mankind, both in ancient and modern societies; they were preserved in written form from very early times. The survival and the loss of these genealogies over the generations has followed the rise and fall of the dynasties, the fortunes of individual families and clans, and the natural and man-made disasters through the centuries. Fortunately, in this day of cultural revival, there is a great deal of enthusiasm for genealogical research on Chinese surnames. However, since most of the documents on the subject were written in vernacular form and without a substantial understanding of the Chinese language, these valuable resources would be incomprehensible to most Western scholars.

So far, there is no basic tool available in English which traces the origin of Chinese surnames. This book is offered as a reference guide to assist East Asian researchers, librarians, bibliographers, students, and scholars in genealogical research on Chinese names.

The book is divided into three major chapters. Chapter 1 details the history and origin of Chinese surnames, the research on Chinese surnames in literature, and the reasons for changes of surnames in Chinese history. Chapters 2 provides the genealogical analysis of popular Chinese surnames found in Surnames of a Hundred Families (Pai chia hsing 百家姓). It is arranged alphabetically, disregarding marks. The treatment of aspirates and diereses, however, follows the arrangement found in Liang Shih-ch'iu's 梁實秋 A New Practical Chinese-English Dictionary. (Tsui hsin shih yüng Han Ying tz'u tien 最新實用漢英辭典. Taipei: The Far East Book Company, 1988.) Some Chinese surnames have more than one pronunciation, with each representing a different genealogical origin. Surnames of this category are listed separately with cross references connecting the related surnames. For example, the surname "樂" is pronounced yüeh[4] and le[4]. Therefore, the same character "樂" is treated as two separate surnames.

In chapter 3, an annotated bibliography, in Chinese and English, that covers materials dating from the imperial China era to the Republican era, is compiled for further research and reference. All published works were eligible for inclusion--books, articles, bibliographies, dictionaries, yearbooks, periodicals, and monographs. Selection was based on the availability of the materials in the United States, and priorities were given to publications of an academic rather than a popular nature. English publications that include Chinese characters transliterated by the author have those transliterations retained in the bibliographical annotations. For convenience, the vernacular forms of the Chinese personal names that appear in the bibliographical citations have been given in the East Asian order (i.e., last names followed by first names) rather than in the western order (i.e., first and middle names followed by last names). A literal translation is provided for Chinese titles and appears at the beginning of the individual bibliographical annotations. There are over 250 entries in this bibliography, and most of them are annotated; approximately four fifths of them are in Chinese, and one fifth is in English.

The volume opens with a Glossary and a Chronology of Chinese History that will help readers in finding genealogical terms and the dates of imperial periods mentioned in this book.

Wade-Giles (the official system of romanization adopted by the Library of Congress to catalog Chinese materials) has been used throughout this writing. For the convenience of those not quite familiar with Wade-Giles, a Pinyin to Wade-Giles Conversion Table will be found after the Chronology of Chinese History. The Family Name and Stroke Number Indexes will facilitate the search for a specific Chinese surname cited in this book. A combined Author and Title Index is located at the end the volume.

The present publication reflects the translation and interpretation of nearly 200 books in ancient Chinese literature. Certain materials may have been omitted because the author is unaware of their existence or availability in the United States. The great majority of materials are located in Columbia University's East Asian Library; the Harvard-Yenching Library at Harvard University found in the <u>Catalogues of the Harvard-Yenching Library, Chinese catalogue</u> (New York: Garland Publishing, Inc., 1986. 39 volumes ); the Library of Congress online catalog and the Online Computer Library Center (OCLC) and were requested through interlibrary loan services.

I wish to thank Mr. Paul Moy and Professor Tansen Sen for their editorial support and bibliographical assistance. I am also grateful to my colleague Mrs. Louisa Moy for her interlibrary loan arrangements. Finally, I would like to thank my husband, Eugene, for supporting and encouraging my efforts throughout the process of researching information for this book.

# Glossary

This glossary contains definitions of the bibliographic terms used in this book. These terms have been defined only within the context of this book. For additional definitions of these terms, consult standard Chinese and English dictionaries.

Chia ming 假名

> Pseudonym, an alias.

Chia p'u 家譜

> The Chinese genealogy, also called Chih p'u 支譜, Tsung p'u 宗譜, Tsu p'u 族譜, or Shih p'u 氏譜. Each family has its own genealogical record, giving the origin of the family, its collateral lines, names and ages of the members, records of marriages, births and deaths, including a brief history of the men. This genealogy is generally revised or supplemented every thirty to fifty years to bring it up to date.

Chiang nan 江南

> South of the Yangtze River (Yangtze chiang 揚子江). Originally the name of one of the administrative circuits of the T'ang 唐 dynasty. The name was used to refer to south central China below the Yangtze. It was a prosperous rice-growing area and its flourishing craft and commercial activities in the Ming 明 dynasty made it one of the key economic areas of China.

Chih p'u 支譜

> See Chia p'u 家譜.

Chün ming 郡名

> Originated during the Han (漢, 206 B.C.-A.D. 220) dynasty. The empire was divided into ninety Commanderies or Chün 郡 administered by a Governor (t'ai- shou 太守) with the assistance of the Defender (wei 尉). Many families or clans assigned to the Chün adopted the name of their Commandery (Chün ming 郡名) as their common surnames.

Feng hao 封號

> The imperially bestowed posthumous titles, also called Shih ming 諡名. In ancient customs, the titles are officially bestowed on persons of distinguished merit after his death.

Feudalism, Feng chien 封建

> Feudalism, the ancient Chinese term of Feng chien 封建, means "to enfeoff (nobles) and so construct (the state)."

It was the governmental practice of the Shang 商 and especially the Chou 周 dynasty.

## Feudal territories

In the Chou dynasty, the Chinese were organized under a King (wang 王) in a varying and changing feudal (feng chien 封建) pattern, dominated by a hereditary aristocracy. Feudal territories outside the directly controlled royal domain were allocated to feudal lords collectively known as "the various marquises" (chu hou 諸侯), whose fiefs were called states (kuo 國). There were five grades of lords, in descending order of eminence as follows: dukes (kung 公), marquises (hou 侯), earls (po 伯), viscounts (tzu 子), and barons (nan 男).

## Genealogy

The study of family pedigrees.

## Hao 號

Literary name, designation, or title of a man.
See also Pieh hao 別號.

## Hsiao ming 小名

Childhood name.
See also Ju ming 乳名 and Nai ming 奶名.

## Hsing 姓

Surname, or family name. The word "姓" made up of two individual characters: nü 女 (woman) and sheng 生 (to give birth). That is to say, the surname of the early Chinese followed the maternal line.

## Hsüeh ming 學名

See Shu ming 書名.

## Ju ming 乳名

Name used during childhood as a "milk name".
See also Nai ming 奶名 and Hsiao ming 小名.

## Kuan ming 官名

Official name assigned to a man upon earning an academic degree or official rank.

## Lineage

A group of individuals tracing descent from the descendants to a common ancestor.
See also Pedigree.

Miao hao 廟號
> Temple name, or dynastic title for emperors

Ming 名
> Generation name.

Nai ming 奶名
> Name used during childhood as a "milk name". See also Hsiao ming 小名 and Ju ming 乳名.

Pedigree
> An ancestral line; a register recording a line of ancestors.
> See also Lineage.

Pi ming 筆名
> Pen name, or nom de plume, name used in writing and publications.

Pieh hao 別號
> Names derived from gardens, studios, etc. are called study name or studio name.
> See also Shih ming 室名

Shih 氏
> Clan name.

Shih ming 謚名
> Posthumous name bestowed on emperors after death.
> see also Feng hao 封號.

Shih ming 室名
> Studio name.

Shih p'u 氏譜
> Family tree; lineage; genealogy.
> See also Chia p'u 家譜.

Shih tsu 氏族
> A family, a clan.

Shih tsu 始祖
> Progenitor; the common ancestor of a group of persons.

Shu ming 書名
> Also called Hsüeh ming 學名; book name or school name used from the first period of education.

Ts'o hao 綽號
>Nickname of a person.
>See also Hao 號 and Pieh hao 別號.

Ts'u t'ang 祠堂
>Ancestral hall; an organization which records, edits and preserves the history and genealogy of the family.

Tsu p'u 族譜
>See Chia p'u 家譜.

Tsung p'u 宗譜
>See Chia p'u 家譜.

Tzu 字
>Courtesy name, or style, a literary appellation by which a man is most usually designated in familiar parlance or in literature, the name is used upon the reaching of adulthood.

## Sources:

Hook, Brian, ed. The Cambridge encyclopedia of China. Cambridge, London; New York: Cambridge University Press, 1982.

Hucker, Charles O. A dictionary of official titles in imperial China. Stanford, CA: Stanford University Press, 1985.

# Chronology of Chinese History

Hsia 夏, ca. 2200 - 1700 B.C.

Shang 商, ca. 1700 - 1122 B.C.

Chou 周, ca. 1122 - 221 B.C.
    Western Chou (Hsi Chou　西周,　1122 - 771 B.C.)
    Eastern Chou (Tung Chou 東周,　770 - 221 B.C.)

    Spring and Autumn (Ch'un ch'iu 春秋, 770 - 476 B.C.) Period
    Warring States　　(Chan kuo　　戰國, 475 - 221 B.C.) Period

Ch'in 秦, 221 - 206 B.C.

Han 漢, 206 B.C. - A.D. 220
    Western Han (Hsi Han　西漢, 206 B.C. - A.D. 9)
    Wang Mang interregnum (Hsin 新, A.D. 9 - 24)
    Eastern Han (Tung Han 東漢, A.D. 25 - 220)

Three Kingdoms (Shan kuo 三國, A.D. 220 - 280)
    Wei 魏, A.D. 220 - 265
    Shu 蜀, A.D. 221 - 263
    Wu　吳, A.D. 222 - 280

Western Chin (Hsi Chin　西晉, A.D. 265 - 316)

Eastern Chin (Tung Chin 東晉, A.D. 317 - 420)

Sixteen Kingdoms (Shih-liu kuo 十六國, A.D. 304 - 439)

Southern and Northern Dynasties (Nan-pei ch'ao 南北朝, A.D. 420 - 581)
    Southern Dynasties (Nan ch'ao 南朝)
      Sung 宋, A.D. 420 - 479
      Ch'i 齊, A.D. 479- 502
      Liang 梁, A.D. 502 - 557
      Ch'en 陳, A.D. 557 - 589
    Northern Dynasties (Pei ch'ao 北朝)
    Northern Wei　(Pei Wei　北魏, A.D. 386 - 534)
    Eastern Wei　(Tung Wei 東魏, A.D. 534 - 550)
    Northern Ch'i (Pei Ch'i 北齊, A.D. 550 - 577)
    Western Wei　　(Hsi Wei　西魏, A.D. 535 - 557)
    Northern Chou (Pei Chou 北周, A.D. 557 - 581)

Sui 隋, A.D. 581 - 618

T'ang 唐, A.D. 618 - 907

Five Dynasties and Ten Kingdoms (Wu-t'ai Shih-kuo 五代十國, A.D. 907 - 59)

   Five Dynasties (Wu-t'ai 五代)
    Later Liang (Hou Liang 後梁, A.D. 907 - 923)
    Later T'ang (Hou T'ang 後唐, A.D. 923 - 936)
    Later Chin (Hou Chin 後秦, A.D. 936 - 946)
    Later Han  (Hou Han  後漢, A.D. 947 - 950)
    Later Chou (Hou Chou, 後周, A.D. 951 - 960)

   Ten Kingdoms (Shih-kuo 十國, A.D. 902 - 979)

Sung 宋, A.D. 960 - 1279
   Northern Sung (Pei Sung 北宋, A.D. 960 - 1127)
   Southern Sung (Nan Sung 南宋, A.D. 1127 - 1279)

Liao 遼, A.D. 916 - 1125

Western Hsia (Hsi Hsia 西夏, A.D. 1032 - 1227)

Chin 金, A.D. 1115 - 1234

Yüan 元, A.D. 1276 - 1368

Ming 明, A.D. 1368 - 1644

Ch'ing 清, A.D. 1644 - 1912

**Sources:**

Hook, Brian, ed. The Cambridge encyclopedia of China. Cambridge, London ; New York: Cambridge University Press, 1982, p. 6-7.

Mayers, William Frederick. The Chinese reader's manual: a handbook of biographical, historical, mythological, and general literary reference. Detroit: Gale Research Co., 1910. Pt. III, p. 387-409, Chronological tables.

# Pinying to Wade-Giles Conversion Table

| Pinyin | Wade-Giles | Pinyin | Wade-Giles | Pinyin | Wade-Giles |
|--------|-----------|--------|-----------|--------|-----------|
| **A** | | chuai | ch'uai | feng | feng |
| a | a | chuan | ch'uan | fo | fo |
| ai | ai | chuang | ch'uang | fou | fou |
| an | an | chui | ch'ui | fu | fu |
| ang | ang | chun | ch'un | | |
| ao | ao | chuo | ch'o | **G** | |
| | | ci | tz'u | ga | ka |
| **B** | | cong | ts'ung | gai | kai |
| ba | pa | cou | ts'ou | gan | kan |
| bai | pai | cu | ts'u | gang | kang |
| ban | pan | cuan | ts'uan | gao | kao |
| bang | pang | cui | ts'ui | ge | ko |
| bao | pao | cun | ts'un | gei | kei |
| bei | pei | cuo | ts'o | gen | ken |
| ben | pen | | | geng | keng |
| beng | peng | **D** | | gong | kung |
| bi | pi | da | ta | gou | kou |
| bian | pien | dai | tai | gu | ku |
| biao | piao | dan | tan | gua | kua |
| bie | pieh | dang | tang | guai | kuai |
| bin | pin | dao | tao | guan | kuan |
| bing | ping | de | te | guang | kuang |
| bo | po | deng | teng | gui | kuei |
| bou | pou | di | ti | gun | kun |
| bu | pu | dian | tien | guo | kuo |
| | | diao | tiao | | |
| **C** | | die | tieh | **H** | |
| ca | ts'a | ding | ting | ha | ha |
| cai | ts'ai | diu | tiu | hai | hai |
| can | ts'an | dong | tung | han | han |
| cang | ts'ang | dou | tou | hang | hang |
| cao | ts'ao | du | tu | hao | hao |
| ce | ts'e | duan | tuan | he | ho |
| cen | ts'en | dui | tui | hei | hei |
| ceng | ts'eng | dun | tun | hen | hen |
| cha | ch'a | duo | to | heng | heng |
| chai | ch'ai | | | hong | hung |
| chan | ch'an | **E** | | hou | hou |
| chang | ch'ang | e | o | hu | hu |
| chao | ch'ao | en | en | hua | hua |
| che | ch'e | er | erh | huai | huai |
| chen | ch'en | | | huan | huan |
| cheng | ch'eng | **F** | | huang | huang |
| chi | ch'ih | fa | fa | hui | hui |
| chong | ch'ung | fan | fan | hun | hun |
| chou | ch'ou | fang | fang | huo | huo |
| chu | ch'u | fei | fei | **J** | |
| chua | ch'ua | fen | fen | ji | chi |

| Pinyin | Wade-Giles | Pinyin | Wade-Giles | Pinyin | Wade-Giles |
|---|---|---|---|---|---|
| jia | chia | liu | liu | nuan | nuan |
| jian | chien | long | lung | nüe | nüeh |
| jiang | chiang | lou | lou | nuo | no |
| jiao | chiao | lu | lu | | |
| jie | chieh | lü | lü | O | |
| jin | chin | luan | luan | ou | ou |
| jing | ching | lüan | lüan | | |
| jiong | chiung | lüe | lüeh | P | |
| jiu | chiu | lun | lun | pa | p'a |
| ju | chü | luo | lo | pai | p'ai |
| juan | chüan | | | pan | p'an |
| jue | chüeh | M | | pang | p'ang |
| jun | chün | ma | ma | pao | p'ao |
| | | mai | mai | pei | p'ei |
| K | | man | man | pen | p'en |
| ka | k'a | mang | mang | peng | p'eng |
| kai | k'ai | mao | mao | pi | p'i |
| kan | k'an | mei | mei | pian | p'ien |
| kang | k'ang | men | men | piao | p'iao |
| kao | k'ao | meng | meng | pie | p'ieh |
| ke | k'o | mi | mi | pin | p'in |
| kei | k'ei | mian | mien | ping | p'ing |
| ken | k'en | miao | miao | po | p'o |
| keng | k'eng | mie | mieh | pou | p'ou |
| kong | k'ung | min | min | pu | p'u |
| kou | k'ou | ming | ming | | |
| ku | k'u | miu | miu | Q | |
| kua | k'ua | mo | mo | qi | ch'i |
| kuai | k'uai | mou | mou | qia | ch'ia |
| kuan | k'uan | mu | mu | qian | ch'ien |
| kuang | k'uang | | | qiang | ch'iang |
| kui | k'uei | N | | qiao | ch'iao |
| kun | k'un | na | na | qie | ch'ieh |
| kuo | k'uo | nai | nai | qin | ch'in |
| | | nan | nan | qing | ch'ing |
| L | | nang | nang | qiong | ch'iung |
| la | la | nao | nao | qiu | ch'iu |
| lai | lai | nei | nei | qu | ch'ü |
| lan | lan | nen | nen | quan | ch'üan |
| lang | lang | neng | neng | que | ch'üeh |
| lao | lao | ni | ni | qun | ch'ün |
| le | le | nian | nian | | |
| lei | lei | niang | niang | R | |
| leng | leng | niao | niao | ran | jan |
| li | li | nie | nieh | rang | jang |
| lia | lia | nin | nin | rao | jao |
| lian | lien | ning | ning | re | je |
| liang | liang | niu | niu | ren | jen |
| liao | liao | nong | nung | reng | jeng |
| lie | lieh | nou | nou | ri | jih |
| lin | lin | nu | nu | rong | jung |
| ling | ling | nü | nü | rou | jou |

| Pinyin | Wade-Giles | Pinyin | Wade-Giles | Pinyin | Wade-Giles |
|--------|-----------|--------|-----------|--------|-----------|
| ru | ju | te | t'e | ye | yeh |
| ruan | juan | teng | t'eng | yi | yi |
| rui | jui | ti | t'i | yin | yin |
| run | jun | tian | t'ien | ying | ying |
| ruo | jo | tiao | t'iao | yong | yung |
| | | tie | t'ieh | you | yu |
| **S** | | ting | t'ing | yu | yü |
| sa | sa | tong | t'ung | yuan | yüan |
| sai | sai | tou | t'ou | yue | yüeh |
| san | san | tu | t'u | yun | yün |
| sang | sang | tuan | t'uan | | |
| sao | sao | tui | t'ui | **Z** | |
| se | se | tun | t'un | za | tsa |
| sen | sen | tuo | t'o | zai | tsai |
| seng | seng | | | zan | tsan |
| sha | sha | **W** | | zang | tsang |
| shai | shai | wa | wa | zao | tsao |
| shan | shan | wai | wai | ze | tse |
| shang | shang | wan | wan | zei | tsei |
| shao | shao | wang | wang | zen | tsen |
| she | she | wei | wei | zeng | tseng |
| shen | shen | wen | wen | zha | cha |
| sheng | sheng | weng | weng | zhai | chai |
| shi | shih | wo | wo | zhan | chan |
| shou | shou | wu | wu | zhang | chang |
| shu | shu | | | zhao | chao |
| shua | shua | **X** | | zhe | che |
| shuai | shuai | xi | hsi | zhen | chen |
| shuan | shuan | xia | hsia | zheng | cheng |
| shuang | shuang | xian | hsien | zhi | chih |
| shui | shui | xiang | hsiang | zhong | chung |
| shun | shun | xiao | hsiao | zhou | chou |
| shuo | shuo | xie | hsieh | zhu | chu |
| si | ssu | xin | hsin | zhua | chua |
| song | sung | xing | hsing | zhuai | chuai |
| sou | sou | xiong | hsiung | zhuan | chuan |
| su | su | xiu | hsiu | zhuang | chuang |
| suan | suan | xu | hsü | zhui | chui |
| sui | sui | xuan | hsüan | zhun | chun |
| sun | sun | xue | hsüeh | zhuo | cho |
| suo | so | xun | hsün | zi | tzu |
| | | | | zong | tsung |
| **T** | | **Y** | | zou | tsou |
| ta | t'a | ya | ya | zu | tsu |
| tai | t'ai | yai | yai | zuan | tsuan |
| tan | t'an | yan | yen | zui | tsui |
| tang | t'ang | yang | yang | zun | tsun |
| tao | t'ao | yao | yao | zuo | tso |

Chapter 1

# HISTORY AND ORIGIN OF CHINESE SURNAMES

# The History of Chinese surnames

A person's name signifies his identity and is subtly related to his self-esteem as well as to the way others regard him. Due to the ancient historical and cultural tradition, Chinese pay great attention in choosing their names. For Chinese, a name could trace not only a person's blood relatives and generation within a family but also his social status. If a person is well-named, he will feel justly proud, and in the same way he may despise his name if it is silly and meaningless and causes him embarrassment. Strange though it may seem, Chinese names generally do have a psychological effect. If a person has a name meaning strong and just, for example, then somehow others will expect him to possess those attributes. If his name connotes failure or deception, then the tendency would be to impute him with these characteristics[1].

The use of a family name or surname by the Chinese people has a very remote origin. Family names were created and used by the Chinese people about 2,800 years ago before the Three Dynasties, Hsia (夏, ca. 2200-700 B.C.), Shang (商, ca. 1700-1122 B.C.) and Chou (周, ca. 1122-221 B.C.)[2]. According to legend, the Chinese surname system was established by the legendary emperor Fu Hsi (伏羲, 2852-2737? B.C.)[3]. Since the accession of the emperor Fu Hsi, all Chinese were required to have a family name; its purpose was to distinguish the families and prevent the marriages between persons of the same family name. From the time of the emperor Fu Hsi 伏羲 until the Chou dynasty, two categories of family names were in use, the first called shih 氏, being an hereditary title from the father side created for the clan given by and held at the pleasure of the emperor, king, or lord. This class of name was used to address the constituents of the clan and the male. The other class was called hsing 姓, to indicate origin of birth from the mother side. This second class was used to address the female.

The major shift of status becomes evident during the Warring States (Chan kuo 戰國, 475-221 B.C.) Period. At this period, the establishment of the agricultural society marked the shift of power from woman to man, plus the Chinese adopted their names (shih 氏) predominantly from their feudal territory during that period. Thus shih became more important than hsing. From the Chou dynasty to the succeeding Ch'in (秦, 221-206 B.C.) dynasty, She Huang-ti 始皇帝 pursued an aggressive policy directed against the remaining feudal states, he had assumed the full control of his government, with the weakening of the power of the nobles, the difference between hsing and shih became less and less prominent. After the Chou dynasty, the classes of shih and hsing were becoming identical, and only surnames or family names were used[4].

Scholars also consider other possibilities such as the legendary emperor Huang-ti (黃帝, 2697-2597? B.C.) and the early Chinese matriarchal societies as possible sources of Chinese family names. From an anthropological point of view, the totems[5] of the ancient Chinese people also had a great impact on the Chinese family names. In all, the family names of legendary emperors, the family names of the ancient matriarchal clans, and the totems of the ancient people fostered the evolution of the Chinese family names[6].

According to Ku Yen-wu 顧炎武, a prominent scholar in the Ming (明, A.D. 1368-1644) dynasty, stated in his book Jih chih lu 日知錄[7]: "When people were discussing family names (hsing), they based their arguments on the Five Emperors, including Shao Hao 少昊, Chuan Hsü 顓頊, Ti K'u 帝嚳, T'ang Ti-yao 唐帝堯 and Yü Ti-shun 虞帝舜. There were twenty-two surnames found in the Ch'un ch'iu 春秋[8]. After the Warring States Period, people identified the shih with the hsing, thus the hsing, which had existed from the age of the Five Emperors, disappeared.[9]" He also said: "Generally speaking, people of the Warring States Period still used a clan (shih tsu 氏族) designation which people of the Han (漢, 206 B.C.-A.D. 220) dynasty period usually called hsing although the shih tsu designation continued...the hsing shih 姓氏 designations have been mixed as one and the same since the time of the Grande Duke of T'ai (T'ai-shih kung 太史公), or Ssu-ma Ch'ien 司馬遷[10]." At present, though hsing and shih are mixed as one and the same, their function is not even slightly diminished. Today people who bear the same surname, though not of the same ancestry, still largely identify themselves as having a clan relationship[11].

## The Origin of Chinese Surnames

There are evidence in at least twenty four sources from which family names originated[12]. They are enumerated with examples in the following:

1. Adopting a dynasty designation, examples are: T'ang 唐, Yü 虞, Hsia 夏, Shang 商, Chou 周, Lu 魯, Sung 宋, etc.

2. Using the name of a feudal territory or state (kuo 國), for

example, Cheng Ch'iao 鄭樵 stated in his <u>Comprehensive history of institutions</u> (T'ung chih 通志, 1149): "Hsiang-yü 項羽 bestowed I-ch'ang 義常 on the grandson of Ch'u Huai-wang 楚懷王 and established the capital in Ch'en 郴, his descendants adopted the surname Ch'en"; other examples include Chiang 江, Huang 黃, Ch'in 秦, Ch'i 齊, Wu 吳, Wei 魏, and Chin 晉, etc.

3. Taking the name of a political district (hsien 縣), similar to county in a state of the United States, examples are: Hung 紅, Ch'i 蘄, and Fan 番, etc.

4. Using the name of a town (ch'eng 城), such as Pien 卞, Feng 馮, Ts'ui 崔, Lu 盧, Pao 鮑, Fei 費, Hsieh 謝, Yang 楊, Liu 柳, Su 蘇, Yeh 葉, Pai 白, Ma 馬, Mao 毛, Lu 鹿, Luan 欒, Pu 步, Chung 鍾, Chan 詹, Miao 苗, Tsou 鄒, P'ing 平, Kan 甘, Shang-kuan 上官, Yin 尹, and Shan 單, etc.

5. From the name of a village (hsiang 鄉), as for examples P'ei 裴, Lu 陸, P'ang 龐, Yen 閻, and Hao 郝, etc.

6. From road stations (ting 亭), such as Mi 糜, Ma 馬, Ou-yang 歐陽, and Ts'ai 采, etc.

7. Taking the name of residence from suburbs of direction, east (tung 東), west (hsi 西), south (nan 南), and north (pei 北), examples are: Tung-kung 東宮, Hsi-men 西門, Nan-kuo 南郭, She-nan 社南, Pei-kuo 北郭, and She-pei 社北, and Tung-meng 東門, etc.

8. Adopting the family name (hsing 姓), of a historical personage, such as Yao 姚, Chiang 姜, Jen 任, Chi 姬, Ssu 姒, Wei 隗, Yün 允, Yu 酉, Ch'i 漆, Feng 風, I 弋, I 伊, and Ssu 巳, etc.

9. Adopting the generation name (ming 名), of a historical personage, such as Jan 冉, Fu 伏, Yü 禹, Chin 金, T'ang 湯, Lung 龍, T'ung 童, Kao 高, Yü 余, K'o 柯, Mo 莫, Tuan 段, Ch'ai 柴, Lien 連, Lo 駱, Hsiung 熊, Hsi 奚, I 易, and Wu 伍, etc.

10. Using a man's social name or courtesy name (tzu 字), for a family name, as for example Yu 游, Fang 方, Chang 張, Tung 董, P'an 潘, Yüan 袁, Shih 石, Shih 施, Sun 孫, Kung 貢, Niu 牛, Ho 賀, Yen 顏, Ch'eng 成, Pao 包, K'ung 孔, and T'ung 童, etc.

11. Adopting the custom of ranking (ts'u 次), by using the appellation applied to a relative, as old brother, young sister,

etc. For example, Meng 孟, the first brother; Chi 季, the last brother; and Tsu 祖, the grandfather.

12. From names of tribes or clans (tsu 族), such as Ching 景, and Tso 左, and So 索, etc.

13. From names of official posts (kuan 官), such as T'iao 調, a civil reconciliator; Shih 史, a historian; Ch'ien 錢, a treasurer; Shih 師, a teacher, Shuai 帥, a general; Chi 籍, a librarian; K'ou 寇, a policeman; and Ssu-ma 司馬 and Ssu-tu 司徒, civil officials.

14. From titles of nobility (chüeh 爵), examples are: Huang 黃, emperor; Wang 王, king; Pa 霸, grand duke; and Hou 侯, duke.

15. Honorary name given by the emperor in appreciation of a man's contribution to the kingdom or country, for example, Cheng Cheng-kung 鄭成功 was given the honorary name Chu 朱 by the Ming 明 Emperor T'ai-tsu 太祖, his name was Chu Yüan-chang 朱元璋 and Hsü Hsün 徐勛 was honored by the name Li 李, given by the emperor T'ang Kao-tsu 唐高祖, his name was Li Yüan 李淵.

16. From occupations or trades (chih yeh 職業), such as Yü 漁, a fisherman and Ch'iao 樵, a woodsman.

17. Using a man's techniques (chi 技), for example, Wu 巫, a magician; T'u 屠, a butcher; T'ao 陶, a potter; Chiang 匠, a builder; and Pu 卜, an astrologer.

18. From the name of a tree (shu 樹), such as Wan 萬, the species of an orange tree.

19. From posthumous titles (shih 謚) of rulers, examples are: Chuang 莊, politeness; Min 閔, kindness; Yen 嚴, strictness; Wen 文, the literary; and Wu 武, the military, etc.

20. From the name of an object (wu 物), as for example Ch'e 車, a carriage; Kuan 冠, a hat; P'u 蒲, grass; and Fu 符, a flower.

21. From the lineage name, adding a diminutive (hsi 系) to the progenitor, such as Wang-sun 王孫, a king's grandson; Kung-sun 公孫, grandson of a duke; and Yüan-po 原伯, the first son of Yüan.

22. Taking the name of a vassal state (i 邑), in which a person

was under the protection of a feudal lord to whom he was vowed homage, examples are: Shen 申, Ch'i 祈, Liu 劉, Yeh 葉, E 鄂, Lin 藺, Chi 冀, Chia 郟, Wen 溫, Yen, 閻, Liu 柳, Fan 范, Feng 馮, Fan 樊, and Chiang 蔣, etc.

23. A man who marries into a woman's family (ju chui 入贅) will combine his surname with his wife's surname to form a joint surname, for example, Mr. Chang marries Ms. Liao and enters her family, their children will have the surname Chang-liao 張廖 and the name Fang-chiang 范姜 is derived from the same process.

24. Name of contempt, derision and opprobrium, given to an evildoer (erh 惡) by the ruler, such as Fu 蝮, poison snake; Mang 蟒, rebel; Ch'ing 黥, branded felon; and Hsiao 梟, an owl. In Chinese, the owl is considered as an evil sign.

## Chinese Surnames in Literature

A number of compilations listing surnames in current use have been made at different stages of Chinese history[13]. During the time of the Five Emperors, only 23 names have been recorded, it grew into 130 names in the Han 漢 dynasty, nearly 400 names existed in the T'ang (唐, A.D. 618-907) dynasty, 2,300 in the Sung (宋, A.D. 960-1279), 3,736 in the Yüan (元, A.D. 1276-1368), 4,600 in the Ming (明, A.D. 1368-1644), and nearly 5,000 in the Ch'ing (清, A.D. 1644-1912) dynasty[14]. The book, Surnames of a Hundred Families (Pai chia hsing 百家姓) which was written in the Northern Sung (Pei Sung 北宋, A.D. 960-1127) dynasty, recorded a total of 438 surnames, of which 408 were single and 30 were multiple surnames[15]. Cheng Ch'iao 鄭樵 listed 2,117 surnames in his Comprehensive history of institutions (T'ung chih 通志, 1149)[16], Ma Tuan-lin 馬端臨 listed 3,736 surnames in his General history of institutions and critical examination of documents and studies (Wen hsien t'ung k'ao 文獻通考, 1224)[17], and Wang Ch'i 王圻 listed 4,657 surnames in his Supplement to General history of institutions and critical examination of documents and studies (Hsü wen hsien t'ung k'ao 續文獻通考)[18]. Till the Republic era, Teng Hsien-ching 鄧獻鯨 listed 3,484 single, 2,032 double, and 146 triple-character names with a total of 5,662 surnames in his book Chung-kuo hsing shih chi (中國姓氏集, 1971)[19]. Chung-kuo hsing shih hui p'ien (中國姓氏匯編, 1984) complied 5,730 surnames[20]. Wang Su-ts'un 王素存 collected a total of 7,720 surnames in his book Chung-hua hsing fu (中華姓府, 1969)[21].

According to the 1982 national census conducted in China, the

8

top four popular Chinese surnames were Li 李 (7.8%), Wang 王 (7.4%), Chang 張 (7.1%), and Liu 劉 (1%+). Additional popular surnames include Chao 趙, Yen 嚴, Ch'en 陳, Sun 孫, Ma 馬, Wu 吳, and Kao 高[22]. In Taiwan, the ten most common Chinese surnames are Ch'en 陳, Lin 林, Huang 黃, Chang 張, Li 李, Wang 王, Wu 吳, Liu 劉, Ts'ai 蔡, and Yang 楊 in that order. According to the 1987 Taiwan census data, these comprise 52% of the total population in Taiwan[23].

## The Change of Surnames

There are various reasons for the changing of surnames during the period of nearly 5,000 years since the system was first inaugurated and the most important ones are enumerated in the following[24]:

1. For merit: The surname bestowed upon worthy statesmen, councilors, or warriors, etc. who have made great contributions to the country. The surname of the emperor's own family was given as a reward of merit, for example, in the Han 漢 dynasty, the surname Liu 劉 was taken from Han Kao-tsu 漢高祖, his name was Liu Pang 劉邦; in the T'ang 唐 dynasty, the surname Li 李 was taken from T'ang Kao-tsu 唐高祖, his name was Li Yüan 李淵; and in the Sung 宋 dynasty, the surname Chao 趙 was taken from Sung T'ai-tsu 宋太祖, his name was Chao K'uang-yin 趙匡胤.

2. For demerit: Names of criminals and conquered rulers were changed as a punishment and the purging of former dynastic appellations. For example, in the Han 漢 dynasty, by imperial decree, the surname of Ying Pu 英布 was changed to Ch'ing 黥, meaning a branded felon; in the T'ang 唐 dynasty, the surname of Tou Huai-cheng 竇懷正, a betrayer of his country, was changed to Tu 毒, meaning poison and the surname of a conquered ruler, Sun Hsiu 孫秀, was changed to Li 厲, meaning devil.

3. To avoid using the surname of the emperor: No one is allowed to speak or write the surname of the ruler during his dynasty. For example, Shih 師 was changed to Shuai 帥, simpler strokes of a different word; Chi 籍 was changed to Hsi 席, bearing nearly the same sound; Chuang 莊 was changed to Yen 嚴, synonyms but two different characters; Shen 沈 was changed to Yu 尤, dropping the radical to avoid conflicting with imperial surname.

4. To escape from enemies: For example, Tuan-mu 端木 changed to Mu 木 by dropping the first word and subsequently changed to Mu

沐 by adding a radical; Chi 姬 changed to Chang 張, both names bear the similar sound; Wu 伍 changed to Wu 五 by dropping a radical; and Niu 牛 changed to Lao 牢 and later to Liao 寮 by dropping a radical and subsequently changing to a word of the similar form.

5. To simplify the writing of the name by dropping a radical: For example, Sui 隨 changed to Sui 隋, the latter has simpler strokes, Chang 鄣 changed to Chang 章, Man 蔓 to Wan 萬, and Mo 幕 to Mo 莫.

6. To simplify the writing of the name by changing from double to single word: For example, Lu-p'u 盧蒲 to Lu 盧, Tuan-kan 段干 to Tuan 段, Ssu-k'ou 司寇 to K'ou 寇, and Chung-li 鍾離 to Chung 鍾.

7. To show the lineage of descent by changing from double to single word: For example, Chi 季 changed to Chi-sun 季孫, meaning the grandson of Chi, and Ko 葛 changed to Chu-ko 諸葛, the latter designates all sons of Ko.

8. By mistakes in the form of characters or sounds: For example, P'ei 裴 was incorrectly changed to Lei 壘, Lü 閭 to Lu 盧, Chan-ko 瞻葛 to Chu-ko 諸葛, Keng 耿 to Chien 簡, Shen-t'u 申屠 to Hsin-tu 信都, P'o-liu 破六 to P'an-liu 潘六, and Tang 黨 to Chang 掌.

9. Through adoption: When a child is adopted, he adds the family name of the person adopting him. For example, Ou-li 歐李 was taken by the son of the Li 李 family who was adopted by the Ou 歐 family, and Hsü-cheng 許鄭 was taken by the son the Cheng 鄭 family who went to the Hsü 許 family.

10. Dissatisfaction with the family name because of its meaning or sound: For example, Ai 哀 changed to Chung 衷, two similar characters with quite different meanings, Ai 哀 means sadness while Chung 衷 means sincereness.

---

Sources:

1.  Lip, Evelyn. Choosing auspicious Chinese names. (Singapore: Times Books International, 1988), p. 7.

2.  Ch'en, Shao-hsing and Morton H. Fried. The distribution of family names in Taiwan (T'ai-wan

jen kou chih hsing shih feng pu
台灣人口之姓氏分佈). (T'ai-pei: New Taiwan
University, the Dept. of Sociology, College of
Law, 1968), p. ii-iii.

3.   Lip, Evelyn, p. 7.

4.   Kiang, K'ang-hu 江亢虎. <u>On Chinese studies</u>.
     (Shang-hai: The Commercial Press Limited, 1934),
     p. 127.

5.   Totem is an object as an animal or plant serving
     as the emblem of a family or clan and often as a
     reminder of its ancestry. See <u>Merriam-Webster's
     collegiate dictionary</u>, 10th ed. (Springfield,
     MA: Merriam-Webster, 1993), p. 1246.

6.   Hu, Qianli.  "How to distinguish and catalog Chinese
     personal names." <u>Cataloging & Classification Quarterly</u>,
     v. 19, no. 1 (1994): p. 30.

7.   <u>The Daily Miscellaneous Notes</u>.  It was a common practice
     among ancient scholars especially in the T'ang and Sung
     dynasties to record their most interesting observations
     in their notebooks.  See Wilkinson, Endymion. <u>The
     history of imperial China: a research guide</u>. (Cambridge,
     MA: Harvard University Press, 1973), p. 173.

8.   <u>The Spring and Autumn Annals</u>.  It was the court
     chronicle of the State of Lu (Lu kuo 魯國) and recorded
     historical events of the years 722-480 B.C.  Editorship
     was traditionally and implausibly ascribed to Confucius.
     The book contains three commentaries: <u>Tso chuan</u> 左傳,
     <u>Kung-yang chuan</u> 公羊傳, and <u>Ku-liang chuan</u> 穀梁傳. See
     Wilkinson, p. 68.

9.   Chen, Shao-hsing and Morton H. Fried, p. ii.

10.  The historian of the Ming 明 dynasty.  His work, <u>Shih
     chi</u> 史記, known in English title as <u>Records of the Grand
     Historian</u>, covering from earliest times to 99 B.C., was
     one of the most important historical writings in Chinese
     literature. See Wilkinson, p. 77-78.

11.  Chen, Shao-hsing and Morton H. Fried, p. ii.

12.  The following sources were consulted:

Kiang, K'ang-hu 江亢虎, p. 128-129.

Jones, Russell. <u>Chinese names: notes on the use of surnames & personal names by the Chinese in Malaysia and Singapore</u>. (Malaysia: Pelanduk, 1984), p. 7-8.

Liao, Fu-peng 廖福本. <u>T'ai-wan pai hsing yüan liu</u> 臺灣百姓源流. (T'ai-pei shih: Tso wen ch'u pan she, 1990), p. 8-12.

Teng, Hsien-ching 鄧獻鯨. <u>Chung-kuo hsing shih chi</u> 中國姓氏集. T'ai-pei shih: Chih ta t'u shu wen chü chiao yü yüng p'ing ku fen yu hsien kung ssu, 1971), p. 65-68.

Wilkinson, Endymion. <u>The history of imperial China: a research guide</u>. (Cambridge, MA: Harvard University Press, 1973).

13.  Jones, Russell, p. 8.

14.  Laio, Fu-peng 廖福本, p. 13.

15.  Lin, Shan. <u>What's in a Chinese name</u>. (Singapore: Federal Publications, 1988), p. 16.

16.  Wilkinson, Endymion, p. 126.

17.  Ibid.

18.  Chen, Shao-hsing, p. iii.

19.  Liao, Fu-peng 廖福本, p. 13.

20.  Wang, Ch'üan-ken 王泉根. <u>Hua-hsia hsing shih chih mi</u> 華夏姓氏之謎. T'ai-pei: Chih shu fang ch'u pan she, 1992), p. 5.

21.  Ibid.

22. Hu, Qianli, p. 31.

23. Liao, Fu-peng 廖福本, p. 14.

24. The following sources were consulted:

   Teng, Hsien-ching 鄧獻鯨, p. 70
   Kiang, K'ang-hu 江亢虎, p. 131-133.

# Chapter 2

# GENEALOGY OF CHINESE SURNAMES

1. Ai[1] 哀

According to Feng shu t'ung 風俗通, the surname Ai 哀 follows the ancestral line of Duke Ai (Ai kung 哀公) from the State of Lu (Lu kuo 魯國) in the Spring and Autumn (Ch'un ch'iu 春秋) Period. During the reign of the Ming 明 Emperor Shih-tsung 世宗 in Chia-ching 嘉靖 Period, the Emperor ordered the change of surname Ai 哀 to Chung 衷. However, both names are still widely used nowadays.

See also Chung[1] 衷.

2. Ai[4] 艾

The surname Ai 艾 derived from two sources: 1. Hsing shih k'ao lüeh 姓氏考略 traces the surname to its founder Ju Aai 汝艾 who was a government minister in the Hsia 夏 dynasty. His descendants adopted Ai as their common surname and settled primarily in T'ien-shui 天水 and Lung-hsi 隴西 in Kan-su 甘肅 province. 2. Ming hsien shih tsu yen hsing lei kao 名賢氏族言行類稿 and T'ung chih Shih tsu lüeh 通志氏族略 describe the name's origin as follows: The surname originated from Ai Kung 艾孔 who was a grand master (ta-fu 大夫) of the State of Ch'i (Ch'i kuo 齊國) in the Spring and Autumn (Ch'un ch'iu 春秋) Period.

3. Ai[4] 愛

According to Hsing shih k'ao lüeh 姓氏考略, the surname Ai 愛 can be traced to the Uigurs (Hui-he 回紇) who were initially a tribe of Hsiung-nus 匈奴, subdued and became part of the Tu-chüehs 突厥. Subsequently, the tribe regained its independence and adopted the name of Hui-he following the rebellion against the Tu-chüehs. During the prosperous period of the T'ang 唐 dynasty, a T'ang Emperor bestowed the honorary surname Ai on the chieftain of Hui-hes, known as Ai Hsieh-wu 愛邪勿. Subsequently, his descendants adopted Ai as their common surname. The family settled in northwestern Shan-hsi 山西 which was the ancient locale of Hsi-ho

Commandery (Hsi-ho chün 西河郡), which became the Ai family's ancestral hall name (t'ang ming 堂名).

4. An¹ 安

According to <u>T'ang shu tsai hsiang shih hsi piao</u> 唐書宰相世系表, An-hsi kuo 安息國 was a politically independent state founded by the grandson of Huang-ti (黃帝, 2697-2597? B.C.) and lasted for three thousand years until it was subdued by the Han 漢 dynasty. An was adopted as a common surname during the Han period and the descendants of the An family settled primarily in the region known as the Western Territories (Hsi-yü 西域) located in the northwestern part of China.

5. Ao² 敖

<u>Ming hsien shih tsu yen hsing lei kao</u> 名賢氏族言行類稿 and <u>Feng shu t'ung</u> 風俗通 trace the origin of the surname Ao 敖 to the ancestral line of Ta Ao 大敖 who was the master of Chuan Hsü 顓頊, during the Legendary Period.

6. Ch'a² 查

<u>Wan hsing t'ung p'u</u> 萬姓統譜 says: The surname Ch'a 查 branched from the surname Chiang 姜 and was adopted from the name of a district (i 邑) in Shan-tung 山東 province at the end of the Five Dynasties (Wu t'ai 五代, A.D. 907-959). The family prospered in Hai-ling 海陵 which was located in the present T'ai hsien 泰縣 in Chiang-su 江蘇 province.

7. Chai² 翟

<u>Yüan ho hsing tsuan</u> 元何姓纂 describes the origin of the surname Chai 翟 as follows: The surname Chai derived from the name of a feudal territory, the State of Chai (Chai kuo 翟國), in the Spring and Autumn (Ch'un ch'iu 春秋) Period. It was adopted as a common surname by its citizens. After the State of Chai was defeated by the State of Chin (Chin kuo 晉國), the family

relocated in Shan-hsi 山西 province and subsequently prospered in Chiang-su 江蘇 and Che-chiang 浙江 provinces.

8. Ch'ai[2] 柴

According to <u>Yüan ho hsing tsuan</u> 元何姓纂, the surname Ch'ai 柴 branched from the surname Chiang 姜 of the ancestral line of Yen-ti 炎帝. The founder of the surname was Kao Ch'ai 高柴, who was a pupil of Confucius (K'ung-tze 孔子) in the Spring and Autumn (Ch'un ch'iu 春秋) Period. The Ch'ai family primarily settled in Tsou-yang hsien 鄒陽縣, Shan-tung 山東 province and they lived there for generations. The family named their ancestral hall (t'ang hao 堂號, or t'ang ming 堂名) P'ing-yang 平陽 (the ancient name of Tsou-yang 鄒陽) in memory of its original settlement in that place.

9. Chan[1] 詹

According to <u>Hsing yüan</u> 姓苑, the founder of the surname Chan 詹 was Chou Hsüan-wang (周宣王, 827-781 B.C.). Because one of his sons was enfeoffed as the Marquise of Chan (Chan hou 詹侯), Chan was later adopted as a common surname by his descendants. The ancestral region of the Chan family was Po-hai 渤海 in Shan-tung 山東 province.

10. Chan[3] 展

The surname Chan 展 derived from three sources. 1. <u>Hsing shih hsün yüan</u> 姓氏尋源 traces the name's origin to Chan Shang-kung 展上公, during the reign of Ti K'u 帝嚳 (Kao-hsin shih 高辛氏) in the Legendary Period. 2. The surname Chan derived from the ancestral line Tzu-chan 子展 who was a son of the Duke Lu Hsiao-kung 魯孝公 in the Spring and Autumn (Ch'un ch'iu 春秋) Period. 3. According to <u>Wei shu kuan shih chih</u> 魏書官氏志, the surname Chan branched from the surname Chan-ch'ih 輾遲 of the tribal group of Hsiung-nu 匈奴. The radical of the character Chan 輾 was later removed and Chan 展 was adopted as a common surname in the Northern Wei

(Pei Wei 北魏) dynasty.

11. Chan³-ch'ih² 輾遲

See Chan³ 展.

12. Chan⁴ 湛

See Ch'en2 諶.

13. Ch'an²-yü² 單于

According to <u>Han shu Hsiung-nu chuan</u> 漢書匈奴傳,
ch'an-yü 單于 literally means the Son of Heaven
or the Emperor. It was originally the name of a
Hsiung-nu cheiftain who invaded China in the Han
漢 dynasty and was adopted as a surname during
the time of the Later Chou (Hou Chou 後周, 951-
960 A.D.) Period. Presently, there are many
Ch'an-yü families residing in places, such as
Li-ch'eng 歷城 and I-tu 益都 in Shan-tung 山東
province.

14. Chang¹ 章

<u>Ku chin hsing shih shu pien cheng</u> 古今姓氏書辨證
says: The surname Chang 章 originated from the
name of a feudal territory, Chang 鄣, in the
Chou 周 dynasty. It was later conquered by the
State of Ch'i (Ch'i kuo 齊國) and the
descendants of the Chang family removed the
radical from the name and adopted the simplified
form, Chang 章, as their common surname. They
settled in Nan-chang hsien 南昌縣, the capital
of Chiang-hsi 江西 province.

15. Chang¹ 張

<u>Yüan ho hsing tsuan</u> 元何姓纂 and <u>Hsing shih k'ao</u>
<u>lüeh</u> 姓氏考略 trace the genealogy of the surname
Chang 張 as follows: The surname Chang came
from the lineage of Huang-ti 黃帝 and traced to
his fifth son Hui 揮 who invented the bow (kung
弓), one of the most important tools for warfare
in ancient times. The motion of bending the bow
and aligning the arrow by stretching (chang 張)

the arms gave rise to the word "chang 張" which is composed of two individual characters: kung 弓 (a bow) and ch'ang 長 (to stretch). Eventually, some offsprings of Hui adopted Kung 弓 while others adopted Chang 張 as their common surnames. The Chang family settled originally in the city of T'ai-yüan 太原 in Shan-hsi 山西 province.

See also Kung[1] 弓, Fu[2] 福.

16. Chang[3] 仉

Hsing shih k'ao lüeh 姓氏考略 and Ming hsien shih tsu yen hsing lei kao 名賢氏族言行類稿 trace the origin of the surname Chang 仉 as follows: The surname Chang follows the ancestral line of Chou Wen-wang 周文王 and first appeared in the Spring and Autumn (Ch'un ch'iu 春秋) Period. It was branched from the surname Tang 黨 of the ancestral line of Tang shih 黨氏 who was a grand master (ta-fu 大夫) from the State of Lu (Lu kuo 魯國). The Chang 仉 family initially settled in Shan-tung 山東 province.

See also Tang[3] 黨.

17. Chang[3] 掌

According to T'ung chih Shih tsu lüeh 通志氏族略, the surname Chang 掌 branched from the surname Tang 黨 and it was evolved by mistake from the similar forms between these surnames.

See also Tang[3] 黨.

18. Ch'ang[1] 昌

According to Feng shu t'ung 風俗通, the surname Ch'ang 昌 belongs to the ancestral line of Huang-ti 黃帝 and its founder, Ch'ang I 昌意, was a son of Huang-ti. The family prospered in Ho-nan 河南, Shan-tung 山東, Chiang-su 江蘇, Kuang-tung 廣東, and Kuang-hsi 廣西 provinces.

19. Ch'ang[2] 常

Yüan ho hsing tsuan 元何姓纂 and T'ung chih Shih tsu lüeh 通志氏族略 trace the origin of the surname Chang 常 as follows: The surname Chang originated from the name of a vassal state, the District of Ch'ang (Ch'ang i 常邑), bestowed on a grandson of K'ang shu 康叔 from the State of Wei (Wei kuo 衛國) in the Chou 周 dynasty. Chang was adopted as a common surname by the descendants of K'ang shu and they settled primarily in T'ai-yüan 太原, Shan-hsi 山西 and P'ing-yüan 平原, Shan-tung 山東 provinces.

20. Chang[3]-sun[1] 長孫

T'ung chih Shih tsu lüeh 通志氏族略 traces the origin of the surname as follows: The surname Chang-sun 長孫 follows the ancestral line of the Hsien-pei 鮮卑 tribe of T'o-pa 拓跋, who ruled during the Northern Wei (Pei Wei 北魏) dynasty. The name's founder, Sha Mo-hsiung 沙莫雄, was the eldest son of Hsien-ti 獻帝 in the Northern Wei period. After his ruling power was past to his eldest son Sung 嵩, the family name was changed to Chang-sun 長孫 (meaning the eldest grandson in the family) and it was subsequently adopted as the common surname by his descendants.

21. Chao[4] 趙

The surnames of a hundred families (Pai chia hsing 百家姓) is the leading authority of Chinese surnames published in the Northern Sung (Pei Sung 北宋) dynasty, in which Chao 趙 was listed as the first surname in memory of the founder and the first emperor in the Northern Sung dynasty, Chao K'uang-yin 趙匡胤. According to Yüan ho hsing tsuan 元何姓纂, Chao originated from the name of a feudal territory, Chao ch'eng 趙城, bestowed on Tsao Fu 造父, in the Chou 周 dynasty and he later adopted Chao as his surname. The family initially settled in the city of T'ai-yüan 太原 in Shan-hsi 山西 province and eventually pervaded Kan-su 甘肅, Ho-nan 河南, and Chiang-su 江蘇 provinces.

22.　Chao⁴ 召

According to <u>T'ung chih Shih tsu lüeh</u> 通志氏族略, the surnames Shao 邵 and Chao 召 branched from the surname Chi 姬 of blood relatives. The surname Chao 召 was traced to the Duke of Chao (Chao kung 召公) who was bestowed with the State of Yen (Yen kuo 鄢國) in the Spring and Autumn (Ch'un ch'iu 春秋) Period. The Chao 召 family initially settled in Fu-feng 扶風, Shen-hsi 陝西 province.

See also Shao⁴ 邵.

23.　Ch'ao² 朝

The following books have documented the origin of the surnames Ch'ao 朝 and Ch'ao 晁: <u>Yüan ho hsing tsuan</u> 元何姓纂, <u>Hsing shih k'ao lüeh</u> 姓氏考略, <u>Feng shu t'ung</u> 風俗通 and <u>T'ung chih Shih tsu lüeh</u> 通志氏族略. According to these sources, the founder of the surname Ch'ao 朝, Wang Tzu-ch'ao 王子朝, was a son of the Chou 周 king, Ching-wang (景王, 544-519 B.C.). And the founder of the surname Ch'ao 晁 was the Grand Master (ta-fu 大夫) Shih Ch'ao 史晁 from the State of Wei (Wei kuo 衛國) in the Spring and Autumn (Ch'un ch'iu 春秋) Period. Although these two surnames came from different sources, they have been used interchangeably as one and the same by the descendants of the founders; many changed their surnames to its homonymous form of Ch'ao 朝 / Ch'ao 晁 and vice versa. Both families initially settled in Ying-ch'uan 潁川 and Ching-chao 京兆 in Ho-nan 河南 province.

24.　Ch'ao² 晁

See Ch'ao² 朝.

25.　Ch'ao² 巢

The surname Ch'ao 巢 derived from two sources. 1. According to <u>Hsing p'u</u> 姓譜, the surname originated from Yu-ch'ao shih 有巢氏 who was a legendary saint during the time of Emperor T'ang Ti-yao 唐帝堯 who lived high up in a tree (before the house was introduced) and was named Yu-ch'ao 有巢 (having a nest or a living quarter). 2. <u>Hsing shih k'ao lüeh</u> 姓氏考略 says: The Lake of Ch'ao (Ch'ao hu 巢湖, located in Ann-hui 安徽 province) was the site of the ancient State of Ch'ao (Ch'ao kuo 巢國) during the Shang 商 and Chou 周 dynasties. After the State of Ch'ao was defeated by the State of Wu (Wu kuo 吳國) at the end of the Spring and Autumn (Ch'un ch'iu 春秋) Period, its descendants adopted Ch'ao as their common surname and settled in P'eng-ch'eng 彭城, Ann-hui 安徽 province.

26. Ch'e¹ 車

The surname Ch'e 車 derived from two sources: 1. According to <u>Yüan ho hsing tsuan</u> 元何姓纂, the name came from T'ien Ch'ien-ch'iu 田千秋, a highly esteemed counselor-in-chief (ch'eng-hsiang 丞相), who was nicknamed Ch'e Ch'eng-hsiang 車丞相, due to his use of a carriage (che 車) as the means of transportion to the Han 漢 palace. And 2. <u>Wei shu kuan shih chih</u> 魏書官氏志 says that the name came from the Hu 胡 people, a nomadic group who invaded northern China during the Southern and Northern dynasties (Nan-pei ch'ao 南北朝). They were later subdued and absorbed by the Han 漢 people and adopted the surname Ch'e.

27. Chen¹ 甄

According to <u>Ch'en Liu Feng su chuan</u> 陳留風俗傳 and <u>Ming hsien shih tsu yen hsing lei kao</u> 名賢氏族言行類稿, the surname Chen 甄 originated from the name of a profession, the potter, during the reign of Yü Ti-shun (虞帝舜, 2255-2205? B.C.). The Cheng family now densely populates Ting hsien 定縣, Ho-pei 河北 province.

28. Chen¹ 真

The surname Chen 真 derived from two sources. 1. According to <u>T'ung chih Shih tsu lüeh</u> 通志氏族略, Chen was one of the eight surnames adopted by the State of Pai-chi 百濟 in Ch'ao-hsien 朝鮮 (the former name of Korea). 2. Feng shu t'ung 風俗通 says: Chen was a popular surname in the Han 漢 dynasty and a representative of this family was the Commander-in-Chief (t'ai-wei 太尉) Chen Yu 真祐 during that period. The ancestral region of the family was in Shang-ku 上谷, located in midwestern Ho-pei 河北 province.

29. Ch'en[1] 郴

According to T'ung chih Shih tsu lüeh 通志氏族略, the surname Ch'en 郴 derived from the place name, Ch'en hsien 郴縣, in Hu-nan 湖南 province. The founder of the surname was Hsiung Hsin 熊心 who was a grandson of Huai-wang 懷王 from the State of Ch'u (Ch'u kuo 楚國) during the Warring States (Chan kuo 戰國) Period. During the civilian revolt at the end of the Ch'in 秦 dynasty, Hsiang-yü 項羽 bestowed I-ch'ang 義常 on Hsiung Hsin and established the capital in Ch'en hsien. Subsequently, Ch'en was adopted as the common surname by Hsiung Hsin's descendants.

30. Ch'en[2] 陳

According to Yüan ho hsing tsuan 元何姓纂 and T'ung chih Shih tsu lüeh 通志氏族略: Ch'en 陳 was initially a region where fortunetelling using the eight diagrams (pa-kua 八卦) flourished and it was bestowed as a feudal territory on Kuei Man 嬀滿 (also known as Hu Kung-man 胡公滿) during the reign of Chou Wu-wang (周武王, 1122-1115 B.C.). Kuei Man and his family originally resided in Huai yang hsien 淮陽縣, Ho-nan 河南 province. Ten generations later, his descendants emigrated from their homeland due to political instability and formally adopted Ch'en 陳 as their common surname. The family settled predominantly in Ho-nan 河南, Chiang-su 江蘇, and Shan-tung 山東 provinces.

See also Yao[2] 姚, T'ien[2] 田, Man[3] 滿, and Hu[2] 胡.

31. Ch'en[2] 諶

The surnames Ch'en 諶 and Chan 湛 came from blood relatives and the predecessor of the surname Chan 湛 was Ch'en 諶. According to <u>Wan hsing t'ung p'u</u> 萬姓統譜 and <u>T'ung chih Shih tsu lüeh</u> 通志氏族略, the surname Ch'en 諶 appeared first in Sung 宋 dynasty when the mother of the Sung minister T'ao K'an 陶侃 adopted Ch'en 諶 from her ancestor. The Ch'en 諶 family initially settled in Yü-chang 豫章 and later moved to Nan-ch'ang 南昌, Chiang-hsi 江西 province. In Nan-ch'ang 南昌, some members of the Ch'en 諶 families changed their surname to Chan 湛 and settled there.

## 32. Cheng⁴ 鄭

According to <u>Yüan ho hsing tsuan</u> 元何姓纂, the surname Cheng 鄭 was adopted from the name of a feudal territory, the State of Cheng (Cheng kuo 鄭國), bestowed on Chou Yu 周友 during the reign of Chou Hsüan-wang (周宣王, 827-781 B.C.). The ancestral region of the family was in Cheng hsien 鄭縣, Ho-nan 河南 province.

## 33. Ch'eng² 程

The surname Ch'eng 程 belong to the lineage of Chuan Hsü 顓頊. The surname came from two sources. 1. <u>Yüan ho hsing tsuan</u> 元何姓纂 and <u>Wan hsing t'ung p'u</u> 萬姓統譜 state that the name originated from the name of a vassal state bestowed on the father of Cheng Po-hsiu 程伯休 who held the post of Ssu-ma 司馬, the Minister of War (hsia-kuan 夏官), in the Chou 周 dynasty and 2. <u>Tso chuan</u> 左傳 says Ch'eng 程 derived from the name of a feudal territory bestowed on Hsün shih 荀氏 from the State of Chin (Chin kuo 晉國) in the Spring and Autumn (Ch'un ch'iu 春秋) Period. Hsün shih 荀氏 later adopted Ch'eng as his family name.

See also Ssu¹-ma³ 司馬.

## 34. Ch'eng² 成

<u>Yüan ho hsing tsuan</u> 元何姓纂 and <u>Wan hsing t'ung p'u</u> 萬姓統譜 trace the origin of the surname

Ch'eng 成 to the feudal territory Ch'eng 郕 which was bestowed on Ch'eng Shu-wu 郕叔武 by his father Chou Wen-wang 周文王. After Ch'eng was defeated by the State of Ch'u 楚, the descendants of Ch'eng Shu-wu adopted the simplified form Ch'eng 成 as their common surname and settled in Kuang-ling 廣陵, Shan-tung 山東 province.

35. Chi¹ 戚

Yüan ho hsing tsuan 元何姓纂 describes the origin of the surname Chi 戚 as follows: The surname Chi originated from the name of a feudal territory located in the State of Wei (Wei kuo 衛國) of the Spring and Autumn (Ch'un ch'iu 春秋) Period. The descendants of the Chi family settled primarily in P'u-yang hsien 濮陽縣, Ho-nan 河南 province.

36. Chi¹ 嵇

According to Yüan ho hsing tsuan 元何姓纂, the surname Chi 嵇 derived from the following two sources: 1. It originated from the name of a feudal territory, initially located in Kuei-chi 會稽 and bestowed on Chi Chu 嵇杼, who was a son of Shao-k'ang (少康, 2079-2057? B.C.) in the Hsia 夏 dynasty. The feudal territory was later relocated to the Chi Mountain (Chi shan 嵇山) in the Han 漢 dynasty and was subsequently adopted as a surname. This branch of the family belongs to the lineage of the Great Yü (大禹, 2205-2197? B.C.). 2. The surname Chi derived from Chi shih 嵇氏 who originally lived in Chi-kang 嵇康 and later settled in Chi shan 嵇山 during the Han 漢 dynasty. The place of origin, Chi shan 嵇山, is located in An-hui 安徽 province.

37. Chi¹ 姬

According to Ming hsien shih tsu yen hsing lei kao 名賢氏族言行類稿, becasue Emperor Ti K'u 帝嚳's birthplace was near the Chi River (Chi shui 姬水), his descendants adopted Chi 姬 as their common surname in memory of him.

See also Hsüan[1]-yüan[2] 軒轅, Jei[4] 芮, Kung[1] 公,
Kung[1]-sun[1] 公孫,, Kung[1]-yang[2] 公羊.

38. Chi[2] 吉

Yüan ho hsing tsuan 元何姓纂 and Hsing shih k'ao
lüeh 姓氏考略 trace the origin the surname Chi
吉 as follows: The surname Chi follows the
lineage of Huang-ti 黃帝 and its founder was
Huang-ti's great grandson Po-shu 伯儵. He was
given the honorary surname Chi and was bestowed
with the vassal state in Nan-yen 南燕, located
in Chi hsien 汲縣, Ho-nan 河南 province.

39. Chi[2] 汲

The surname Chi 汲 originated from the following
two sources during the Spring and Autumn (Ch'un
ch'iu 春秋) Period: 1. According to Feng shu
t'ung 風俗通, the feudal prince of the Duke of
Hsüan (Hsüan kung 宣公) of the State of Wei (Wei
kuo 衛國) was bestowed with the vassal state of
Chi 汲, so he adopted it as his surname. The
State of Wei was located in the area of the
present Ho-pei 河北 and Ho-nan 河南 provinces.
2. Lu shih 路史 points out that the grandson of
the Duke of Hsüan (Hsüan kung 宣公) of the State
of Ch'i (Ch'i kuo 齊國) was bestowed with the
vassal state of Chi 汲 and Chi was subsequently
adopted as a common surname by his descendants.
The State of Ch'i (Ch'i kuo 齊國) was located in
Shan-tung 山東 province.

40. Chi[2] 籍

According to Kuang yün 廣韻 and Ming hsien shih
tsu yen hsing lei kao 名賢氏族言行類稿, Po Yen
伯黶, the Grand Master (ta-fu 大夫) of the State
of Chin (Chin kuo 晉國), was the Manager of the
Imperial Library (tien-chi 典籍) in the Spring
and Autumn (Ch'un ch'iu 春秋) Period. Some of
his descendants later adopted Tien 典 and others
adopted Chi 籍 as their common surname. The
family originally settled in Shan-hsi 山西,
later moved to Ho-nan 河南 and finally prospered
in Yüng-nein hsien 永年縣 which was the ancient
Kuang-p'ing Commandery (Kuang-p'ing chün 廣平郡)

in Ho-pei 河北 province. Since Chi 藉 and Chi 籍 were used interchangeably in ancient times, the former name was also recognized as a common surname in place of the surname Chi 籍. <u>Shang yu lu</u> 尚友錄 details the change of surname to Hsi 席 as follows: Chi Huan 籍環, a descendant of the Chi 籍 family, changed his surname to Hsi to avoid conflicting with the name used by Han Kao-tsu 漢高祖 as his forename.

See also Hsi² 席, Tien³ 典, Po² 伯, T'an² 談.

41. Chi² 藉

See Chi² 籍.

42. Chi⁴ 薊

<u>Hsing shih k'ao lüeh</u> 姓氏考略 traces the origin of the surname Chi 薊 as follows: In Fan-yang hsien 范陽縣 of the Ho-pei 河北 province, the prickly plants of thistles (chi 薊) are so prolific that poeple living there changed the name of the area to Chi hsien 薊縣 and eventually adopted Chi 薊 as their common surname.

43. Chi⁴ 冀

The surname Chi 冀 derived from two sources. 1. <u>Lu shih</u> 路史 points out that the surname belongs to the lineage of T'ang Ti-yao 唐帝堯 and was adopted as a common surname from the State of Chi (Chi kuo 冀國) in the Chou 周 dynasty. The Chi family initially settled in Ho-chin hsien 河津縣, Shan-hsi 山西 province, where the State of Chi was located. 2. According to <u>Yüan ho hsing tsuan</u> 元何姓纂, Chi was adopted as a common surname after the State of Chi 冀 was defeated by the State of Chin 晉 and became one of its district (vassal state), the District of Chi (Chi i 冀邑) where the Grand Master (ta-fu 大夫) Ch'üeh Jei 郤芮 was enfeoffed. His descendants later adopted Chi as their common surname and the family settled primarily in Ho-pei 河北 province.

44. Chi[4] 暨

According to Hsing shih k'ao lüeh 姓氏考略, the surname Chi 暨 came from the ancestral line of P'eng-tsu 彭祖 who belongs to the lineage of Huang-ti 黃帝. The descendants of P'eng-tsu adopted the surname Chi from either a place named Chi-yang 暨陽, located in Chiang-ying hsien 江陰縣, Chiang-su 江蘇 province or a place named Chu-chi hsien 諸暨縣 in Che-chiang 浙江 province. Both places are now densely populated with the descendants of the Chi families.

45. Chi[4] 祭

Lu shih 路史 describes the origin of the surname Chi 祭 as follows: The surname Chi derived from the name of the feudal territory, the State of Chi (Chi kuo 祭國), which was bestowed on the Earl of Chi (Chi po 祭伯) in the Chou 周 dynasty. Chi was later adopted as a common surname by his descendants and they settled in Cheng hsien 鄭縣, Ho-nan 河南 province.

See also Tzu[3] 訾.

46. Chi[4] 紀

According to Wan hsing t'ung p'u 萬姓統譜 and T'ang shu tsai hsiang shih hsi piao 唐書宰相世系表, the surname Chi 紀 branched from the surname Chiang 姜 of the lineage of Yen-ti 炎帝 (Shen-nung shih 神農氏) and originated from the name of a feudal territory bestowed on a descendant of Yen-ti. The feudal territory was later defeated by the State of Ch'i 齊 and subsequently Chi was adopted as the common surname by its citizens. The family originally settled in T'ien-shui 天水, Kan-su 甘肅 province.

47. Chi[4] 計

According to Wan hsing t'ung p'u 萬姓統譜 and Shang yu lu 尚友錄, the surname Chi 計 originally came from the name of the Ch'i Commandery (Ch'i chün 齊郡) and was later

adopted as the common surname by the descendants
living in the locale. A notable person of the
family was Chi Jan 計然 whose military schemes
helped the Grand Minister (ta-ch'en 大臣) Fan Li
范蠡 and his master Kou Chien 句踐 from the
State of Yüeh (Yüeh kuo 越國) in the defense of
their State and eventually conquered the State
of Wu (Wu kuo 吳國) in the Spring and Autumn
(Ch'un ch'iu 春秋) Period.

48. Chi⁴ 季

According to <u>Yüan ho hsing tsuan</u> 元何姓纂, the
founder of the surname was Chi Lien 季連 who was
a great grandson of Chu-jung shih 祝融氏 of the
lineage of Huang-ti 黃帝. The descendants of
the family initially settled in Lung-ch'üan
龍泉, Che-chiang 浙江 province.

See also Kuei⁴ 桂, Kung¹-yeh³ 公冶.

49. Ch'i¹ 漆

See Ch'i¹-tiao¹ 漆雕.

50. Ch'i² 蘄

According to <u>Hsing yüan</u> 姓苑, the surname Ch'i 蘄
derived from the place name Ch'i-ch'un 蘄春,
located in the present Ch'i-ch'un hsien 蘄春縣,
Hu-pei 湖北 province. Ch'i was later adopted as
a common surname by its residents.

51. Ch'i² 齊

<u>T'ung chih Shih tsu lüeh</u> 通志氏族略 says: The
surname Ch'i 齊 originated from the name of a
feudal territory, the State of Ch'i (Ch'i kuo
齊國), bestowed on Chiang T'ai-kung 姜太公
during the Chou 周 dynasty. The State of Ch'i
was located in the present Ling-tzu hsien
臨淄縣, Shan-tung 山東 province.

52. Ch'i² 祈

According to <u>T'ung chih Shih tsu lüeh</u> 通志氏族略, the surname Ch'i 祈 branched from the surname Chi 姬 of the ancestral line of Huang-ti 黃帝 and originated from the name of a vassal state, the District of Ch'i (Ch'i i 祈邑), bestowed on the Grand Master (ta-fu 大夫) Ch'i Hsi 祈奚, of the State of Chin (Chin kuo 晉國) in the Spring and Autumn (Ch'un ch'iu 春秋) Period and was later adopted as the common surname by his descendants. The family settled initially in Ch'i hsien 祈縣 (near T'ai-yüan 太原, Shan-hsi 山西 province) where the District of Ch'i was located.

See also Yang²-she² 羊舌.

53. Chi¹-kuan¹ 丌官

<u>Hsing shih hsün yüan</u> 姓氏尋源 describes the origin of the surname Chi-kuan 丌官 as follows: Chi 丌 is the synonym of Chi 笄, the hairpin used for fastening hair. In antiquity, women who reached maturity at the age of fifteen, a ceremony would be held and they would start wearing hairpins from that moment on. Chi-kuan 笄官 were the officials in charge of these ceremonies which were established in the Chou 周 dynasty. The name of the official post was later adopted as a common surname by the descendants whose senior family members were on the post.

54. Chi⁴-sun¹ 季孫

According to <u>Shih pen</u> 世本, the surname Chi-sun 季孫 came from the ancestral line of the Duke Huan (Huan kung 桓公), from the State of Lu (Lu kuo 魯國) in the Spring and Autumn (Ch'un ch'iu 春秋) Period and its founder was Chi Yu 季友, who was the youngest son of the Duke Huan. Chi-sun (meaning the grandson of Chi) was adopted as the common surname by the grandson of Chi Yu and the family originally settled in Shan-tung 山東 province.

See also Kung¹-hsi¹ 公西.

## 55. Ch'i¹-tiao¹ 漆雕

According to Lu shih 路史, the surname Ch'i-tiao 漆雕 follows the ancestral line of the Earl of T'ai (T'ai po 泰伯) who was an uncle of Chou Wen-wang 周文王 from the State of Wu (Wu kuo 吳國) in the Spring and Autumn (Ch'un ch'iu 春秋) Period. A representative of this family was Ch'i-tiao K'ai 漆雕開 who was a disciple of Confucius. After the Han 漢 dynasty, this surname was rarely encountered and the reason was explained in Ming hsien shih tsu yen hsing lei kao 名賢氏族言行類稿 as follows: Following the generation of Ch'i-tiao K'ai 漆雕開 from the State of Lu (Lu kuo 魯國), many of his descendants adopted the single surname Ch'i 漆 which caused the decline of the multiple surname Ch'i-tiao.

## 56. Chia¹ 家

The surname came from two sources: 1. According to Ming hsien shih tsu yen hsing lei kao 名賢氏族言行類稿, the surname originated from Chia Fu 家父, a grand master (ta-fu 大夫) under the reign of Yu-wang (幽王, 781-770 B.C.) in the Western Chou (Hsi Chou 西周) dynasty. 2. Hsing shih k'ao lüeh 姓氏考略 points out that the surname Chia originated from Chia shih 家氏 of the State of Lu (Lu kuo 魯國) in Shan-tung 山東 province. The Chia family settled primarily in Kan-su 甘肅 province.

## 57. Chia² 郟

The surname Chia 郟 derived from two sources: 1. According to Yüan ho hsing tsuan 元何姓纂, Chou Ch'eng-wang 周成王 was enthroned in Chia and its residents adopted the locale name as their common surname and settled in K'ai-feng 開封, Ho-nan 河南 province. The Chia family later pervaded Ch'eng-kao 成皋, Ho-nan 河南 and Wu-ling 武陵, Hu-nan 湖南 provinces. 2. Hsing yüan 姓苑 points out that the founder of the surname was Chia Chang 郟張 who was a grand master (ta-fu 大夫) in the Spring and Autumn (Ch'un ch'iu 春秋) Period. The surname Chia was adopted from the name of a vassal state, the District of Chia (Chia i 郊邑), which was bestowed on his progenitor.

58. Chia³ 賈

According to Yüan ho hsing tsuan 元何姓纂, Chia 賈 originated as the name of a feudal territory, the State of Chia (Chia kuo 賈國), bestowed on a son of T'ang Shu-yü 唐叔虞 during the reign of Chou K'ang-wang (周康王, 1078-1052 B.C.). The State of Chia (Chia kuo 賈國) was later defeated by the State of Chin (Chin kuo 晉國) and Chia 賈 became a common surname since that time. The State of Chia was located in Wu-wei 武威, Kan-su 甘肅 province where the Chia family initially settled.

59. Chia³ 甲

According to Feng shu t'ung 風俗通 and Tso chuan 左傳, the surname Chia 甲 branched from the surname 甲父 and initially derived from the name of an ancient state, the State of Chia-fu 甲父.

60. Chia³-fu³ 甲父

See Chia³ 甲.

61. Chiang¹ 江

According to Yüan ho hsing tsuan 元何姓纂, Chiang 江 originated from the name of the feudal territory, Chiang-ling 江陵, bestowed on Po I 伯益, who was a great grandson of Chuan Hsü 顓頊. After the State of Chiang (Chiang kuo 江國) was defeated by the State of Ch'u (Ch'u kuo 楚國) during the Spring and Autumn (Ch'un ch'iu 春秋) Period, the descendants of Po I adopted Chiang as their common surname in his memory.

62. Chiang¹ 姜

The founder of the family name Chiang 姜 was Yen-ti (炎帝, 2737-2697? B.C.). Chiang originated from the name of his birthplace which was near the Chiang River (Chiang-shui 姜水). It is a branch of the Chi River (Chi-shui 岐水) and both of them are located in Chi-shan hsien 岐山縣, Shen-hsi 陝西 province.

See also Lu² 盧, Po² 伯.

63. Chiang³ 蔣

According to <u>Tso chuan</u> 左傳, the founder of the surname Chiang 蔣 was Po Ling 伯齡 who was the third son of the Duke of Chou (Chou kung 周公). The surname originated from the name of a vassal state located in the Village of Chiang (Chiang hsiang 蔣鄉) and it was bestowed on Po Ling and later adopted as a common surname by his descendants. The family initially settled in the northeastern part of Ho-nan 河南 province where Chiang hsiang 蔣鄉 was located.

64. Ch'iang² 強

The surname Ch'iang 強 derived from the following two sources traced in <u>Hsing yüan</u> 姓苑: 1. The surname came from the ancestral line of Huang-ti 黃帝 and its founder was Yü Ch'iang 禹彊. Since Ch'iang 彊 and Ch'iang 強 were used interchangeably in ancient times, both names were later adopted as common surnames by his descendants. 2. The surname Ch'iang 強 derived from the ancestral line of Yen-ti 炎帝. Many of his descendants were marquises (chu-hou 諸侯) in the State of Ch'i (Ch'i kuo 齊國) of the Spring and Authum (Ch'un ch'iu 春秋) Period. Ch'iang was adopted as a common surname by Yen-ti's descendant Kung Shu-ch'iang 公叔強 from the State of Ch'i (Ch'i kuo 齊國) and the family settled primarily in Kan-su 甘肅 province.

65. Ch'iang² 彊

See Ch'iang² 強.

66. Chiao¹ 焦

According to both <u>Kuang yün</u> 廣韻 and <u>T'ung chih Shih tsu lüeh</u> 通志氏族略, Chiao 焦 derived from two sources: 1. The surname Chiao came from the name of a feudal territory, the State of Chiao (Chiao kuo 焦國), bestowed on a descendant of Huang-ti 黃帝 and located in Ho-nan 河南 province. 2. The surname Chiao branched from the surname Chou 周 and was the name of a feudal territory bestowed on a descendant of Yen-ti 炎帝 by Chou Wu-wang 周武王.

See also Chou[1] 周.

## 67. Ch'iao[2] 喬

The predecessor of the surname Ch'iao 喬 was Ch'iao 橋. <u>Yüan ho hsing tsuan</u> 元何姓纂 and <u>Wan hsing t'ung p'u</u> 萬姓統譜 state that both Ch'iaos came from blood relatives and were branched from the surname Chi 姬 of the ancestral line of Huang-ti 黃帝. According to these sources: After Huang-ti's death, he was burried on the Mountain of Ch'iao (Ch'iao shan 橋山) and his descendants adopted Ch'iao 橋 as their common surname in memory of him. In the Later Chou (Hou Chou 後周) period, an emperor commanded the change of surname Ch'iao 橋 to its simplified form Ch'iao 喬 and it was adopted as a common surname since that time. The Ch'iao 喬 family originally settled in Ssu-ch'uan 四川 and Shan-hsi 山西 provinces.

See also Ch'iao[2] 橋.

## 68. Ch'iao[2] 橋

<u>Yüan ho hsing tsuan</u> 元何姓纂 and <u>Wan hsing t'ung p'u</u> 萬姓統譜 state that both Ch'iaos came from blood relatives and were branched from the surname Chi 姬 of the ancestral line of Huang-ti 黃帝. According to these sources, Huang-ti was burried on the Mountain of Ch'iao (Ch'iao shan 橋山), his descendants adopted Ch'iao 橋 as their common surname in memory of him. The surname Ch'iao 橋 was changed to Ch'iao 喬 by an emperor in the Later Chou (Hou chou 後周) period.

See also Ch'iao[2] 喬.

## 69. Ch'iao[2] 譙

The surname Ch'iao 譙 derived from two sources. 1. According to <u>Hsing shih k'ao lüeh</u> 姓氏考略, the surname Ch'iao 譙 branched from the surname Chi 姬 of the royal lineage of Chou Wen-wang 周文王 and derived from the name of the feudal territory, the State of Ch'iao (Ch'iao kuo 譙國) which was bestowed on Duke Chao-kung Shih 召公奭 in the Chou 周 dynasty. Ch'iao was adopted as the common surname by his descendants and they settled initially in Ssu-ch'uan 四川 province where the State of Ch'iao was located. 2. <u>Yüan ho hsing tsuan</u> 元何姓纂 states the origin of the surname as follows: The surname derived from the name of the feudal territory, the State of Ch'iao (Ch'iao kuo 譙國), which was bestowed on Chou Wen-wang's 周文王 thirteenth son Chen To 振鐸. After the State of Ch'iao was defeated by the State of Sung 宋, the descendants of Chen To adopted Ch'iao as their common surname.

## 70. Chien[3] 簡

The surname Chien 簡 originated from two sources. 1. <u>Yüan ho hsing tsuan</u> 元何姓纂 and <u>Fan-yang Chien shih chia p'u</u> 范陽簡氏家譜 trace the surname to the ancestral line of Earl of Chien (Chien po 簡伯), whose real name was Hu Chü-chü 狐鞠居, from the State of Chin (Chin kuo 晉國) in the Spring and Authum (Ch'un ch'iu 春秋) Period. He was bestowed on the vassal state of Hsü (Hsü i 續邑) and named Hsü Chien-po 續簡伯. Chien was adopted as a common surname by his descendants and the family settled in Fan-yan 范陽 and Cho Commandery (Cho chün 涿郡) in Ho-pei 河北 province. 2. According to <u>Hsing yüan</u> 姓苑, the surname Chien 簡 branched from the surname Chien 檢 due to the change of surname by Chien Ming 檢明 in the Han 漢 dynasty. This branch of the Chien 簡 family originally settled in Ho-pei and later expanded to provinces in southern China including Chiang-hsi 江西, Fu-chien 福建, and Kuang-tung 廣東.

See also Chien[3] 檢, Hsü[4] 續.

71.  Chien[3] 檢

According to the Ch'ing 清 scholar Chang Shu
張澍, the surname Chien 檢 derived from the name
of the official post, chien-ch'a-kuan 檢察官,
the Inspector General, whose prescribed duty was
to keep watch over the officialdom and impeach
or otherwise discipline those who violated the
law, proper administrative procedures, customary
morality, etc. In the Han 漢 dynasty, Chien Ming
檢明 changed his surname to Chien 簡 and it was
later adopted as a common surname by his
descendants.

See also Chien[3] 簡.

72.  Ch'ien[2] 錢

T'ung chih Shih tsu lüeh 通志氏族略 states: The
surname Ch'ien 錢 originated from the name of
the official post, the treasurer (ch'ien-fu-
shang-shih 錢府上士).    It was adopted as a
common surname ever since a descendant of Chuan
Hsü (顓頊，2513-2435? B.C.), whose forename was
Fu 孚, assumed the position in the Chou 周
dynasty.    The family initially settled in Hsü-
chou 徐州, Chiang-su 江蘇 province.

73.  Ch'ih[1] 郗

Yüan ho hsing tsuan 元何姓纂 states: The surname
Ch'ih 郗 follows the ancestral line of Chuan Hsü
顓頊 and originated from the name of a vassal
state, the District of Ch'ih (Ch'ih i 郗邑),
bestowed on a son of Su Fen 蘇忿 in the Chou 周
dynasty.    Ch'ih was adopted as a common surname
by the descendants of Su Fen and they settled
initially in Ch'in-yang hsien 沁陽縣, Ho-nan
河南 province where the District of Ch'ih was
located and later prospered in Kao-p'ing hsien
高平縣, Shan-hsi 山西 province.

See also Su[1] 蘇.

## 74. Ch'ih² 池

According to <u>Feng shu t'ung</u> 風俗通 and <u>Ming hsien shih tsu yen hsing lei kao</u> 名賢氏族言行類稿, the origin of the surname Ch'ih (meaning pond 池) was traced to the residence of its founder. The person lived near a pond so that he adopted Ch'ih 池 as his surname. The Ch'ih family initially settled in Ch'en-liu 陳留 and Hsi-p'ing 西平 of the Ho-nan 河南 province and later expanded to Fu-chien 福建, Kuang-tung 廣東 and Yün-nan 雲南 provinces.

## 75. Chin¹ 金

According to <u>Ming hsien shih tsu yen hsing lei kao</u> 名賢氏族言行類稿, the surname Chin 金 came from two sources: 1. It originated from Chin-t'ien shih 金天氏, the social name (hao 號) of Shao Hao (少昊, 2597-2513? B.C.) who was a son of Huang-ti 黃帝. Chin-t'ien shih established the system of trade based on gold (chin 金) and was named for his contribution. The family first settled in C'hü-fu hsien 曲阜縣, Shan-tung 山東 province and later expanded to the city of Hsü-chou 徐州 in Chiang-su 江蘇 province. 2. The surname derived from Jin Jih-ch'an 金日磾. He was originally a Hsiung-nu 匈奴 prince who later surrendered to Han Wu-ti (漢武帝, 140-86 B.C.) and became his grand minister (ta-ch'en 大臣). He was awarded the honorary title Jin Jih-ch'an 金日磾 for his loyalty to the Han dynasty. This branch of the Chin family settled in Ch'ang-an 長安, the ancient capital of Shen-hsi 陝西 province.

## 76. Chin⁴ 靳

According to <u>Feng shu t'ung</u> 風俗通 and <u>T'ung chih Shih tsu lüeh</u> 通志氏族略, the surname Chin 靳 originated from the name of a vassal state, the District of Chin (Chin i 靳邑), bestowed on Chin Shang 靳尚, who was a grand master (ta-fu 大夫) in the State of Ch'u (Ch'u kuo 楚國) during the Warring States (Chan kuo 戰國) Period. The ancestral settlement of the family was in Hsi-ho 西河, Shang-tung 山東 province.

## 77. Chin⁴ 晉

Yüan ho hsing tsuan 元何姓纂 and Hsing shih k'ao lüeh 姓氏考略 trace the genealogy of the surname Chin 晉 as follows: The founder of the surname Chin was T'ang Shu-yü 唐叔虞. He was the third son of Chou Wu-wang 周武王 and was bestowed with the feudal territory of the State of T'ang (T'ang kuo 唐國) during the reign of Chou Ch'eng-wang 周成王 and later his descendants adopted T'ang as their common surname. The State of T'ang was changed to the name of the State of Chin (Chin kuo 晉國) due to the Chin River (Chin shui 晉水) which ran through. Following the name change, Chin 晉 was subsequently adopted as the common surname by its citizens. The family initially settled in Shan-hsi 山西 and lately expanded to Kuo Commandery (Kuo chün 虢郡, presently Ssu-shui hsien 汜水縣 in Ho-nan 河南) and P'ing-yang 平陽 (presently Lin-fen hsien 臨汾縣 in Shan-hsi 山西 province).

See also T'ang² 唐.

## 78. Ch'in¹ 欽

Wei shu 魏書 traces the origin of the surname Ch'in 欽 to the tribe of Wu-huan 烏桓 of the Hu 胡 People. The tribe lived in the region of Ho-pei 河北 and Shan-hsi 山西 provinces in the Han 漢 dynasty. According to the book, Ch'in Chih-shang 欽志賞 was the chieftain of the tribe and the name of the tribe was inspired by the Wu-huan Mountain (Wu-huan shan 烏桓山) where the tribe originally settled. Many of the Ch'in families later expanded to Che-chiang 浙江 and An-hui 安徽 provinces.

## 79. Ch'in² 秦

The surname Ch'in 秦 belongs to the ancestral line of Huang-ti 黃帝 and it came from two different sources: 1. Yüan ho hsing tsuan 元何姓纂 says the name originated in Kan-su 甘肅 province of the lineage of Chuan Hsü 顓頊 and 2.

<u>Ku chin hsing shih shu pien cheng</u> 古今姓氏書辨證
states that the name derived from the city of
T'ai-yüan 太原 in Shan-hsi 山西 province.

80. Ch'in² 琴

The word "ch'in 琴" literally means a Chinese
lute or guitar with seven or five strings and
the name's origin is closely tied to its
literary meaning. According to <u>Hsing shih k'ao</u>
<u>lüeh</u> 姓氏考略, the surname Ch'in 琴 derived from
the name of the profession, ch'in-shih 琴師,
who was the master or player of stringed
instrument. Ch'in was later adopted as a common
surname by the descendants of the family whose
ancestor was a ch'in-shih. The family
originally settled in T'ien-shui 天水, Kan-su
甘肅 and later expanded to the south, in Kuang-
tung 廣東 province.

81. Ching¹ 荆

The surname Ching 荆 originated the place named
Ching chou 荆州. It was the former name of the
State of Ch'u (Ch'u kuo 楚國) in the Spring and
Authum (Ch'un ch'iu 春秋) Period during its pre-
feudal stage. <u>Hsing shih k'ao lüeh</u> 姓氏考略 and
<u>T'ung chih Shih tsu lüeh</u> 通志氏族略 trace the
name's origin to the following two sources. 1.
The surname Ching branched from the surname Hua
華 and was the former name of the State of Ch'u.
It was adopted as the common surname by a son of
Lu Chung 陸終 from the Hua family and originally
came from the ancestral line of the Emperor
Chuan Hsü 顓頊. The family settled primarily in
Kuang-ling 廣陵, presently in Chiang-tu hsien
江都縣, Chiang-su 江蘇 province. 2. The surname
Ching branched from the surname Ch'ing 慶 and
originated in Shan-tung 山東 province. Its
founder was Ching K'e 荆軻 who changed his
surname from Ch'ing 慶 to Ching 荆 during the
Warring States (Chan kuo 戰國) Period.

See also Ch'ing⁴ 慶, Hua² 華.

82. Ching¹ 經

According to Hsing shih k'ao lüeh 姓氏考略, the founder of the surname Ching 經 was the Marquise of Ching (Ching hou 經侯) from the State of Wei (Wei kuo 魏國) in the Warring States (Chan kuo 戰國) Period. The ancestral region of the family was P'ing-yang 平陽, located in the present Ling-feng hsien 臨汾縣, Shan-hsi 山西 province.

83. Ching³ 井

According to Shang yu lu 尚友錄 and Yüan ho hsing tsuan 元何姓纂, the surname Ching 井 originated from the Earl of Ching (Ching po 井伯) who was a grand master (ta-fu 大夫) in the State of Yü (Yü kuo 虞國) during the Chou 周 dynasty. The Ching family originally settled in P'ing-lu hsien 平陸縣, Shan-hsi 山西 province and later expanded to Fu-feng hsien 扶風縣, Shen-hsi 陝西 province.

84. Ching³ 景

The surname Ching 景 derived from two sources during the Spring and Authum (Ch'un ch'iu 春秋) Period. 1. According to Yüan ho hsing tsuan 元何姓纂, the surname Ching was traced to Ching shih 景氏, who was a duke (kung 公) of the State of Ch'u (Ch'u kuo 楚國) and belongs to the lineage of Chuan Hsü 顓頊. The Ching family prospered in Shen-hsi 陝西 province. 2. Hsing shih k'ao lüeh 姓氏考略 says the surname was adopted from the posthumous title of Ch'i Ching-kung 齊景公 who belongs to the lineage of Yen-ti 炎帝.

85. Ch'ing² 黥

Chung-kuo hsing shih chi 中國姓氏集 traces the origin of the surname Ch'ing 黥 to Ying Pu 英布 in the Han 漢 dynasty. He was demoted by the Han 漢 Emperor Kao-tsu 高祖 (Liu Pang 劉邦) and was penalized by the punishment of tattooing his face (ch'ing mien 黥面) and demanding the change of name into Ch'ing Pu 黥布.

See also Ying¹ 英.

## 86. Ch'ing⁴ 慶

The founder of the surname Ch'ing 慶 was Ch'ing Ch'un 慶純 of the Eastern Han (Tung Han 東漢, A.D. 25-220) dynasty. T'ung chih Shih tsu lüeh 通志氏族略 and Hsing shih k'ao lüeh 姓氏考略 both trace the evolution of the surname Ch'ing to the surname Ho 賀 as follows: The surname Ch'ing branched to the surname Ho during the Eastern Han dynasty, when Ch'ing Ch'un 慶純 changed his surname into Ho 賀 to avoid the taboo name of Ch'ing 慶 used by the father of the Emperor An-ti (安帝, A.D. 107-126).

See also Ho⁴ 賀, Ching¹ 荊.

## 87. Ch'iu¹ 邱

The adoption of the surname Ch'iu 邱 was the result of the change of name from the surname Ch'iu 丘. The name change occurred during the reign of the Ch'ing 清 Emperor Yüng-cheng (雍正, A.D. 1723-1736) to pay his respects to the great Chinese philosopher, Confucius, whose surname was Ch'iu 丘.

See also Ch'iu¹ 丘.

## 88. Ch'iu¹ 秋

According to Lu shih 路史, the founder of the family name Ch'iu 秋 was Shao Hao (少昊, 2597-2513? B.C.) who was a son of Huang-ti 黃帝. Because of the lack of historical documentation, the original settlement of the Ch'iu family was unknown.

## 89. Ch'iu¹ 丘

The surname Ch'iu 丘 originated from two sources. 1. According to Yüan ho hsing tsuan 元何姓纂, the Grand Duke of Ch'i (Ch'i t'ai-kung 齊太公) was enfeoffed at the feudal territory of Ying-ch'iu 營丘, located in the present Chang-le hsien 昌樂縣, Shan-tung 山東 province. The descendants of his family adopted Ch'iu as their common surname and the family prospered in Fu-fung 扶風, Shen-hsi 陝西 province.    2. <u>Wei shu kuan shih chih</u> 魏書官氏志 says the name appeared during the Southern and Northern Dynasties (Nan-pei ch'ao 南北朝).  Ch'iu-tun shih　丘敦氏, who belongs to the nomadic group of the Hu 胡 People, was the origin of the surname and Ch'iu was in use as a common surname since that time.

See also Ch'iu[1] 邱.

## 90.  Ch'iu[2] 裘

The surname Ch'iu 裘 derived from two sources: 1. <u>Hsing shih chi chiu p'ien</u> 姓氏急就篇 says the name originated from the name of a vassal state, the District of Ch'iu (Ch'iu i 裘邑), bestowed on a grand master (ta-fu 大夫) of the State of Wei (Wei kuo 衛國) in the Chou 周 dynasty.   The State of Wei was located in the area comprised of Ho-nan　河南 and Ho-pei 河北 provinces, where the Ch'iu family initially settled and later prospered in southern China. 2. According to <u>T'ung chih</u> 通志 and <u>Hsing shih k'ao lüeh</u> 姓氏考略, the surname Ch'iu 裘 branched from the surname Ch'ou 仇.  The change to the name Ch'iu 裘 was to avoid revenge on the family from its rivals.  This Ch'iu family originally settled in Po-hai 渤海, Shan-tung 山東 province.

See also Ch'ou[2] 仇.

## 91.  Cho[2] 卓

<u>Chan kuo ts'e</u> 戰國策 states the origin of surname Cho 卓 as follows: The surname Cho follows the ancestral line of Cho Hua 卓滑 who was a grand master (ta-fu 大夫) of the State of Ch'u (Ch'u kuo 楚國) during the Spring and Autumn (Ch'un ch'iu 春秋) Period.   The family initially settled in Ch'iung-lai hsien 邛崍縣 (presently called Lin-ch'iung hsien 臨邛縣) and later prospered in Yang-ch'eng hsien 陽城縣 (presently called Hsi-ho hsien 西河縣) of the Ssu-ch'uan 四川 province.

## 92.  Chou[1] 周

According to Yüan ho hsing tsuan 元何姓纂, Chou
周 originated from the name of the feudal
territory, the State of Chou (Chou kuo 周國),
bestowed on T'ai-wang 太王 and was later adopted
by his son, Wen-wang 文王 as his surname. The
State of Chou was located in the present Ch'i-
shan hsien 岐山縣, Shen-hsi 陝西 province where
the family initially settled and later expanded
eastward to Ho-nan 河南 province.

See also Chiao¹ 焦.

93. Ch'ou² 仇

Yüan ho hsing tsuan 元何姓纂 states: The
surname Ch'ou 仇 derived from Ch'ou Mu 仇牧, a
grand master (ta-fu 大夫) of the State of Sung
(Sung kuo 宋國) in the Spring and Autumn (Ch'un
ch'iu 春秋) Period. The original settlement of
the family was in Nan-yang hsien 南陽縣, Ho-nan
河南 province.

See also Ch'iu² 裘.

94. Chu¹ 朱

According to Yüan ho hsing tsuan 元何姓纂, the
surname Chu 朱 originated from the name of a
feudal territory, the State of Chu (Chu kuo
邾國), bestowed on Ts'ao Chia 曹挾, who was a
descendant of Chuan Hsü 顓頊; this took place
during the reign of Chou Wu- wang 周武王. The
State of Chu (Chu kuo 邾國) was renamed the
State of Chu-lou (Chu-lou kuo 邾婁國) in the
Spring and Autumn (Ch'un ch'iu 春秋) Period and
further changed into the State of Tsou (Tsou kuo
鄒國). The location of Tsou kuo was in Tsou
hsien 鄒縣, Shan-tung 山東 province. After Ch'u
Hsüan-wang 楚宣王 defeated the State of Chu, the
descendants of Ts'ao Chia's family removed the
radical on the right side of Chu 邾 and adopted
朱 as their common surname. Kung-yang chuan
公羊傳 has the following paragraph: The Chu
family's place of origin was in Tsou hsien 鄒縣,
Shan-tung 山東 province where Chu kuo 邾國 was
located.

See also Lou² 婁, Lü²-ch'iu¹ 閭丘, Ts'ao² 曹, Tsou¹ 鄒.

## 95. Chu¹ 諸

The surname Chu 諸 derived from the following two sources in the Spring and Autumn (Ch'un ch'iu 春秋) Period: 1. According to <u>Hsing yüan 姓苑</u>, the surname originated from the name of a vassal state, the District of Chu (Chu i 諸邑), in the State of Lu (Lu kuo 魯國), located in the present Chu-chang hsien 諸城縣, Shan-tung 山東 province. 2. <u>Ming hsien shih tsu yen hsing lei kao</u> 名賢氏族言行類稿 says: The founder of the surname was Chu Chi-ying 諸稽郢, who was a grand master (ta-fu 大夫) of the State of Yüeh (Yüeh kuo 越國). This branch of the Chu family originally settled in Kuei-chi hsien 會稽縣, Shan-tung 山東 province.

## 96. Chu² 竺

The surname Chu 竺 derived from two sources. 1. T'ien-chu 天竺 was the ancient name of India. According to <u>Hsing shih k'ao lüeh 姓氏考略</u>, the founder of the surname Chu was Chu T'zu 竺次 who came from T'ien-chu. He stayed in China during the reign of Han Hsüan-ti (漢宣帝, 73-48 B.C.) for Buddhist preaching. The monks adopted "Chu 竺" as part of their names to distinguish themselves. As the Buddhist doctrine gradually takes root in the people's minds, many of them adopted Chu as their common surname as well. The initial settlement of the families was Tung-hai 東海 located near the border of Shan-tung 山東 and Chiang-su 江蘇 provinces. At the end of the Sung 宋 and Ming 明 dynasties, the Chu families expanded to Ning-p'o 寧波 and Feng-hua 奉化 in Che-chiang 浙江 province. 2. <u>Hsing yüan</u> 姓苑 says: The surname Chu 竺 was trnasformed from the surname Chu 竹 and the founder the surname was Chu Yen 竺晏 in the Han 漢 dynasty.

See also Chu² 竹.

## 97. Chu² 竹

According to <u>Wan hsing t'ung p'u</u> 萬姓統譜, <u>Ming
hsien shih tsu yen hsing lei kao</u>
名賢氏族言行類稿 and <u>T'ung chih Shih tsu lüeh</u>
通志氏族略, the surname Chu 竹 follows the
lineage of King Ku-chu 孤竹 (Ku-chu chün 孤竹君)
who was bestowed in Liao-hsi 遼西 (in western
Liao-ning 遼寧 province) by the Shang 商 king
Ch'eng-t'ang 成湯. The descendants of Ku-chu
chün adopted Chu as their common surname and
they settled initially in Tung-p'ing 東平,
Kuang-hsi 廣西 province and later populated Yün-
nan 雲南 and Kuei-tsou 貴州 provinces.

See also Chu² 竺.

98. Chu² 儲

<u>Hsing shih k'ao lüeh</u> 姓氏考略 describes the
genealogy of the surname Chu 儲 as follows: Chu
originated from the Grand master (ta-fu 大夫)
Chu Tzu 儲子 of the State of Ch'i (Ch'i kuo
齊國) in the Warring States (Chan kuo 戰國)
Period. The family prospered in Shan-tung 山東
province.

99. Chu⁴ 祝

<u>Yüan ho hsing tsuan</u> 元何姓纂 and <u>T'ang shu tsai
hsiang shih hsi piao</u> 唐書宰相世系表 trace the
origin of the surname Chu 祝 from the following
two sources: 1. The surname Chu 祝 branched from
the surname Chi 姬 of the ancestral line of
Huang-ti 黃帝 and originated from the name of a
feudal territory bestowed on his descendant by
Chou Wu-wang 周武王 in the Shang 商 dynasty.
After the State of Chu 祝 merged with the State
of Ch'i 齊, the descendants from the State of
Chu adopted Chu 祝 as their common surname. 2.
The surname Chu 祝 derived from the title of the
official post, chu-shih 祝史, who was charged
as the Supplication Scribe in the Court of the
Imperial Sacrifices during the Northern Wei (Pei
Wei 北魏) and T'ang 唐 dynasties. 3. <u>T'ung chih
Shih tsu lüeh</u> 通志氏族略 further points out the
name's origin to the change of surname from the
surname Hua-lu 化盧. It was initially the
surname of the tribesmen who lived on the

borderland, particularly referring to the Mongolians, Tibetans and other ethnic minorities. They relocated and settled in China and changed their surname to Chu 祝.

100. Chü¹ 居

Yüan ho hsing tsuan 元何姓纂 and Ming hsien shih tsu yen hsing lei kao 名賢氏族言行類稿 describe the origin of the surname Chü 居 as follows: The surname Chü was adopted from the name of the Grand master (ta-fu 大夫) Hsien Ch'ieh-chü 先且居 of the State of Chin (Chin kuo 晉國) in the Spring and Autumn (Ch'un ch'iu 春秋) Period. The Chü family originally settled in Po-hai 渤海, Ho-pei 河北 province and later prospered in Chiang-su 江蘇 and Hu-pei 湖北 provinces.

101. Chü² 鞠

The surnames Chü 鞠 and Ch'ü 麴 derived from the same blood line. According to Yüan ho hsing tsuan 元何姓纂 and Ming hsien shih tsu yen hsing lei kao 名賢氏族言行類稿, Chü 鞠 was a grandson of Hou Chi 后稷 who was the founding father of the Chou 周 dynasty. By the time of the Han 漢 dynasty, a descendant of the Chü family, Chü Pi 鞠閟, relocated to Wen-chung 溫中 to escape from his enemies. He changed his surname to Ch'ü 麴 and settled in Hsi-p'ing hsien 西平縣, Ho-nan 河南 province.

See also Ch'ü² 麴.

102. Ch'ü¹ 曲

Wan hsing t'ung p'u 萬姓統譜 and T'ung chih Shih tsu lüeh 通志氏族略 trace the origin of the surname Ch'ü 曲 from the ancestral line of Chou Wen-wang 周文王 to his descendant, a son of the Marquise of Mu (Mu hou 穆侯) of the State of Chin (Chin kuo 晉國) who was enfeoffed at Ch'ü-wo 曲沃 by his father. Subsequently, the descendants of the family adopted Ch'ü as their common surname and settled in Yen-men 雁門, Shen-hsi 陝西 province where the site of the feudal territory Ch'ü-wo 曲沃 was located.

## 103. Ch'ü[1] 屈

According to <u>Shang yu lu</u> 尚友錄 and <u>Wan hsing t'ung p'u</u> 萬姓統譜, the surname Ch'ü 屈 branched from the surname Mieh 芈 of the lineage of Wu-wang 武王 of the State of Ch'u (Ch'u kuo 楚國) in the Spring and Autumn (Ch'un ch'iu 春秋) Period and originated from the name of a vassal state, the District of Ch'ü (Ch'ü i 屈邑), which was bestowed on Wu-wang's son. Ch'ü was later adopted as the common surname by his descendants and the family settled in Ho-nan 河南 province.

## 104. Ch'ü[2] 麹

According to <u>Yüan ho hsing tsuan</u> 元和姓纂 and <u>Ming hsien shih tsu yen hsing lei kao</u> 名賢氏族言行類稿, the surname Ch'ü 麹 branched from the surname Chü 鞠 during the Han 漢 dynasty. The evolution of the surnames is as follows: The surname Chü 鞠 first appeared in the Chou 周 dynasty. During the Han 漢 dynasty, a descendant from the Chü family, Chü Pi 鞠閟, relocated to Wen-chung 溫中 to escape from his enemies. He changed his surname to Ch'ü 麹 and settled in Hsi-p'ing hsien 西平縣, Ho-nan 河南 province.

See also Chü[2] 鞠.

## 105. Ch'ü[2] 瞿

According to <u>Hsing shih k'ao lüeh</u> 姓氏考略, the surname Ch'ü 瞿 derived from Ch'ü t'ang hsia 瞿唐峽, the name of the famous gorge in the Middle Yangtze, which passes through the area of Feng-chieh 奉節, Ssu-ch'uan 四川 province. Ch'ü was adopted initially by the people living in that area and the family later expanded to Sung-yang hsien 松陽縣, Che-chiang 浙江 province.

## 106. Ch'u[3] 楚

The surname Ch'u 楚 derived from two sources.

1. According to <u>Hsing yüan</u> 姓苑 and <u>Ming hsien shih tsu yen hsing lei kao</u> 名賢氏族言行類稿: The surname Ch'u branched from the surname Mi 芈 of the ancestral line of Chou Wen-wang 周文王 and originated from the name of the feudal territory, the State of Ch'u (Ch'u kuo 楚國), which was bestowed on Hsiung I 熊繹 by Chou Ch'eng-wang 周成王. Ch'u was adopted as the common surname by the descendants of Hsiung I and the family settled in Hu-nan 湖南 and Hu-pei 湖北 provinces where the site of Ch'u kuo was originally located. 2. The second source of the surname Ch'u 楚 came from the surname Lin 林. <u>Wan hsing t'ung p'u</u> 萬姓統譜 traces the name's origin to Lin Ch'u 林楚 of the State of Ch'i (Ch'i kuo 齊國) in the Spring and Autumn (Ch'un ch'iu 春秋) Period. Ch'u was later adopted as the common surname by his descendants.

See also Mi$^3$ 芈, Lin$^2$ 林.

## 107. Ch'u$^3$ 褚

The surname Ch'u 褚 was traced to two different sources. 1. <u>Hsing shih k'ao lüeh</u> 姓氏考略 and <u>Tso chuan</u> 左傳 both state that the name came from the road station, Ch'u shih t'ing 褚氏亭, which was located in Lo-yang hsien 洛陽縣, Ho-nan 河南 province. 2. Ch'u derived from the name of the official post, ch'u-shih 褚師, a position similar to county chief or city mayor and existed in the states (kuo 國) of the various marquises (chu-hou 諸侯) during the Spring and Autumn (Ch'un ch'iu 春秋) Period.

## 108. Chu$^1$-ko$^3$ 諸葛

The following books have documented the origin of the multiple surname Chu-ko 諸葛: <u>San kuo chih Wu chih Chu-ko Chin chuan</u> 三國志吳志諸葛瑾傳, <u>Feng shu t'ung</u> 風俗通 and <u>T'ung chih Shih tsu lüeh</u> 通志氏族略. According to these sources, the multiple surname was branched from the surname Ko 葛 and the founder of the surname was Ko Ying 葛嬰. He and his descendants resided in Chu-chang hsien 諸城縣, Shan-tung 山東 province and later his offsprings adopted the combination of Chu 諸 and Ko 葛 as their common surname. Because of the site of their original settlement, Chu-chang hsien 諸城縣, was located in Lang-yeh Commandery (Lang-yeh chün 瑯琊郡), the Chu-ko clan adopted Lang-yeh 瑯琊 as its ancestral hall name (t'ang hao 堂號) in memory of their progenitor.

See also Ko[3] 葛.

109. Ch'üan[2] 全

The Ch'üan 全 surname branched from the homonymous surname Ch'üan 泉. According to the prominent Ch'ing 清 scholar Ch'üan Tsu-wang 全祖望 in his book, <u>Chieh ch'i t'ing chi</u> 鮚琦亭集, the surname Ch'üan 泉 derived from the official title of ch'üan-fu 泉府, serving under the head of the Ministry of Education (ti-kuan 地官) and oversees civil administration and social welfare in the Chou 周 dynasty. It was adopted as a common surname and changed into the homonymous surname Ch'üan 全 several generations later. The Ch'üan 全 family originally settled in Ch'ien-t'ang 錢塘, Che-chiang 浙江 province.

See also Ch'üan[2] 泉.

110. Ch'üan[2] 泉

According to <u>Chieh ch'i t'ing chi</u> 鮚琦亭集, the surname Ch'üan 泉 derived from the official title of ch'üan-fu 泉府, serving under the head of the Ministry of Education (ti- kuan 地官) and oversees civil administration and social welfare in the Chou 周 dynasty.

See also Ch'üan[2] 全.

111. Ch'üan[2] 權

The surname Ch'üan 權 derived from two sources. 1. According to <u>T'ang shu tsai hsiang shih hsi piao</u> 唐書宰相世系表, the Shang 商 king Wu-ting 武丁 bestowed the State of Ch'üan (Ch'üan kuo 權國) on his grandson, whose descendants

adopted Ch'üan as their common surname and
settled in the State of Ch'üan which was located
in the present Tang-yang hsien 當陽縣, Hu-pei
湖北 province.    2. <u>Ming hsien shih tsu yen hsing
lei kao</u> 名賢氏族言行類稿 further elaborates the
status of the State of Ch'üan as follows:    The
State of Ch'üan had existed for nearly seven
hundred years until it was defeated by the State
of Ch'u (Ch'u kuo 楚國) in the Spring and Autumn
(Ch'un ch'iu 春秋) Period.    At that time, the
nobleman Tou Min 鬥緡 from the State of Ch'u 楚
assumed the position of District Magistrate
(ling-yin 令尹) of the State of Ch'üan and
subsequently, his descendants adopted Ch'üan as
their common surname.    The family settled and
prospered in T'ien-shui 天水, Kan-su 甘肅
province.    The descendants of Ch'üan families
adopted T'ien-shui as their ancestral hall name
(t'ang ming 堂名) to commemorate their
ancestors.

See also Na¹ 那.

## 112.  Chuan¹-sun¹ 顓孫

According to <u>Shang yu lu</u> 尙友錄 and <u>Feng shu
t'ung</u> 風俗通, the multiple surname Chuan-sun
顓孫 follows the lineage of Yü Ti-shun 虞帝舜.
During the Spring and Autumn (Ch'un ch'iu 春秋)
Period, the feudal prince Chuan Sun 顓孫 of the
State of Ch'en (Ch'en kuo 陳國) took an official
post in the State of Chin (Chin kuo 晉國) and
his descendants later adopted his whole name as
their common surname.    A representative of the
family was Chuan-sun Shih 顓孫師 who was one of
the famous disciples of Confucius in the Spring
and Autumn  Period.

## 113.  Chuang¹ 莊

According to <u>Ming hsien shih tsu yen hsing lei
kao</u> 名賢氏族言行類稿 and <u>Yüan ho hsing tsuan</u>
元何姓纂, the surname Chuang 莊 came from the
ancestral line of Chuang-wang (莊王, 696-681
B.C.) in the State of Ch'u (Ch'u kuo 楚國) of
the Spring and Autumn (Ch'un ch'iu 春秋) Period.
It was adopted posthumously by the descendants

of Chuang-wang in memory of him.  <u>Hsing shih
k'ao lüeh</u> 姓氏考略 further points out that
Chuang Kuang 莊光, a Grand Minister (ta-ch'en
大臣) to Han Ming-ti (A.D. 58-76, 漢明帝),
changed his name to Yen Kuang 嚴光 to avoid
using the same name as that of the Emperor. This
marked the beginning of the surname Yen 嚴.  The
Yen family initially settled in Che-chiang 浙江
province.

See also Nien² 年, Yen² 嚴.

114.  Ch'üeh⁴ 闕

> <u>Hsing shih k'ao lüeh</u> 姓氏考略 traces the
> genealogy of surname Ch'üeh 闕 as follows:  The
> surname Ch'üeh derived from the place name
> Ch'üeh-tang 闕黨 (located in the present Ch'ü-fu
> 曲阜, Shan-tung 山東 province) where the great
> Chinese philosopher Confucius (K'ung-tzu 孔子)
> came from. The Ch'üeh family originally settled
> in Shan-tung and later expanded to P'ei hsien
> 邳縣, Chiang-su 江蘇 province.

115.  Ch'üeh⁴ 卻

> See Pu⁴ 步.

116.  Ch'un²-yü² 淳于

> According to <u>Ku chin hsing shih shu pien cheng</u>
> 古今姓氏書辨證, the surname Ch'un-yü 淳于
> originated from the name of a feudal territory
> bestowed on Duke Ch'un-yü (Ch'un-yü kung 淳于公)
> by Chou Wu-wang 周武王 and was later  adopted as
> a common surname by his descendents.  The family
> initially settled in Shan-tung 山東 province.

117.  Chung¹ 衷

> The surname Chung 衷 came from the following two
> sources: 1. According to <u>Hsing p'u</u> 姓譜, during
> the period of Southern and Northern Dynasties
> (Nan-pei ch'ao 南北朝), the family of Ai Ching-
> yüan 哀景元 escaped from its homeland to Ning-tu
> hsien 寧都縣, Chiang-hsi 江西 province to avoid

revenge by enemies and subsequently changed its surname to Chung 衷. 2. According to <u>Feng shu t'ung</u> 風俗通, the surname Chung 衷 was evolved from the surname Ai 哀 during the reign of Ming Shih-tsung 明世宗 in the Chia-ching 嘉靖 Period. The Ai 哀 family was dissatisfied with its family name because of its meaning. Ai 哀 was changed into Chung 衷, two similar characters with quite different meanings. Ai 哀 means sadness while Chung 衷 means sincereness.

See also Ai[1] 哀.

## 118. Chung[1] 鍾

According to <u>Ming hsien shih tsu yen hsing lei kao</u> 名賢氏族言行類稿, the surnames Chung 鍾 and Chung-li 鍾離 are two branches of the same blood line and were both traced to the place known as Chung-li 鍾離. The Chung family belongs to the ancestral line of Wei-tzu 微子 of the State of Sung (Sung kuo 宋國) in the Spring and Autumn (Ch'un ch'iu 春秋) Period and the founder of the surname was Po Chieh 伯接. The surname Chung-li 鍾離 originated from the name of the vassal state bestowed on his fater, Po Chou-li 伯州犁, and was adopted as a common surname by his son Po Chieh. The family originally settled in Yin-ch'uan 穎川, Ho-nan 河南 province.

See also Chung[1]-li[2] 鍾離.

## 119. Chung[1] 終

<u>Yüan ho hsing tsuan</u> 元何姓纂 traces the origin of the surname Chung 終 to the ancestral line of Huang-ti 黃帝 and the name was derived from his descendant Lu Chung 陸終, who was a son of Chu-jung shih 祝融氏. Chung was later adopted as a common surname and the family settled in Chi-nan 濟南 and Nan-yang 南陽 in Shan-tung 山東 province.

## 120. Chung[4] 仲

The Chung 仲 surname derived from the following sources: 1. According to <u>Yüan ho hsing tsuan</u>

元何姓纂, the founder of the surname Chung was Chung-k'an 仲堪 who was a prominent scholar during the reign of Ti K'u (帝嚳, 2435-2365? B.C.) in the Legendary Period. 2. <u>Ming hsien shih tsu yen hsing lei kao</u> 名賢氏族言行類稿 describes the genealogy of the surname as follows: During the Spring and Autumn (Ch'un ch'iu 春秋) Period, Ch'i Huan-kung's 齊桓公 son Ch'ing Fu 慶父 was nicknamed Chung-sun 仲孫, a lineage name attributed to him according to Chinese genealogical order. Both Chung and Chung-sun were later adopted as common surnames by his descendants. 3. <u>Hsing shih k'ao lüeh</u> 姓氏考略 says the founder of the surname was Chung Chi 仲幾 of the Sung 宋 dynasty and the place of origin was located in Le-an 樂安 and Chung-shan 中山 in Ssu-ch'uan 四川 province.

See also Chung⁴-sun¹ 仲孫, Meng⁴ 孟, Meng⁴-sun¹ 孟孫.

121. Ch'ung¹ 充

<u>Hsing p'u</u> 姓譜 traces the origin of the surname to the name of the official post, ch'ung-jen 充人, the fattener of sacrificial animals. According to <u>Chou li</u> 周禮, ch'ung-jen was a member of the Ministry of Rites (ch'un-kuan 春官) who received animals from the breeders of sacrificial animals (mu-jen 牧人) and tended them in the final stages of their preparation as sacrificial victims in important state ceremonies. Ch'ung was later adopted as a common surname by the descendants of the family who originally held the position and the family settled primarily in T'ai-yüan 太原, Shan-hsi 山西 province.

122. Chung¹-li² 鍾離

The origin of the multiple surname Chung-li 鍾離 was cited in <u>Wan hsing t'ung p'u</u> 萬姓統譜, <u>Shang yu lu</u> 尚友錄 and <u>Ku chin hsing shih shu pien cheng</u> 古今姓氏書辨證. According to these books, the surnames Chung 鍾 and Chung-li 鍾離 are two branches of the same blood line. Both surnames branched from the surname Chi 姬 and were traced to the place name known as Chung-li 鍾離. The Grand Master (ta-fu 大夫) Po Tsung 伯宗 was murdered while in office in the State of Chin (Chin kuo 晉國). His son, Po Chou-li 伯州犁, escaped to the State of Ch'u 楚 and was bestowed with the vassal state in Chung-li 鍾離. Subsequently, Po Chou-li's two sons, Po Fa 伯發, the elder son, adopted Chung-li 鍾離 as his common surname and settled in Chiu-chiang 九江, Chiang-hsi 江西 and Po Chieh 伯接, the younder son, adopted Chung 鍾 as his common surname and settled initially in Ch'ang-she 長社, Chiang-hsi 江西 province and later in Yin-ch'uan 潁川, Ho-nan 河南 province.

See also Chung[1] 鍾.

123. Chung[4]-sun[1] 仲孫

According to T'ung chih Shih tsu lüeh 通志氏族略, the founder of the surname Chung-sun 仲孫 was Ch'ing Fu 慶父 from the State of Lu (Lu kuo 魯國) in the Spring and Autumn (Ch'un ch'iu 春秋) Period. According to Chinese genealogical order, chung 仲 is designated as the second eldest son within a family rank following po 伯. For this reason, Ch'ing Fu was nicknamed Chung-sun 仲孫 and subsequently the name was adopted as the common surname by his descendants. The initial settlement of the family was Kao-yang 高陽 in Ho-pei 河北 province. The surname Meng 孟 branched from the surname Chung-sun 仲孫. T'ung chih Shih tsu lüeh 通志氏族略 states the evolution of the surname as follows: Ch'ing Fu 慶父 murdered the Duke of Min (Min kung 閔公). In order to hide his identity, he later changed his surname to Meng.

See also Chung[4] 仲, Meng[4] 孟, Meng[4]-sun[1] 孟孫, Nan[2]-kung[1] 南宮.

124. E[4] 鄂

E 鄂 is the geographical abbreviation of the Hu-pei 湖北 province. In antiquity, Hu-pei was the domain of the State of Ch'u (Ch'u kuo 楚國) during the Spring and Autumn (Ch'un ch'iu 春秋)

Period. The surname E 鄂 derived from the following three sources: 1. According to <u>Shih chi Ch'u shih chia</u> 史記楚世家, the surname originated from the name of a vassal state in the State of Ch'u 楚, the District of E (E i 鄂邑), and was later adopted as a common surname by its citizens. The family settled in Wu-ch'ang 武昌, Hu-pei 湖北 province. 2. <u>Ming hsien shih tsu yen hsing lei kao</u> 名賢士族言行類稿 describes the origin of the surname as follows: The founder of the sunrame E was the Marquise of E (E hou 鄂侯) originally from the State of Chin 晉. E was later adopted as a common surname by his descendants and the family settled in Hsiang-ning hsien 鄉寧縣, Shan-hsi 山西 province. 3. <u>Hsing shih k'ao lüeh</u> 姓氏考略 traces the genealogy of the surname E to the lineage of Yüeh Fei 岳飛, a patriotic hero in the Sung 宋 dynasty. He was honored posthumously with the title of the King of E (E wang 鄂王) by Sung Ning-tsung (宋寧宗, 1195-1225 A.D.) and later his descendants adopted E as their common surname in memory of him.

125. Erh⁴ 佴

The first documented source regarding the genealogy of the surname Erh 佴 appeared in <u>Shan ku chi</u> 山谷集, which was written by the Sung 宋 scholar Huang T'ing-chien 黃庭堅. The book traces the surname Erh to some 1,600 years ago with real people of the family, such as the prominent educator Erh Chan 佴湛 of the Chin 晉 dynasty. The ancestral region of the family was Yün-nan 雲南 province and its ancestral hall name (t'ang ming 堂名) was Ku-tien Commandery (Ku-tien chün 古滇郡).

126. Fa³ 法

The origin of the surname Fa 法 was detailed in <u>Hou Han shu Fa hsiung chuan</u> 後漢書法雄傳 and <u>Yüan ho hsing tsuan</u> 元何姓纂. According to these documents, Ch'i 齊 was one of the strongest States during the Spring and Autumn (Ch'un ch'iu 春秋) Period. Its political status had lasted for three hundred years until

the T'ien 田 family seized power from the State
of Ch'i 齊. T'ien was adopted as the common
surname since the family took the ruling power
of the State of Ch'i and this was lasted for
about one hundred and fifty years. The founder
of the surname Fa was Ch'i Hsiang-wang 齊襄王
whose name was T'ien Fa-chang 田法章. It was
not until the Ch'in 秦 Emperor Shih Huang-ti
始皇帝 overthrew the State of Ch'i that the
descendants of Ch'i Hsiang-wang 齊襄王 changed
their surname from T'ien 田 into Fa 法 to avoid
further persecutions under the Ch'in's reign.
The Fa family initially settled in Shan-tung
山東 and later expanded to Fu-fung 扶風, Shen-
hsi 陝西 province.

See also T'ien² 田.

127. Fan² 樊

According to Yüan ho hsing tsuan 元何姓纂, the
founder of the surname Fan 樊 was Fan Chung-pi
樊仲皮 who was a son of Chou Wen-wang 周文王.
The surname Fan originated from the name of a
vassal state, the District of Fan (Fan i 樊邑),
bestowed on Fan Chung-pi and was later adopted
as a common surname by his descendants. The
family initially settled in Yang-fan 陽樊,
located in the present Nan-yang hsien 南陽縣,
Ho-nan 河南 province.

See also Pi² 皮.

128. Fan⁴ 范

Yüan ho hsing tsuan 元何姓纂 and Lu shih 路史
describes the genealogy of the surname Fan 范 as
follows: The surname Fan was traced to its
founder, Liu Lei 劉累, of the lineage of T'ang
Ti-yao (唐帝堯, 2356-2255? B.C.). He founded the
ancient State of T'ang (T'ang kuo 唐國), located
in I ch'eng 翼城, Shan-hsi 山西, and later was
known as T'ang-tu shih 唐杜氏. In the Chou 周
dynasty, the State of T'ang was defeated by Chou
Ch'eng-wang 周成王 and a descendant of Liu Lei
was enfeoffed at Tu ch'eng 杜城 (located in Hsi-
an 西安, Shen-hsi 陝西) as the Earl of Tu (Tu po

杜伯). Subsequently Tu 杜 was adopted as a common surname by his descendants. After the feudal territory Tu ch'eng was defeated by Chou Hsüan-wang 周宣王, Hsi Shu 隰叔, a son of the Earl of Tu, escaped to the State of Chin (Chin kuo 晉國) and was appointed Serviceman (shih-shih 士師), he changed his surname into Shih 士. Not until his great grandson Ssu-hui 士會 was appointed Minister (ch'ing 卿) and later enfeoffed at the vassal state of the District of Fan (Fan i 范邑) did the family changed its surname again into that of the locale. The Fan family prospered in Kao-p'ing hsien 高平縣, Shan-hsi 山西 province.

See also Shih⁴ 士, Tu⁴ 杜.

## 129. Fan⁴ 範

According to <u>Hsing shih k'ao lüeh</u> 姓氏考略, the surname Fan branched from the surname Fan-shih 範師, which was traced to an occupational title in the Chou 周 dynasty. Two representatives from the Fan family were Fan I 範依 of the Han 漢 dynasty and Fan Hsien 範顯 of the Sung 宋 dynasty.

## 130. Fan⁴-shih¹ 范師

According to <u>Hsing shih k'ao lüeh</u> 姓氏考略, the surname Fan-shih 范師 derived from the occupational title of fan-shih kung-shih 范師供事, who was a government employee (kung-shih 供事) in the Chou 周 dynasty for casting gold to make instruments for official use. <u>Li chih</u> 禮記 states that Fan-shih 范師, also known as fan-shih 範師, was an experienced gold caster. The title was later adopted a common surname by the descendants of the family whose ancestor was a fan-shih.

## 131. Fan⁴-shih¹ 範師

See Fan⁴-shih¹ 范師.

## 132. Fang¹ 方

<u>Yüan ho hsing tsuan</u> 元何姓纂 says: the Fang 方 surname originated from Fang Shu 方叔, a grand master (ta-fu 大夫) under the reign of Chou Hsüan-wang (周宣王, 827-781 B.C.). The descendants of his family settled initially in Ho-nan 河南 and later moved to Chiang-hsi 江西, Kuang-tung 廣東, and Fu-chien 福建 provinces.

133. Fang² 房

<u>Yüan ho hsing tsuan</u> 元何姓纂 and <u>Kuang yün</u> 廣韻 describe the genealogy of the surname Fang 房 as follows: Yü Ti-shun 虞帝舜 bestowed Tan Chu 丹朱 (a son of T'ang Ti-yao 唐帝堯) with Fang-ling 房陵 and appointed him the Marquise of Fang-i (Fang-i hou 房邑侯) and Fang was adopted as a common surname by his descendants. The Fang family has Ch'ing-ho 清河 as its ancestral hall name (t'ang ming 堂名) because a descendant has appointed the governor (t'ai-shou 太守) of the Ch'ing-ho Commandery (Ch'ing-ho chün 清河郡). The family prospered in Ch'ing-ho 清河 for generations.

134. Fei³ 費

The surname "費" materialized from three sources according to its phonetic variations. According to <u>Yüan ho hsing tsuan</u> 元何姓纂, the surname Fei³ 費 belongs to the ancestral line of the Great Yü (Ta Yü 大禹) and derived from Fei Chung 費仲, a grand minister (ta-ch'en 大臣) of Cho-hsin (紂辛, 1154-1122 B.C.) in the Shang 商 dynasty. The family settled in Chiang-hsia 江夏 which was located in the present areas of Wu-ch'ang 武昌 and Han-k'ou 漢口 in Hu-pei 湖北 province.

See also Fei⁴ 費, Pi⁴ 費.

135. Fei⁴ 費

The surname "費" materialized from three sources according to its phonetic variations. The earlist reference of the surname Fei⁴ 費 was from the name of a vassal state, the District of Fei (Fei i 費邑). It was bestowed on the father of Fei Ling 費庈 who was the Grand Master (ta-fu

大夫) of the State of Lu (Lu kuo 魯國) during the Spring and Autumn (Ch'un ch'iu 春秋) Period. His descendants settled in Yü-t'ai hsien 魚台縣, Shan-tung 山東 province where the District of Fei was located. A road station, Fei t'ing 費亭, was established there in memory of the family's history.

See also Lang[2] 郎, Fei[3] 費, Pi[4] 費.

136.  Feng[1] 封

According to Hsing yüan 姓苑 and Yüan ho hsing tsuan 元何姓纂, the surname Feng 封 belongs to the ancestral line of Yen-ti 炎帝. His grandson, Chü 鉅, who had been a tutor for Huang-ti 黃帝 and was graciously bestowed with the feudal territory, Feng 封, which was the present Feng-ch'iu hsien 封丘縣 in Ho-nan 河南 province. Chü 鉅 adopted Feng as his surname and the family prospered in Feng-ch'iu hsien 封丘縣, Ho-nan 河南 province.

137.  Feng[1] 豐

According to Yüan ho hsing tsuan 元何姓纂, the surname Feng 豐 came from the ancestral line of Chou Wen-wang 周文王 and derived from his descendant Feng 豐, who was a son of the Duke of Mu (Mu kung 穆公) from the State of Cheng (Cheng kuo 鄭國) in the Spring and Autumn (Ch'un ch'iu 春秋) Period. The family prospered in Ch'ang-an 長安, Shen-hsi 陝西 province.

138.  Feng[1] 風

The surname Feng 風 originated from the name of the ancient state, the State of Feng (Feng kuo 風國). It was cited in Ch'un ch'iu 春秋 as Hsü-chü kuo 須句國. According to the document, the surname Feng 風 derived from the ancestral line of T'ai Hao 太昊 (Fu-hsi shih 伏羲氏) and adopted as a common surname by his descendants. The State of Feng was located in the areas of the present Shou-chang hsien 壽張縣 and Tung-p'ing hsien 東平縣 in Shan-tung 山東 province where the family initially settled.

See also Hsü[1] 須, Kou[1] 句, Fu[2] 伏.

## 139. Feng[1] 酆

According to <u>Yüan ho hsing tsuan</u> 元何姓纂, the surname Feng 酆 belongs to the ancestral line of Chou Wen-wang 周文王 and originated from the name of the feudal territory, Feng 酆, bestowed on his seventeenth son, the Marquise of Feng (Feng hou 酆侯) and later adopted as a common surname by his descendants. The family prospered in Ch'ang-an 長安, Shen-hsi 陝西 province.

## 140. Feng[2] 馮

According to <u>Yüan ho hsing tsuan</u> 元何姓纂, the surname Feng 馮 was traced to the ancestral line of Chou Wen-wang's 周文王 fifteenth son, Pi Kung-kao 畢公高, who was bestowed with the vassal state of Feng i 馮邑, located in Feng ch'eng 馮城, by his father. Feng was adopted as a common surname by his descendants and the family initially settled in Yin-ch'uan 穎川, Honan 河南 and later migrated to Shang-tang 上黨, Shan-hsi 山西 and Ch'ang-le 長樂, Ho-pei 河北 provinces.

## 141. Feng[2] 逢

According to <u>Hsing shih k'ao lüeh</u> 姓氏考略, the surname Feng 逢 originated from Feng Po-ling 逢伯陵 who was a member of the royal family in the Shang 商 dynasty. The family initially settled in Pei-hai 北海, Kuang-hsi 廣西 province.

## 142. Feng[4] 鳳

"Feng 鳳", meaning the male phoenix, has long been considered as the emblem of joy and good luck by the Chinese people. <u>T'ung chih Shih tsu lüeh</u> 通志氏族略 describes the genealogy of the surname Feng 鳳 as follows: The founder of the surname Feng was Feng-niao shih 鳳鳥氏 who was appointed to the official post, li-cheng 歷正, Calendrical Administrater, during the reign of

Ti K'u 帝嚳. The major responsibility of li-cheng 歷正 was to maintain social and political peace and harmony within the kingdom through the observation of the four seasons. The Feng family settled and prospered in P'ing-yang 平陽 and T'ai-yang 邰陽 of the Shen-hsi 陝西 province.

143. Fu² 符

According to Yüan ho hsing tsuan 元何姓纂, the surname Fu 符 belongs to the lineage of Chou Wen-wang 周文王 and came from the name of the official post, fu-hsi-lang 符璽郎, Court Gentleman for the Imperial Seals, in charge of the imperial insignias. The title was held by a grandson of Ch'i Ch'ing-kung 齊頃公 during the Spring and Autumn (Ch'un ch'iu 春秋) Period and his descendants later adopted Fu as their common surname. The family's ancestral home was in Huai-yang hsien 淮陽縣, Ho-nan 河南 province.

144. Fu² 扶

According to Lu shih 路史, the surname Fu 扶 originated from a Grand Minister (ta-ch'en 大臣) of the Great Yü (Ta Yü 大禹) named Fu-teng shih 扶登氏. The Fu family initially settled in Ho-nan 河南 province.

145. Fu² 伏

The surname Fu 伏 originated from two sources. 1. According to Wei shu kuan shih chih 魏書官氏志, the surname Fu branched from the surname Hou-fu 侯伏 in the Northern Wei (Pei Wei 北魏) dynasty. 2. Wan hsing t'ung p'u 萬姓統譜 and Shang yu lu 尚友錄 describe the origin of the surname as follows: The surname Fu 伏 branched from the surname Feng 風 of the ancestral line of T'ai Hao 太昊 (Fu-hsi shih 伏羲氏) and was adopted as a common surname by his descendants. The Fu family originally settled in Kao-yang 高陽, Ho-pei 河北 province.

See also Hou²-fu² 侯伏, Feng¹ 風, Fu² 宓.

146. Fu[2] 福

The surname Fu 福 derived from three sources. 1.
<u>Hsing shih k'ao lüeh</u> 姓氏考略 traces the name's
origin to the Grand Master (ta-fu 大夫) Fu Tzu-
tan 福子丹 from the State of Ch'i (Ch'i kuo
齊國) in the Spring and Autumn (Ch'un ch'iu
春秋) Period. 2. <u>T'ung chih Shih tsu lüeh</u>
通志氏族略 describes the source of the name as
follows: The surname Fu 福 branched from the
triple surname Fu-fu-shun 福富順 as a result of
the change of surname by the people of the State
of Pai-chi (Pai-chi kuo 百濟國) in the T'ang 唐
dynasty. Fu was adopted as a common surname
after the State of Pai-chi was absorbed by the
T'ang dynasty. 3. The third branch of the Fu
family originated from Chang Fu-shih 張福時, who
was a minister to Ming Shih-tsung 明世宗 and was
notable for his archery and military tactics.
Since he was widely known by his forname Fu-shih
福時 in his life, Fu was later adopted as a
common surname by his descendants.

See also Chang[1] 張.

147. Fu[2] 宓

According to <u>Shih chi</u> 史記, the surnames Fu 宓
and Fu 伏 were interchangeably in ancient times.
The founder of the surname Fu was T'ai Hao 太昊
(Fu-hsi shih 伏羲氏, also known as Fu-hsi shih
宓羲氏) who was the chieftain of a tribe during
the Legendary Period. A representative of the
family was Fu Pu-ch'i 宓不齊 who was a disciple
of Confucius and a music player of stringed
instruments.

See also Fu[2] 伏

148. Fu[4] 傅

According to <u>Yüan ho hsing tsuan</u> 元何姓纂 and
<u>Ming hsien shih tsu yen hsing lei kao</u>
名賢氏族言行類稿, the founder of the family name
Fu 傅 was Fu Yüeh 傅說. He was the Counselor-
in-Chief (ch'eng-hsiang 丞相) to the Shang 商
king Wu-ting (武丁, 1324-1265 B.C.) and Fu was

adopted as his surname from the name of his
residence in Fu-yen 傅巖, which was located in
the present P'ing-lu hsien 平陸縣, Shan-hsi 山西
province. The family settled and prospered in
many places, including Ning-hsia 寧夏, Kan-su
甘肅, Ho-pei 河北, and Shan-tung 山東 provinces.

149. Fu⁴ 富

The surname Fu 富 originated from two sources.
1. According to Tso chuan 左傳 and T'ung chih
Shih tsu lüeh 通志氏族略, Fu Ch'en 富辰, a grand
master (ta-fu 大夫) in the Chou 周 dynasty, was
the founder of the surname Fu. The native place
of the family was in Ch'en-liu hsien 陳留縣, Ho-
nan 河南 province. 2. Hsing shih k'ao lüeh
姓氏考略 and Yüan ho hsing tsuan 元何姓纂
describe the genealogy of the surname as
follows: The surname Fu derived from Fu Fu 富父,
who was a marquise of the State of Lu (Lu kuo
魯國) during the Spring and Autumn (Ch'un ch'iu
春秋) Period. The original settlement of this
branch of the family was Shan-tung 山東
province.

150. Ha¹ 哈

According to Cheng tzu t'ung 正字通, the surname
Ha 哈 appeared before the Ming 明 dynasty and
was a popular surname in Hu-pei 湖北 province.
Many of the prominent figures from the Ha family
originally came from either Hu-pei or Ho-pei
河北 provinces.

151. Hai³ 海

Wan hsing t'ung p'u 萬姓統譜 traces the origin
of the surname Hai 海 to its founder Hai Ch'un
海春 who was a grand minister (ta-ch'en 大臣) to
Duke Wei-ling (Wei-ling kung 衛靈公) during the
Spring and Autumn (Ch'un ch'iu 春秋) Period.
Hai Ch'un adopted the surname Hai due to his
deep affection for the sea (hai 海). The family
initially settled in the State of Wei (Wei kuo
衛國) and later expanded to Hsüeh Commandery
(Hsüeh chün 薛郡), located in the area of the
present southwestern Shan-tung 山東 and northern

Chiang-su 江蘇 provinces.

## 152. Han² 韓

According to <u>Feng shu t'ung</u> 風俗通, the surname Han 韓 originated from the name of the feudal territory, Han-yüan 韓原, bestowed on Wu Tzu 武子, who was a descendant of Chou Wen-wang 周文王 during the Spring and Autumn (Ch'un ch'iu 春秋) Period. Han-yüan 韓原 was located in the present Han-ch'eng hsien 韓城縣, Shen-hsi 陝西 province. The descendants of the Han family had been grand masters (ta-fu 大夫) of the State of Han (Han kuo 韓國) for generations and they lived in the State of Han, located in P'ing-yang 平陽, which is the present Lin-fen hsien 臨汾縣, Shan-hsi 山西 province. They later migrated to Yin-ch'uan 穎川 and Nan-yang 南陽 in Ho-nan 河南 province.

See also Ho² 何, Yen² 言.

## 153. Hang² 杭

The surname Hang 杭 branched from the surname K'ang 抗. According to <u>Hsing shih k'ao lüeh</u> 姓氏考略, the surname K'ang 抗 frist appeared in Tan-yang hsien 丹陽縣, Hu-nan 湖南 province with K'ang Hsü 抗徐 as the Governor (t'ai-shou 太守) of the Han 漢 dynasty. Most of the descendants of K'ang Hsü changed their surname into Hang 杭 during the Sung 宋 dynasty and at the present, more people bear the surname Hang 杭 than K'ang 抗.

See also K'ang⁴ 抗.

## 154. Hao³ 郝

<u>T'ung chih Shih tsu lüeh</u> 通志氏族略 describes the origin of the surname Hao 郝 as follows: Since Ti-yi (帝乙, 1191-1154 B.C.) was enthroned as the twenty-seventh king of the Shang 商 dynasty, he bestowed his son with the feudal territory, the Village of Hao (Hao-hsiang 郝鄉), located in the present T'ai-yüan 太原, Shan-hsi

山西 province. His descendants adopted the territorial name as their common surname and settled in T'ai-yüan 太原, Shan-hsi 山西 province.

## 155. Heng[2] 衡

The surname Heng 衡 derived from three sources. 1. According to Yüan ho hsing tsuan 元何姓纂, the surname originated from the feudal prince Heng 衡 of the State of Lu (Lu kuo 魯國) in the Chou 周 dynasty. This branch of the Heng family prospered in Shang-tung 山東 province. 2. Ming hsien shih tsu yen hsing lei kao 名賢氏族言行類稿 describes the origin of the surname as follows: The surname Heng derived from a-heng 阿衡, the unofficial reference to the official post of Counselor-in-Chief (ch'eng-hsiang 丞相) in the Shang 商 dynasty. I I 伊尹 held this administrative post during the reign of Ch'eng-t'ang 成湯 and subsequently his descendants adopted Heng as their common surname. 3. Wan hsing t'ung p'u 萬姓統譜 states that the surname Heng was the result of a change of name from Yüan 袁 to Heng 衡 and the evolution of the name was as follows: At the end of the Eastern Han (Tung Han 東漢, 25-220 A.D.) dynasty, Yüan Shao 袁紹's military was defeated by the enemies. Subsequently, his family and relatives escaped from their homes and hid in the Heng Mountain (Hen shan 衡山). They changed their surname to Heng and settled primarily in Ju-nan 汝南, Ho-nan 河南 province.

## 156. Ho[2] 何

According to Yüan ho hsing tsuan 元何姓纂, the surname Ho 何 came into existence in the Ch'in 秦 dynasty and it branched from the surname Han 韓 of the linage of Chou Wen-wang 周文王. The founder of the surname Ho was Han Ann 韓安, who lived in the State of Han (Han kuo 韓國) located in P'ing-yang 平陽 of the present Lin-fen hsien 臨汾縣, Shan-hsi 山西 province. When the State of Han was defeated by the Emperor Ch'in Shih-huang 秦始皇, Han Ann 韓安 escaped, changed his family name into Ho 何 and relocated to Chiang-su 江蘇 province. The Ho family later populated the area along the Yangtze and Huai 淮 Rivers which pass through Chiang-su 江蘇 and An-hui 安徽 provinces.

See also Han[2] 韓.

157. Ho[2] 和

Yüan ho hsing tsuan 元何姓纂 and T'ung chih Shih tsu lüeh 通志氏族略 describe the origin of the surname as follows: The surname Ho 和 originated from the name of the official post, hsi-ho 羲和, the Astrologer, in charge of calendrical calculations and harmonizing heavenly and earthly matters in high antiquity. According to the legend, families named Hsi 羲 and Ho 和 were put in hereditary charge of this position. The founder of the surname Ho was Ch'ung Li 重黎. He was appointed to Hsi-ho during the reign of T'ang Ti-yao 唐帝堯 and later some of his descendants adopted Hsi and others adopted Ho as their common surname. The families settled primarily in Hsi-ling 西陵, Shen-hsi 陝西 province.

See also Hsi[1] 羲.

158. Ho[4] 賀

T'ung chih Shih tsu lüeh 通志氏族略 and Hsing shih k'ao lüeh 姓氏考略 both describe the origin the surname Ho 賀 as follows: The surnme Ho branched from the surname Ch'ing 慶 during the Eastern Han (Tung Han 東漢) dynasty when Ch'ing Ch'un 慶純 changed his surname into Ho 賀 to avoid the taboo name Ch'ing 慶 used by the father of An-ti (安帝, A.D. 107-126). The descendants of the Ho family settled in Kuei-chi 會稽, Ho-nan 河南 province.

See also Ch'ing[4] 慶.

159. Ho[4]-lien[2] 赫連

Chin shu Ho-lien Po-po tsai chi 晉書赫連勃勃載記

says the surname Ho-lien 赫連 appeared during the Southern and Northern Dynasties (Nan-pei ch'ao 南北朝). During that time, many tribes of the Hu 胡 People declared their sovereign power over northwestern territories in China. Po-po 勃勃, who belongs to the nomadic group of Hsiung-nu 匈奴, named himself the Emperor of Ta Hsia 大夏 and adopted Ho-lien 赫連 ("ho 赫" means "grandeur, the Heavenly Master" and "lien 連" means "to connect"; therefore ho-lien means "to connect with the Heavenly Master, or to God") as the common surname. The surname was later adopted by his descendants and the Ho-lien families settled primarily in southern China.

160. Hou² 侯

During the Chou 周 feudal age, fringe territories bordering the royal domain were allocated to feudal lords collectively known as "the various marquises" (chu-hou 諸侯). According to Yüan ho hsing tsuan 元何姓纂, The Hou 侯 surname was first adopted by Min 緡, who was the Marquise (hou 侯) of the State of Chin (Chin kuo 晉國) in the Chou 周 dynasty. The family originally settled in Shan-hsi 山西 and later expanded to Ho-pei 河北 province.

See also Lien⁴ 練.

161. Hou⁴ 後

According to Hsing shih k'ao lüeh 姓氏考略, the surname Hou 後 follows the ancestral line of T'ai Hao 太昊 (Fu-hsi shih 伏羲氏) and the founder of the surname was his grandson Hou Chao 後照. Hou was adopted as the common surname by the descendants of Hou Chao and the family prospered in Shan-tung 山東 and Chiang-su 江蘇 provinces.

162. Hou⁴ 后

The surname Hou 后 derived from the following two sources: 1. It derived from the name of the official post, Hou-tu 后土, the Land Official, who was the principal of the territorial administration in high antiquity. The title was established and dated during the reign of Chuan Hsü 顓頊 in the Legendary Period. <u>Yüan ho hsing tsuan</u> 元何姓纂 documented that Chuan Hsü's son Li 黎 was appointed to the position and later his descendants adopted Hou as their common surname. 2. The founder of the surname Hou was Hou Chi 后稷 who was also the founding father of the royal families in the Chou dynasty. Both <u>Hsing shih k'ao lüeh</u> 姓氏考略 and <u>Ch'ien fu lun</u> 潛夫論 trace the Hou 后 surname from Hou Chi 后稷 to the Duke of Chou (Chou kung 周公) and followed by his descendants, feudal lords of the State of Lu (Lu kuo 魯國) located in Shan-tung 山東 province. Today, many of the Hou families were originally from Shan-tung 山東.

163.  Hou$^2$-fu$^2$ 侯伏

The surnames Fu 伏 and Hou-fu 侯伏 came from the same blood line. According to <u>Pei shih</u> 北史, Hou Chih 侯植 was honored and given the family name of Hou-fu 侯伏 by the Emperor Hsiao-wu 孝武 in the Northern Wei (Pei Wei 北魏) dynasty. Some of his descendants later adopted the surname Hou-fu 侯伏 and others adopted the surname Fu 伏 as their common surname.

See also Fu$^2$ 伏.

164.  Hsi$^1$ 西

The surname Hsi 西 branched from the surname Hsi-men 西門. According to <u>Hsing yüan</u> 姓苑, the founder of the surname Hsi was Hsi-men Pao 西門豹 from the Western Chin (Hsi Chin 西晉, A.D. 265-316) dynasty. He changed his multiple surname to the single surname Hsi 西 and later his descendants adopted it as their common surname.

See also Hsi$^1$-men$^2$ 西門.

165.  Hsi$^1$ 羲

The surname Hsi 羲 derived from two sources.  1.

<u>Yüan ho hsing tsuan</u> 元何姓纂 and <u>T'ung chih Shih tsu lüeh</u> 通志氏族略 describe the origin of the surname as follows: The surname Hsi originated from the name of the official post, hsi-ho 羲和, the Astrologer, in charge of calendrical calculations and harmonizing heavenly and earthly matters in high antiquity. The founder of the surname was Ch'ung Li 重黎. He was appointed to Hsi-ho during the reign of T'ang Ti-yao 唐帝堯 and later some of his descendants adopted Hsi and others adopted Ho as their common surname. The families settled primarily in Hsi-ling 西陵, Shen-hsi 陝西 province. 2. According to <u>Feng su t'ung</u> 風俗通, the surname Hsi 羲 follows the ancestral line of Hsi Chung 羲仲 who was a grand minister (ta-ch'en 大臣) during the reign of T'ang Ti-yao 唐帝堯 in the Legendary Period. The Hsi family setled primarily in Pei-ching 北京, Hu-pei 湖北 and Ch'eng-tu 成都, Ssu-ch'uan 四川 provinces.

See also Ho² 和.

166. Hsi¹ 奚

According to <u>Shuo wen chieh tzu</u> 說文解字 and <u>Ku chin hsing shih shu pien cheng</u> 古今姓氏書辨證: Hsi Chung 奚仲, a descendant of the Jen 任 family from the lineage of Huang-ti 黃帝, was the inventor of the carriage in the Hsia 夏 dynasty. Hsi was later adopted as the common surname by him and his descendants because of his contribution to the Hsia dynasty.

See also Jen² 任.

167. Hsi² 習

<u>Hsing shih k'ao lüeh</u> 姓氏考略 traces the origin of the surname Hsi 習 to the place name, Shao-hsi 少習, located in Wu-kuan 武關, where the residents adopted Hsi as their common surname. The family originally settled in Hsiang-yang 襄陽, Hu-pei 湖北 province.

168. Hsi² 席

The surname Hsi 席 derived from two sources. 1. Wan hsing t'ung p'u 萬姓統譜 says the surname Hsi first appeared during the reign of T'ang Ti-yao 唐帝堯. In Hsiang-ling 襄陵 (the present Sui hsien 睢縣, Ho-nan 河南 province), a farmer, Hsi Shih 席氏, wrote the song Chi jan ko 擊壤歌 to describe a farmer's life working in the rice field was appraised by T'ang Ti-yao 唐帝堯 and was honored with the title of Hsi Teacher (Hsi lao shih 席老師). Subsequently, Hsi was adopted as the common surname by his descendants. 2. According to Yüan ho hsing tsuan 元何姓纂 and Hsing yüan 姓苑, the descendants of the Chi 籍 family changed their surname into Hsi 席 in the Han 漢 dynasty and this branch of the Hsi family settled in Shan-hsi 山西 province.

See also Chi² 籍.

169. Hsi⁴ 郤

Ku chin hsing shih shu pien cheng 古今姓氏書辨證 and Ming hsien shih tsu yen hsing lei kao 名賢氏族言行類稿 describe the origin of the surname Hsi 郤 as follows: The surname Hsi derived from a place name, the Village of Hsi (Hsi-hsiang 郤鄉), located in Ho-nan 河南 province. It was the name of a vassal state bestowed on Shu-hu 叔虎, a grand master (ta-fu 大夫) of the State of Chin (Chin kuo 晉國) during the Spring and Autumn (Ch'un ch'iu 春秋) Period. Hsi was adopted as the common surname by his descendants and the family settled primarily in Ting-t'ao 定陶 and Chin-hsiang hsien 金鄉縣 in Shan-tung 山東 province.

170. Hsi¹-kuo¹ 西郭

See also Tung¹-kuo¹ 東郭.

171. Hsi¹-men² 西門

T'ung chih Shih tsu lüeh 通志氏族略 traces the origin of the surname Hsi-men 西門 to a grand master (ta-fu 大夫) of the State of Cheng (Cheng kuo 鄭國) in the Spring and Autumn (Ch'un ch'iu 春秋) Period because Hsi-men was the site of his residence.

See also Hsi[1] 西, Tung[1]-men[2] 東門, Nan[2]-men[2] 南門,
Pei[3]-men[2] 北門.

172. Hsia[4] 夏

> <u>Yüan ho hsing tsuan</u> 元何姓纂 describes the
> origin of the surname Hsia 夏 as follows: The
> surname originated from the founder of the Hsia
> 夏 dynasty, the Great Yü (Ta Yü 大禹), who was
> called Hsia hou shih 夏后氏. The family's place
> of origin was Kuei-chi hsien 會稽縣, Che-chiang
> 浙江 province.

See also Hsia[4]-hou[2] 夏侯.

173. Hsia[4]-hou[2] 夏侯

> <u>Hsing p'u</u> 姓譜 and <u>T'ang shu tsai hsiang shih</u>
> <u>hsi piao</u> 唐書宰相世系表 describe the genealogy
> of the surname Hsia-hou 夏侯 as follows: The
> multiple surname branched from the surname Hsia
> 夏 of the ancestral line of the Great Yü (Ta Yü
> 大禹) in the Hsia 夏 dynasty. In the Chou 周
> dynasty, Wu-wang 武王 bestowed the feudal
> territory Ch'i 杞 on his descendant. After Ch'i
> was defeated by the State of Ch'u 楚, the
> brother of the Duke of Chien (Chien kung 簡公)
> whose name was T'o 佗 escaped to the State of Lu
> 魯. Since T'o 佗 came from the royal family of
> the Great Yü (Ta Yü 大禹), he was treated with
> great respect and was enfeoffed as the Marquise
> of Hsia (Hsia hou 夏侯). Subsequently, Hsia-hou
> was adopted as the common surname by the
> descendants of T'o.

See also Hsia[4] 夏.

174. Hsiang[4] 相

> According to <u>Hsing p'u</u> 姓譜, the surname Hsiang
> 相 derived from the Hsia 夏 dynasty's fifth king
> Hsiang (相, 2146-2118 B.C.) and was traced
> originally from the ancestral line of the
> surname Hsia 夏 of the Great Yü (Ta Yü 大禹).

175. Hsiang⁴ 項

The origin of the surname Hsiang 項 was cited in Wan hsing t'ung p'u 萬姓統譜, T'ung chih Shih tsu lüeh 通志氏族略, and Ming hsien shih tsu yen hsing lei kao 名賢氏族言行類稿. According to these books, the surname Hsiang derived from the name of the feudal territory, the State of Hsiang (Hsiang kuo 項國), which was later defeated by the State of Ch'i 齊 and its residents adopted Hsiang as their common surname and settled in Hsiang-ch'eng hsien 項城縣 where the State of Hsiang was originally located.

See also Liu² 劉.

176. Hsiang⁴ 向

The surname Hsiang 向 originated from two sources. 1. According to T'ung chih Shih tsu lüeh 通志氏族略, the surname Hsiang 向 branched from the surname Ch'i 祁 of the ancestral line of Huang-ti 黃帝 and the founder of the surname was Hsiang Chih 向摯 who was the Grand Scribe (t'ai-shih 太史) to Chou Wu-wang 周武王, in charge of recording and interpreting celestial and other remarkable natural phenomena, weather forecasting, and other esoteric aspects of astronomy. 2. Yüan ho hsing tsuan 元何姓纂 says: The surname Hsiang belongs to the lineage of the Shang 商 king Ch'eng T'ang 成湯 and derived from Hsiang Fu 向父. He was a descendant of Ch'eng T'ang and a son of the Duke Sung Huan (Sung Huan-kung 宋桓公) in the Spring and Autumn (Ch'un ch'iu 春秋) Period.

177. Hsiao¹ 蕭

Yüan ho hsing tsuan 元何姓纂 and T'ung chih Shih tsu lüeh 通志氏族略 describe the genealogy of the surname Hsiao 蕭 in detail as follows: The surname Hsiao originated from the name of a feudal territory bestowed on a grandson of Wei-tzu 微子 in the Chou 周 dynasty. Hsiao was later adopted as a common surname by Wei-tzu's descendants and the family settled primarily in Hsiao hsien 蕭縣, Chiang-su 江蘇 province where the feudal territory was located. <u>Hsing shih k'ao lüeh</u> 姓氏考略 mentions the surname's place of origin as follows: The surname Hsiao first appeared in Lan-ling 蘭陵 (located in the present I hsien 嶧縣, Shang-tung 山東 province) and Kuang-ling 廣陵 (located in the present Chiang-tu hsien 江都縣, Chiang-su 江蘇 province).

178. Hsieh[4] 謝

<u>Yüan ho hsing tsuan</u> 元何姓纂 says: The Hsieh 謝 surname branched from the Chiang 姜 surname of the ancestral line of Yen-ti 炎帝 and originated from the name of the feudal territory, the State of Hsieh (Hsieh kuo 謝國), bestowed on the Earl of Shen (Shen po 申伯), who was a brother-in-law of Chou Hsüan-wang (周宣王, 827-781 B.C.). Hsieh was later adopted as the common surname by the descendants of Shen po and the family settled in T'ang-ho hsien 唐河縣, Ho-nan 河南 province where the State of Hsieh was located.

179. Hsieh[4] 解

<u>Wan hsing t'ung p'u</u> 萬姓統譜 and <u>Hsing shih chi chiu p'ien</u> 姓氏急就篇 state that the surname Hsieh 解 belongs to the lineage of Huang-ti 黃帝 and originated from the name of the vassal state, Hsieh-ch'eng 解城, located in the present Lou-yang hsien 洛陽縣, Ho-nan 河南 province. The vassal state was enfeoffed at T'ang Shu-yü's 唐叔虞 son Liang 良 in the Chou 周 dynasty. Hsieh was later as the common surname by Liang's descendants an the family settled primarily in Lou-yang hsien 洛陽縣, Ho-nan 河南 province.

180. Hsien[1]-yü[2] 鮮于

According to <u>Shang yu lu</u> 尚友錄 and <u>Ku chin hsing shih shu pien cheng</u> 古今姓氏書辨證: Chou Wu-wang 周武王 bestowed Chi-tzu 箕子 in Ch'ao-hsien 朝鮮 and subsequently enfeoffed his son at the feudal territory named Yü 于. The combined form of Hsien 鮮 and Yü 于 was later adopted as the common surname by the descendants of Chou Wu-wang and the family settled primarily in Yü-yang 漁陽, Ho-pei 河北 province.

181. Hsien² 咸

> According to Hsing yüan 姓苑, the founder of the
> surname Hsien 咸 was Wu Hsien 巫咸, who was a
> sorcerer, a subordinate of the Directors of
> Sorcery (ssu-wu 司巫) under the Ministry of
> Rites (ch'un-kuan 春官) in the Shang 商 dynasty.
> Hsien was later adopted as a common surname by
> his descendants.

182. Hsin¹ 辛

> The surname Hsin 辛 originated from two sources:
> 1. According to Yüan ho hsing tsuan 元何姓纂 and
> Ming hsien shih tsu yen hsing lei kao
> 名賢氏族言行類稿, the King Ch'i (啓, 2197-2188?
> B.C.) of the Hsia 夏 dynasty bestowed his son
> with the feudal territory called the State of
> Hsin (Hsin kuo 莘國). His descendants dropped
> the radical and adopted Hsin 辛 as their
> surname. The family initially settled in T'ai-
> yang 邰陽, Shen-hsi 陝西 and later prospered in
> T'ien-shui 天水, Kan-su 甘肅 province. 2. Ch'ien
> fu lun 潛夫論 says: Hsin 辛 was one of the
> eight surnames branched from the ancestral line
> of Chu-jung shih 祝融氏 and its place of origin
> was western Kan-su 甘肅 province.

> See also Hsin¹ 莘.

183. Hsin¹ 莘

> The surname Hsin 莘 derived from two sources.
> 1. According to Wan hsing t'ung p'u 萬姓統譜,
> the surname Hsin 莘 came from the place name Yu-
> hsin 有莘, located in the present Ts'ao hsien
> 曹縣, Shan-tung 山東 province. 2. Yüan ho hsing
> tsuan 元何姓纂 and Ming hsien shih tsu yen hsing
> lei kao 名賢氏族言行類稿 trace the surname to
> the King Ch'i 啓 of the Hsia 夏 dynasty. He
> bestowed his son with the feudal territory
> called the State of Hsin (Hsin kuo 莘國), and
> later his descendants dropped the radical and
> adopted Hsin 辛 as their common surname. The
> family initially settled in T'ai-yang 邰陽,

Shen-hsi 陝西 and later prospered in T'ien-shui 天水, Kan-su 甘肅 province.

See also Hsin[1] 辛.

184.  Hsing[2] 邢

The surname Hsing 邢 was traced to the lineage of Chou Wen-wang 周文王 and originated from the following two sources:  1. According to <u>Yüan ho hsing tsuan</u> 元何姓纂, the origin of the surname Hsing derived from the name of a vassal state, the District of Hsing (Hsing kuo 邢邑), bestowed on the fourth son of the Duke of Chou (Chou kung 周公) and was adopted as the common surname by his descendants. The family settled in Hsing-t'ai hsien 邢台縣, Ho-pei 河北 province where the District of Hsing was located.  2. <u>Yüan ho hsing tsuan</u> 元何姓纂 traces the surname to Chou Wen-wang's descendant T'ang Shu-yü 唐叔虞 and attributes its origin to the name of a vassal state in P'ing-hsing 平邢. This branch of the family initially settled in Wen hsien 溫縣, Ho-nan 河南 province where the vassal state was located.

185.  Hsing[4] 幸

According to the Ch'ing 清 scholar Chang Shu 張澍 in his book, <u>Hsing shih we shu</u> 姓氏五書, the surname Hsing derived from the meaning of the word "hsing 幸".  In ancient China, it was common for the concubines who were favored (hsing 幸) by the emperor to adopt Hsing as their common surname.  The descendants from this branch of the family settled primarily in Nan-ch'ang 南昌, Chiang-hsi 江西 province.

186.  Hsing[4] 姓

According to <u>Hsing shih hsün yüan</u> 姓氏尋源, the surname Hsing 姓 was traced to the following two sources: 1. The progenitor of the family was a common citizen who was nameless so he took the word "name (Hsing 姓)" as his common surname. 2. The Hsing families possibly came from the lineage of the Duke of Ts'ai in the State of

Ts'ai (Ts'ai kuo 蔡國) of the Chou 周 dynasty and they settled primarily in Nan-hai 南海, Kaung-tung 廣東 province.

187. Hsiung[2] 熊

According to <u>Shang yu lu</u> 尚友錄 and <u>T'ung chih Shih tsu lüeh</u> 通志氏族略, the surname Hsiung 熊 was traced to the following two sources: 1. The founder of the surname was Yü Hsiung 鬻熊 from the State of Ch'u (Ch'u kuo 楚國) and Hsiung was adopted as the common surname by his descendants. The family originally settled in Nan-chang 南昌, Chiang-hsi 江西 province. 2. The origin of the surname was attributed to Huang-ti 黃帝 whose name was Yu-hsiung shih 有熊氏.

See also Nai[4] 能.

188. Hsü[1] 須

The surname Hsü 須 derived from two sources. 1. It branched from the surname Feng 風 of the ancestral line of T'ai Hao 太昊 (Fu-hsi shih 伏羲氏). The surname Feng 風 originated from the name of the ancient State of Feng (Feng kuo 風國), which was cited in <u>Ch'un ch'iu</u> 春秋 as Hsü-kou kuo 須句國. For this reason, both Hsü 須 and Kou 句 were adopted as common surnames from the name of the above feudal state and the families initially settled in Shan-tung 山東 province where the State of Feng was located. 2. According to <u>Ming hsien shih tsu yen hsing lei kao</u> 名賢氏族言行類稿, the surname Hsü 須 was traced to the State of Mi-hsü (Mi-hsü kuo 密須國) in the Shang 商 dynasty. Mi-hsü kuo was affiliated with the State of Yen (Yen kuo 燕國), located in Ling-t'ai hsien 靈臺縣, Kan-su 甘肅 province. After Mi-hsü kuo was defeated by Chou Wen-wang 周文王, Mi-hsü 密須, Hsü 須 and Mi 密 were subsequently adopted as common surnames and the families settled in Kan-su 甘肅 province.

See also Feng[1] 風, Kou[1] 句.

189. Hsü[1] 胥

According to <u>Tso chuan</u> 左傳, the founder of the
family name Hsü 胥 was Hsü Ch'en 胥臣. He was
the head of the Ministry of Works (Ssu-k'ung
司空) in the State of Chin (Chin kuo 晉國) to
Chin wen-kung 晉文公 during the Spring and
Autumn (Ch'un ch'iu 春秋) Period. The family
initially settled in Shan-hsi 山西 province.

190. Hsü[2] 徐

<u>Yüan ho hsing tsuan</u> 元何姓纂 describes the
origin of the surname Hsü 徐 as follows: The
founder of the surname Hsü was Po I 伯益. He
was the Grand Minister (ta-ch'en 大臣) to Yü Ti-
shun 虞帝舜. The surname Hsü derived from the
name of the fedudal territory, the State of Hsü
(Hsü kuo 徐國), bestowed on Po I's son during
the reign of the Great Yü (Ta Yü 大禹) in the
Hsia 夏 dynasty. After the State of Hsü was
defeated by the State of Ch'u (Ch'u kuo 楚國),
Hsü was adopted as the common surname by the
descendants of Po I to commemorate their loss
and the family settled primarily in Shan-tung
山東 province.

191. Hsü[3] 許

According to <u>Yüan ho hsing tsuan</u> 元何姓纂, the
surname Hsü 許 branched from the surname Chiang
姜 of the descent of Yen-ti 炎帝. Wen-shu 文叔,
a descendant of Yen-ti, was bestowed with the
feudal territory of the State of Hsü (Hsü kuo
許國) by Chou Wu-wang 周武王, which was later
defeated by the State of Ch'u (Ch'u kuo 楚國)
and Hsü was adopted as the common surname by his
descendtants to commemorate their loss. The
State of Hsü was located in the present Hsü-
chang hsien 許昌縣 in Ho-nan 河南 province.

192. Hsü[4] 續

The surname Hsü 續 derived from two sources. 1.
<u>Yüan ho hsing tsuan</u> 元何姓纂 and <u>T'ung chih Shih
tsu lüeh</u> 通志氏族略 trace the genealogy of

surname to Hsü Ya 續牙 in the Legendary Period during the reign of Yü Ti-shun 虞帝舜. 2. <u>Wan hsing t'ung p'u</u> 萬姓統譜 and <u>T'ung chih Shih tsu lüeh</u> 通志氏族略 describe the origin of the surname as follows: The surname Hsü originated from the name of a vassal state, the Disctrict of Hsü (Hsü i 續邑), bestowed on the Grand Master (ta-fu 大夫) Hu Chü 狐鞠 of the State of Chin (Chin kuo 晉國) in the Spring and Autumn (Ch'un ch'iu 春秋) Period. Hsü was adopted as a common surname by his descendtants and the family settled primarily in Shan-hsi 山西 province.

See also Chien[3] 簡.

193. Hsüan[1] 宣

<u>T'ung chih Shih tsu lüeh</u> 通志氏族略 describes the origin of the surname Hsüan 宣 as follows: The surname Hsüan originated from Ch'iao Ju 僑如 who was a descendant of a grand master (ta-fu 大夫) from the State of Lu (Lu kuo 魯國) and was bestowed poshumously as the Earl of Hsüan (Tsüan po 宣伯) in the Chou 周 dynasty. His descendants adopted Hsüan as their common surname and settled in Tung-chün 東郡, located in the area of southern Ho-pei 河北 and western Shan-tung 山東 provinces.

194. Hsüan[1]-yüan[2] 軒轅

According to <u>Shih chi so yin</u> 史記索引, Huang-ti 黃帝 was born near the hillside of Hsüan-yüan 軒轅 so that he adopted the place name as his first name as well as his social name (hao 號). The site where Huang-ti was born was located in Hsin-cheng 新鄭, Ho-nan 河南 province.

See also Chi[1] 姬, Kung[1]-sun[1] 公孫.

195. Hsüeh[1] 薛

The surname Hsüeh 薛 derived from two sources: 1. <u>Yüan ho hsing tsuan</u> 元何姓纂 and <u>Hsing shih k'ao lüeh</u> 姓氏考略 describe the genealogy of the surname as follows: The surname Hsüeh 薛 branched from the surname Jen 任 of the ancestral line of Huang-ti 黃帝. Hsi Chung 奚仲, a descendant of the Jen 任 family from the lineage of Huang-ti, was bestowed with the feudal territory of the State of Hsüeh (Hsüeh kuo 薛國). His family members have served as marquises (chu-hou 諸侯) through the Hsia 夏, Shang 商, and Chou 周 periods until the State of Hsüeh was defeated by the State of Ch'u (Ch'u kuo 楚國) at the end of the Chou 周 dynasty and Hsüeh was adopted as the common surname since that time. The family settled in the areas of Kao-p'ing hsien 高平縣 (in Shan-hsi 山西), Hsin-Ts'ai hsien 新蔡縣 (in Ho-nan 河南), and Su hsien 宿縣 (in An-hui 安徽). 2. <u>Wu lu</u> 吳錄 says: The name attributed to the feudal territory, Hsüeh, bestowed on Meng Chang-chün 孟嘗君 at the end of the Chou dynasty. The location of this feudal territory was the present Hsüeh-cheng 薛城 in Shan-tung 山東 province.

See also Jen² 任, P'ei² 邳.

## 196. Hsün² 荀

<u>T'ung chih Shih tsu lüeh</u> 通志氏族略 and <u>Yüan ho hsing tsuan</u> 元何姓纂 trace the genealogy of the surname Hsün 荀 as follows: The surname Hsün branched from the surname Chi 姬 of the ancestral line of Chou Wen-wang 周文王 and originated from the name of the feudal territory Hsün 荀, bestowed on the Marquise of Hsün (Hsün hou 郇侯) who was the seventeenth son of Wen-wang 文王. His descendants modified the character Hsün 郇 and adopted the form of Hsün 荀 as their common surname and settled in He-nei 河內, Kan-su 甘肅 province.

## 197. Hu¹ 呼

The surname Hu 呼 originated from two sources. 1. <u>Hsing shih hsün yüan</u> 姓氏尋源 traces the name's origin to Hu Tzu-hsieh 呼子先 who was a diviner in the Han 漢 dynasty and originally came from Hu-pei 湖北 province. Hu was later adopted as a common surname by his descendants and the family settled primarily in Shan-hsi 山西 and Shen-hsi 陕西 provinces. 2. According to T'ung chih Shih tsu lüeh 通志氏族略 and Hsing shih k'ao lüeh 姓氏考略, the surname Hu-yen 呼延 derived from Hu-yen shih 呼衍氏 of the Hsiung-nus 匈奴. It changed to the present form after Hu-yen shih 呼衍氏 emigrated to China. The surname Hu 呼 branched from the surname Hu-yen 呼延 as the result of the change of surname. Many Hu families populate Shan-hsi 山西 province today.

See also Hu$^1$-yen$^2$ 呼延.

198. Hu$^1$-yen$^3$ 呼衍

See Hu$^1$-yen$^2$ 呼延.

199. Hu$^1$-yen$^2$ 呼延

According to T'ung chih Shih tsu lüeh 通志氏族略, the surname Hu-yen 呼延 derived from the surname Hu-yen 呼衍 of the Hsiung-nus 匈奴. It changed to the present surname after Hu-yen shih 呼衍氏 emigrated to China. The Hu-yen 呼延 family has populated T'ai-yüan 太原, Shan-hsi 山西 province for generations.

See also Hu$^1$ 呼.

200. Hu$^2$ 胡

According to Yüan ho hsing tsuan 元何姓纂, the Hu 胡 surname belongs to the lineage of Yü Ti-shun 虞帝舜 and its founder was Hu Kung-man 胡公滿. The surname originated from the name of a vassal state, the District of Ch'en (Ch'en i 陳邑), bestowed on him by Chou Wu-wang 周武王 and Hu was adopted posthumously as the common surname by Hu Kung-man's descendants. The family's place of origin was Huai-yang hsien 淮陽縣 in Ho-pei 河北 province.

See also Ch'en$^2$ 陳, Man$^3$ 滿, T'ien$^2$ 田, Yao$^2$ 姚.

## 201. Hu² 狐

The surname Hu 狐 originated from two sources.
1. <u>Hsing shih k'ao lüeh</u> 姓氏考略 says: The
surname Hu follows the ancestral line of Chou
Ch'eng-wang 周成王 and its founder was a
descendant of T'ang Shu-yü 唐叔虞 from the State
of Chin (Chin kuo 晉國) in the Spring and Autumn
(Ch'un ch'iu 春秋) Period. 2. <u>T'ung chih Shih
tsu lüeh</u> 通志氏族略 traces the origin of the
surname to a son of Chou P'ing-wang 周平王 who
was known as Prince Hu (Hu Kung-tze 狐公子).

## 202. Hu⁴ 扈

<u>Feng shu t'ung</u> 風俗通 describes the origin of
the surname Hu 扈 as follows: The surname Hu
originated from the place name, Yu Hu 有扈. It
was an indendent state which was subdued by the
Hsia 夏 dynasty during the reign of Ch'i (啓,
2197-2188 B.C.). After Hu was adopted as the
common surname, the family settled in Hu hsien
鄠縣, Shen-hsi 陝西 province.

## 203. Hua¹ 花

The origin of the Hua 花 surname was only
scantily mentioned in ancient documents and
according to <u>Hsing yüan</u> 姓苑, it branched from
the Ho 何 surname. <u>Hsing shih k'ao lüeh</u> 姓氏考略
further elaborates: the appearance of the
surname took place before the T'ang 唐 dynasty
and initially came from Tung-p'ing hsien 東平縣,
Shan-tung 山東 province.

## 204. Hua² 滑

In the Chou 周 feudal age, Chou Wu-wang 周武王
had aggressively bestowed feudal territories to
protect the Chou kingdom, and these territories,
located outside the direct control of the royal
dominion, were allocated to feudal lords.
According to <u>Wan hsing t'ung p'u</u> 萬姓統譜, the
surname Hua 滑 came from the feudal territory of
the State of Hua (Hua kuo 滑國) whose feudal
lord held the post of earl (po 伯) under the
reign of Chou Wu-wang 周武王. The ancient State

of Hua was located in the present Yen-shih hsien 偃師縣, Ho-nan 河南 province.

## 205. Hua⁴ 華

The surname Hua 華 was traced to two different sources. 1. <u>Hsing shih k'ao lüeh</u> 姓氏考略 says: Chung-k'ang (仲康, 2159-2146? B.C.) of the Hsia 夏 dynasty held religious ceremony in the Hua Mountain (Hua shan 華山 ), Shen-hsi 陝西 province and his descendants later adopted Hua as their common surname. 2. According to <u>Ming hsien shih tsu yen hsing lei kao</u> 名賢氏族言行類稿, Hua Tu 華督, the son of a gand master (ta-fu 大夫) of the State of Sung (Sung kuo 宋國) from the Spring and Autumn (Ch'un ch'iu 春秋) Period, was the founder of the Hua surname. He adopted Hua when he was enfeoffed at the feudal territory named Hua. The descendants of this branch of the Hua family settled in Ho-nan 河南 and Chiang-su 江蘇 provinces where the State of Sung was located.

See also Ching¹ 荊.

## 206. Hua⁴-lu² 化盧

See Chu⁴ 祝.

## 207. Huai² 懷

The origin of the surname Huai 懷 was only scantily mentioned in <u>Han shu Kao-ti chi</u> 漢書高帝紀. According to the book, the founder of the surname Huai came from the royal family of the State of Ch'u (Ch'u kuo 楚國) during the reign of Kao-tsu (高祖, 206-194 B.C.) in the Western Han (Hsi Han 西漢) dynasty.

## 208. Huan² 桓

<u>T'ung chih Shih tsu lüeh</u> 通志氏族略 traces the origin of the surname Huan 桓 to the following two sources: 1. The surname Huan adopted posthumously from the Duke Ch'i-huan (Ch'i-huan kung 齊桓公) of the Warring States (Chan kuo 戰國) Period and the Huan family originally

settled in Shan-tung 山東 province. 2. The Duke Sung-huan (Sung-huan kung 宋桓公) was another originator of the surname Huan and this branch of the family initially settled in Ho-nan 河南 province. Wei shu kuan shih chih 魏書官氏志 further elaborates that some of the Huan families initially came from the nomadic group of Hsien-pei 鮮卑 during the Southern and Northern Dynasties (Nan-pei ch'ao 南北朝).

209. Huan⁴ 宦

According to Shuo wen chieh tzu 說文解字, the surname Huan 宦 originated from the name of the official post Eunuch (huan-kuan 宦官), the common name for castrated males in palace service. Huan was adopted as a common surname by the adopted children of these officials. The families settled primarily in Tsun-i 遵義, Kuei-chou 貴州 and Tan-yang 丹陽, Chiang-su 江蘇 areas.

210. Huang² 黄

Yüan ho hsing tsuan 元何姓纂 describes the genealogy of the surname Huang 黄 as follows: The surname Huang originated from the name of the feudal territory, the State of Huang (Huang kuo 黄國), bestowed on a descendant of Lu Chung 陸終 by Chou Wu-wang 周武王. The State of Huang was located in Huang-ch'uan hsien 潢川縣, Ho-nan 河南 province, which was later defeated by the State of Ch'u (Ch'u kuo 楚國), setting the stage for the adoption of Huang as a surname by Lu Chung's descendants in commemoration. Huang shih tsu p'u 黄氏族譜 further elaborates that the surname's place of origin was I-yang hsien 弋陽縣 in Chiang-hsi 江西 province.

See also K'uang⁴ 況.

211. Huang²-fu³ 皇甫

The origin of the multiple surname Huang-fu 皇甫 was documented in T'ang shu tsai hsiang shih hsi piao 唐書宰相世系表 and T'ung chih Shih tsu lüeh 通志氏族略. It was summarized as follows:

84

The surname Huang-fu branched from the surname Chi 姬 of the ancestral line of the Shang 商 king Ch'eng-t'ang 成湯 and its origin was traced to the social name Huang-fu 皇父 of Ch'ung Shih 充石. He was a son of the Duke of Tai (Tai kung 戴公) from the State of Sung (Sung kuo 宋國) in the Spring and Autumn (Ch'un ch'iu 春秋) Period. Huang-fu 皇父 was changed into Huang-fu 皇甫 by Huang-fu Luan 皇甫鸞, a descendant of Ch'ung Shih in the Eastern Han (Tung Han 東漢) dynasty. The name was subsequently adopted as a common surname and the family first settled in Ho-nan 河南 (at the site of the State of Sung 宋), relocated to Shang-tung 山東 (at the site of the State of Lu 魯), and moved to Mao-ling 茂陵, located in the present Hsing-p'ing hsien 興平縣, Shen-hsi 陝西 province.

212.  Hui[4] 惠

According to Ming hsien shih tsu yen hsing lei kao 名賢氏族言行類稿, the surname Hui 惠 derived posthumously from the title of Chou Hui-wang (周惠王, 676-651 B.C.) who ruled the Chou dynasty for twenty-five years during his reign. The descendants of the Hui family settled primarily in the south of Chiang-su 江蘇 and Che-chiang 浙江 provinces. A new branch to the Hui family tree emerged in the Ch'ing (清, A.D. 1583-1908) dynasty; a large percentage of the core of Manchu soldiers known as the Banners (Ch'i jen 旗人) also adopted Hui as their surname while serving in the imperial Ch'ing military organizations.

213.  Hung[2] 弘

According to Lü shih ch'un ch'iu 呂氏春秋, the founder of the surname Hung 弘 was Hung Yen 弘演, a grand master (ta-fu 大夫) of the State of Wei (Wei kuo 魏國) in the Warring States (Chan kuo 戰國) Period. Hung was adopted as the common surname by the descendants of Hung Yen and the family settled in Chiang-su 江蘇 and An-hui 安徽 provinces. Yüan ho hsing tsuan 元何姓纂 further states the evolution of the surname Hung as follows: The surname Hung became less common after the T'ang 唐 dynasty because many people changed their surname to Li 李 to avoid the taboo name Hung during the T'ang period.

See also Hung² 洪.

214. Hung² 紅

According to <u>Ming hsien shih tsu yen hsing lei kao</u> 名賢氏族言行類稿, the surname Hung 紅 follows the ancestral line of Chuan Hsü 顓頊 and the founder of the surname was the Marquise Hung (Hung hou 紅侯) whose name was Liu Fu 劉富. He was a descendant of the Emperor Ch'u-yüan (Ch'u-yüan wang 楚元王) in the Han 漢 Dynasty. Hung was adopted as the common surname by the descendants of Liu Fu and the family settled in Shan-hsi 山西 province.

215. Hung² 洪

The surname Hung 洪 derived from three different sources. 1. According to <u>Yüan ho hsing tsuan</u> 元何姓纂, it originated from Kung-kung shih 共工氏 during the Legendary Period and later the surname was changed to Kung 共 after he was sent into exile by Yü Ti-shun 虞帝舜. The name was changed subsequently by adding the radical of water (shui 水) on its left side, thus the appearence of the present family name Hung 洪. 2. <u>Hsing shih k'ao lüeh</u> 姓氏考略 describes the origin of the surname as follows: The name originated from Hung shih 宏氏 of Nan-Ch'ang hsien 南昌縣, Chiang-hsi 江西 province. To avoid the taboo name of T'ang T'ai-tsung (唐太宗, A.D. 627-650), he changed his surname into Hung 洪. And 3. <u>Yüan ho hsing tsuan</u> 元何姓纂 says: Hung shih 弘氏 from Wu-ching 武進, Chiang-su 江蘇 province, was the Censor-in-Chief (yü-shih 御史) of T'ang Te-tsung (唐德宗, A.D. 780-805), he changed his surname into 洪 to avoid using the taboo name of Hung 弘.

See also Ko³ 葛, Kung³ 龔.

216. Huo⁴ 霍

According to both <u>Kuang Yün</u> 廣韻 and <u>Yüan ho hsing tsuan</u> 元何姓纂, the founder of the family name Huo 霍 was Huo Shu-ch'u 霍叔處, the sixth son of Chou Wen-wang 周文王. He was bestowed with the State of Huo (Huo kuo 霍國) and later his descendants adopted Huo as their common surname. The State of Huo was located in the present T'ai-yüan 太原, Shan-hsi 山西 province.

217. I¹ 伊

<u>Yüan ho hsing tsuan</u> 元何姓纂 traces the origin the surname to the birth place of T'ang Ti-yao 唐帝堯. It was near the I River (I-shui 伊水), located in I-ch'uan 伊川, Ho-nan 河南 province.

218. I² 頤

<u>Chung-kuo hsing shih ta chüan</u> 中國姓氏大全 traces the origin of the surname I 頤 to the following two sources: 1. The surname I derived from the ancient State of I (I kuo 頤國) in the Hisa 夏 dynasty. The State was located in the present Fan hsien 范縣, Ho-nan 河南 province where the descendants of the I family were originally settled. 2. The surname came from the place name, the Village of I (I hsiang 頤鄉), which was located in the State of Ch'u (Ch'u kuo 楚國) of the Spring and Autumn (Ch'un ch'iu 春秋) Period. I was adopted as a common surname by its citizens and the family settled primarily in the District of Lu (Lu i 鹿邑) in Ho-nan 河南 province where the Village of I was located.

219. I⁴ 易

According to <u>Hsing shih k'ao lüeh</u> 姓氏考略, the surname I 易 belongs to the ancestral line of Chiang T'ai-kung 姜太公 and the founder of the surname was a feudal prince from the State of Ch'i (Ch'i kuo 齊國) in the Spring and Autumn (Ch'un ch'iu 春秋) Period. The family originally settled in Chi-yang 濟陽, Shang-tung 山東 province where the State of Ch'i was located. The I clan adopted the ancestral hall name (t'ang ming 堂名) Chi-yang 濟陽 to commemorate their ancestors.

## 220. I⁴ 益

The surname I 益 originated from two sources. 1. <u>Yüan ho hsing tsuan</u> 元何姓纂 says: The surname I branched from the surname Ying 嬴 and the founder of the name was Po I 伯益. <u>Hsing shih k'ao lüeh</u> 姓氏考略 mentions that the original settlement of the family was Feng-i 馮翊 in Shen-hsi 陝西 province. 2. According to <u>T'ai p'ing huan yü chi</u> 太平寰宇記, the surname was traced to the place name I-tu hsien 益都縣 which was the ancient site of Ch'eng-yang Commandery (Ch'eng-yang chün 成陽郡) in Shan-tung 山東 province. This branch of the family prospered primarily in Shan-tung province.

See also Ying² 嬴.

## 221. I⁴ 羿

According to <u>Lu shih</u> 路史, the founder of the family name Yi 羿 was Ho Yi 后羿 who was the chieftain of the tribe of Tung-i 東夷 in the Hsia 夏 dynasty.

## 222. Jan³ 冉

The surname Jan 冉 originated from two sources. 1. <u>Hsing shih hsün yüan</u> 姓氏尋源 traces the name's origin to Chou Wen-wang 周文王's son Chi-tsai 季載 who was bestowed with the feudal territory Jan 冉 and later his descendants adopted Jan as their common surname. The family initially settled in Shan-tung 山東 province. 2. <u>Ming hsien shih tsu yen hsing lei kao</u> 名賢氏族言行類稿 traces the origin of the surname as follows: The surname Jan originated from the Grand Master (ta-fu 大夫) Shu Shan-jan 叔山冉 of the State of Ch'u (Ch'u kuo 楚國) and was later adopted as the common surname by his descendants. The family initially settled in Ssu-ch'uan 四川 province.

## 223. Jang³ 壤

According to <u>Hsing shih k'ao lüeh</u> 姓氏考略, the surname Jang 壤 branched from the surname Jang-ssu 壤駟 and its founder was Jang-ssu Ch'ih 壤駟赤. The Jang family prospered in T'ien-shui 天水, Kan-su 甘肅 province.

See also Jang³-ssu⁴ 壤駟.

### 224. Jang³-ssu⁴ 壤駟

According to <u>Hsing shih k'ao lüeh</u> 姓氏考略, the surname Jang-ssu 壤駟 follows the ancestral line of Jang-ssu Ch'ih 壤駟赤 who was a disciple of Confucius and originally came from the State of Ch'in (Ch'in kuo 秦國) in the Spring and Autumn (Ch'un ch'iu 春秋) Period. Jang-ssu 壤駟 was initially adopted as a common surname by his descendants and the family settled primarily in Kan-su 甘肅 and Shen-hsi 陝西 provinces. The surname Jang-ssu later branched to the surname Jang 壤 due to the change of surname to its simplified form by the members of the Jang-ssu family.

See also Jang³ 壤.

### 225. Jao² 饒

According to <u>Ku chin hsing shih shu pien cheng</u> 古今姓氏書辨證, the surname Jao 饒 originated from the name of a vassal state, the District of Jao (Jao i 饒邑), located in the State of Chao (Chao kuo 趙國) during the Warring States (Chan kuo 戰國) Period. The family originally settled in Jao-yang 饒陽, Ho-pei 河北 province and later expanded to Jao-chou 饒州, Chiang-hsi 江西 province.

### 226. Jei⁴ 芮

According to <u>Ming hsien shih tsu yen hsing lei kao</u> 名賢氏族言行類稿 and <u>T'ung chih Shih tsu lüeh</u> 通志氏族略, the surname Jei 芮 branched from the surname Chi 姬 and the founder of the name was the Earl of Jei (Jei Po 芮伯), who was the head of the Ministry of Education (ssu-t'u 司徒) in the Chou 周 dynasty. The original settlement of family was Fu-fung 扶風 in Shen-hsi 陝西 province.

See also Chi[1] 姬.

227.  Jen[2] 任

According to <u>T'ang shu tsai hsiang shih hsi piao</u> 唐書宰相世系表, the surname Jen 任 originated from the place name, Jen-ch'eng 任城, which was bestowed on Huang-ti 黃帝's twenty-fifth son Yü Yang 禹陽 and was later adopted as a common surname.

See also Hsi[1] 奚, Hsüeh[1] 薛.

228.  Ju[2] 茹

<u>T'ung chih Shih tsu lüeh</u> 通志氏族略 and <u>Ming hsien shih tsu yen hsing lei kao</u> 名賢氏族言行類稿 trace the origin of the surname Ju 茹 as follows: During the Southern and Northern Dynasties (Nan-pei ch'ao 南北朝, A.D. 420-581), the Hu 胡 People pervaded northern China. One of the the strongest tribes among the Hu People was Jou-jan 柔然 in Mongolia. The tribe was renamed Juan-juan 蠕蠕 during the Northern Wei Period (Pei Wei 北魏, 386-534 A.D.) by the Emperor Shih-tsu 世祖. After the tribe was defeated by T'u-chüehs 突厥, those Juan-juans who remained adopted Ju 茹, a word similar in sound, but more simpler in writing than Juan-juan, as their common surname and they settled in Ho-nan 河南 province.

229.  Ju[3] 汝

<u>Hsing yüan yün p'u</u> 姓源韻譜 says: The surname Ju 汝 originated from the name of the feudal territory Ju Ch'uan 汝川 (also known as Ju Ho 汝河) bestowed on the youngest son of Chou P'ing-wang 周平王 in the Eastern Chou (Tung Chou 東周) dynasty. His descendants later adopted Ju as their common surname and settled in Ho-nan 河南 province.

230. Juan³ 阮

According to Yüan ho hsing tsuan 元何姓纂 and Wan hsing t'ung p'u 萬姓統譜, the surname Juan 阮 derived from the name of the feudal territory, the State of Juan (Juan kuo 阮國), in the Shang 商 dynasty and it was adopted as the common surname by the citizens of Juan kuo. The family originally settled in Ch'en-liu 陳留, Ho-nan 河南 province. A representative of the family was Juan Chi 阮籍, who was a prominent poet and literary author in the Eastern Chin (Tung Chin 東晉, A.D. 317-420) dynasty from Ch'en-liu 陳留, Ho-nan 河南 province.

231. Jung² 榮

The surname Jung 榮 originated from two sources. 1. Hsing shih k'ao lüeh 姓氏考略 says: The surname derived from Jung Yüan 榮援 who was the Grand Minister (ta-ch'en 大臣) to Huang-ti 黃帝 from Shang-ku 上谷 in Ho-pei 河北 province. 2. Ming hsien shih tsu yen hsing lei kao 名賢氏族言行類稿 describes the origin of the surname as follows: The surname Jung originated from the name of a vassal state, the District of Jung (Jung i 榮邑), bestowed on the Earl of Jung (Jung po 榮伯), who was a Minister (ch'ing 卿) to Chou Ch'eng-wang (周成王, 1115-1078 B.C.). The descendants from this branch of the family settled in Le-an 樂安, Shan-tung 山東 province.

232. Jung² 戎

Ch'ien fu lun 潛夫論 and Hsing shih k'ao lüeh 姓氏考略 traces the origin the surname Jung 戎 to its founder Sung Wei-tzu 宋微子, who was the eldest brother of the Shang 商 King Chou-hsin (紂辛, 1154-1122 B.C.). The family initially settled in Chiang-ling 江陵, Hu-pei 湖北 and later expanded to Fu-feng 扶風, Shen-hsi 陝西 province.

233. Jung² 融

According to Shih pen 世本, the surname Jung 融 follows the ancestral line of Chuan Hsü 顓頊 and derived from the title of the official post, chu-jung 祝融, Director of Fire Defense. The title was established by Ti K'u 帝嚳 (Kao-hsin shih 高辛氏) and given to Chuan Hsü's descendant Ch'ung Li 重黎, who was appointed to Chu-jung during the reign of Ti K'u. Jung was subsequently adopted as the common surname by his descendants and the family prospered in Nan-k'ang 南康, Chiang-hsi 江西 province. They adopted Nan-k'ang 南康 as their ancestral hall name (t'ang ming 堂名) to commemorate their ancestray.

234. Jung² 容

The surname Jung 容 came from two sources. 1. Ming hsien shih tsu yen hsing lei kao 名賢氏族言行類稿 says: The founder of the surname was Jung Ch'eng 容成 who invented Chinese calendars and was appointed to the Grand Minister (ta-ch'en 大臣) to Huang-ti 黃帝. The Jung family settled primarily in Chiang-su 江蘇 and in other areas of southern China. 2. Hsing shih k'ao lüeh 姓氏考略 traces the origin of the surname to either the name of the ancient state, Jung shih kuo 容氏國, or to the title, jung-kuan 容官, an unofficial reference to the Minister of Rites. Jung kuan was in charge of music rituals in government ceremonies during the Chou 周 period. This branch of the Jung family originally settled in Tun-huang 敦煌, Kan-su 甘肅 province.

235. Kai⁴ 蓋

According to Ku chin hsing shih shu pien cheng 古今姓氏書辨證, the surname Kai 蓋 originated from the name of a vassal state, the District of Kai (Kai i 蓋邑), located in the State of Ch'i (Ch'i kuo 齊國) of the Warring States (Chan kuo 戰國) Period. The Kai family initially settled in Yih-shui hsien 沂水縣, Shan-tung 山東 province where the District of Kai was located.

236. Kan¹ 甘

The surname Kan 甘 derived from two sources. 1.

_Yüan ho hsing tsuan_ 元何姓纂 traces the surname to Kan P'an 甘盤 who was the Grand Minister (ta-ch'en 大臣) to the Shang 商 King Wu Ting (武丁, 1324-1265 B.C.).   2. _Ming hsien shih tsu yen hsing lei kao_ 名賢氏族言行類稿 describes the origin of the surname as follows:  The surname Kan branched from the surname Chi 姬 of the lineage of Chou Wen-wang 周文王.  Kan originated from the name of a vassal state, the District of Kan (Kan i 甘邑), bestowed on a descendant of Chou Wen-wang and later adopted as a common surname.   This  branch  of  the  Kan  family originally settled in Hu hsien 鄠縣, Shen-hsi 陝西 province where the District of Kan was located.

237.  Kan[1] 干

_Wan hsing t'ung p'u_ 萬姓統譜 says: The surname Kan 干 branched from the surname Chi 姬 of the lineage of Chou Wen-wang 周文王 and originated from the name of the feudal territory, the State of Han (Han kuo 邗國), bestowed on a descendant of Chou Wu-wang 周武王 during the Spring and Autumn (Ch'un ch'iu  春秋) Period. When the State of Han was defeated by the State of Wu (Wu kuo 吳國), the residents of the State of Han escaped and relocated to the District of Kan (Kan i 干邑) and subsequently adopted Kan 干 as their common surname.  The family settled in Chiang-tu hsien 江都縣, Chiang-su 江蘇 province where the District of Kan was located.

238.  K'an[4] 闞

According to _Yüan ho hsing tsuan_ 元何姓纂, the surname K'an 闞 originated from a place name located in the State of Lu (Lu kuo 魯國) during the Spring and Autumn (Ch'un ch'iu  春秋) Period.   It was later adopted as a common surname by those who lived in that locale and they settled in Shan-tung 山東 province.

239.  K'ang[1] 康

The surname Kang 康 generated from two sources. 1. According to _Yüan ho hsing tsuan_ 元何姓纂 and

<u>Hsing yüan</u> 姓苑, the surname was adopted posthumously from Kang Shu 康叔 who was initially enfeoffed by his brother Chou Wu-wang 周武王 at the State of Kang (Kang kuo 康國) and later re-enfeoffed at the State of Wei (Wei kuo 衛國). The State of Wei was located in Ch'i hsien 淇縣, Ho-nan 河南 province, where the descendants of the Kang family initially settled and later expanded to Ho-pei 河北 province. 2. <u>Liang shu K'ang Hsüan chuan</u> 梁書康絢傳 attributes the origin of the surname to the tribal state Kang-chü kuo 康居國 which was located in the Western Territories (Hsi-yü 西域) and later subdued by the Emperor Wu-ti (武帝, 140-86 B.C.) of the Western Han (Esi Han 西漢) dynasty. The people of Kang-chü kuo adopted Kang as their common surname and settled in Shen-hsi 陝西 and Kan-su 甘肅 provinces.

240. K'ang⁴ 抗

According to <u>Hsing shih k'ao lüeh</u> 姓氏考略, the surname K'ang 抗 frist appeared in Tan-yang hsien 丹陽縣, Hu-nan 湖南 province with K'ang Hsü 抗徐 as the Governor (t'ai-shou 太守) of the Han 漢 dynasty. The surname K'ang 抗 was changed into Hang 杭 during the Sung 宋 dynasty. The evolution of the surname was listed under Hang² 杭.

See also Hang² 杭.

241. K'ang⁴ 亢

<u>Hsing shih hsün yüan</u> 姓氏尋源 traces the origin of the surname K'ang 亢 to the following two sources: 1. The surname K'ang 亢 branched from the surname K'ang 伉 as the result of a change of name to its simplified form. K'ang 亢 was a popular surname adopted by the feudal lords in the State of Wei (Wei kuo 衛國) during the Spring and Autumn (Ch'un ch'iu 春秋) Period. 2. The surname K'ang 亢 originated from the ancient place name K'ang-fu 亢父, located in the present Chi-ning hsien 濟寧縣, Shan-tung 山東 province. The K'ang families primarily settled in Shan-hsi 山西 province and they adopted T'ai-

yüan 太原 as their ancestral hall name (t'ang ming 堂名).

See also K'ang⁴ 伉.

242. K'ang⁴ 伉

Lu shih 路史 traces the origin of the surname K'ang 伉 to the Grand Master (ta-fu 大夫) Shan K'ang 三伉 of the State of Wei (Wei kuo 衛國) in the Spring and Autumn (Ch'un ch'iu 春秋) Period. The K'ang family settled primarily in Kuang-chou 廣州, Kuang-tung 廣東 province.

See also K'ang⁴ 亢.

243. Kao¹ 高

According to Kuang yün 廣韻, the surname Kao 高 originated in Shan-tung 山東 province and follows the ancestral line of the Grand Duke of Ch'i (Ch'i T'ai-kung 齊太公) in the Chou 周 dynasty. Kao originated from the name of a vassal state bestowed on a descendant of Ch'i T'ai-kung. The family settled originally in Po-hai 渤海, Shan-tung 山東 province where the State of Ch'i was located.

244. Kao⁴ 郜

T'ung chih Shih tsu lüeh 通志氏族略 describes the origin of the surname Kao 郜 as follows: the surname Kao originated from the name of a feudal territory bestowed on the eleventh son of Chou Wen-wang 周文王. It was later adopted as the common surname by his descendants. The Kao family initially settled in Ch'eng-wu hsien 城武縣, Shan-tung 山東 province.

245. Ke¹ 戈

Hsing p'u 姓譜 and Ming hsien shih tsu yen hsing lei kao 名賢氏族言行類稿 trace the origin of the surname Ke 戈 to the lineage of the Great Yü (Ta Yü 大禹) in the Hsia 夏 dynasty. The surname derived from the name of the feudal territory, the State of Ke (Ke kuo 戈國), bestowed on a descendant of Ta Yü and later adopted as a common surname. The family settled and populated Lin-hai 臨海, Che-chiang 浙江 province.

246. Keng³ 耿

The surname Keng 耿 derived from two sources. 1. According to Yüan ho hsing tsuan 元何姓纂, it originated from the name of the feudal state Keng 耿 in the Shang 商 dynasty. The State was later defeated by the State of Chin (Chin kuo 晉國) and Keng was adopted as the common surname since that time. 2. Hsing shih k'ao lüeh 姓氏考略 traces the genealogy of the surname Keng as follows: After the Shang King Tsu-i (祖乙, 1525-1506 B.C.) was enthroned, he relocated the dynastic capital to Keng 耿 and subsequently Keng was adopted as the common surname by the residents living in that locale. There is disagreement in terms of the family's original place of settlement. Some say it was located in Ho-chin hsien 河津縣, Shan-hsi 山西 province while others say it was in Hsing-t'ai hsien 邢台縣, Ho-pei 河北 province.

247. Ko³ 葛

The surname Ko 葛 originated from two sources. 1. According to T'ung chih Shih tsu lüeh 通志氏族略, the founder of the family name was the Earl of Ko (Ko po 葛伯) in the Hsia 夏 dynasty and the family originally settled in Ts'ai-ch'iu hsien 蔡丘縣, Ho-nan 河南 province. 2. Hsing shih k'ao lüeh 姓氏考略 says: The surname Ko branched from the surname Hung 洪 in the Eastern Han (Tung Han 東漢) dynasty during the reign of Kuang Wu-ti 光武帝 and the family settled in Chiang-nan 江南, south of the Yangtze River.

See also Ch¹-ko² 諸葛, Hung² 洪.

248. K'o¹ 柯

According to Kuang yün 廣韻, the surname K'o 柯

originated from the name of the feudal prince
K'o Lu 柯盧, of the State of Wu (Wu kuo 吳國)
during the Spring and Autumn (Ch'un ch'iu 春秋)
Period. K'o is a popular surname in southern
China.

249. Kou¹ 勾

Ming hsien shih tsu yen hsing lei kao
名賢氏族言行類稿 and Lu shih 路史 trace the
origin of the surname Kou 勾 to the official
title of kou-mang 勾芒, Manager of the Bamboo
and Lumber Services. The position was in
existence during the reign of T'ai Hao 太昊 (Fu-
hsi shih 伏羲氏) when Shao Hao 少昊's cousin was
appointed to the position and subsequently Kou
was adopted as the common surname by his
descendants. Tz'u hai 辭海 further elaborates
the name's relationship with the surname Kou 句
as follows: Kou-mang 勾芒 was also written as
kou-mang 句芒. Both characters were used
interchangeably in ancient times.

See also Kou¹ 句.

250. Kou¹ 緱

According to Wan hsing t'ung p'u 萬姓統譜, the
surname Kou 緱 originated from the name of a
vassal state, the Kou shih District (Kou shih i
緱氏邑), bestowed on a minister (ch'ing 卿) of
Chou Wen-wang 周文王 and was later adopted as a
common surname. The Mountain of Kou (Kou shih
shan 緱氏山), located in Kou shih District, was
named after the surname Kou 緱. The Kou family
settled primarily in Ho-nan 河南 province where
the Kou shih District was located.

251. Kou¹ 句

According to Lu shih 路史, the surname Kou 句
was traced to the official title of Kou-mang
句芒 (also written as kou-mang 勾芒), Manager of
the Bamboo and Lumber Services. The description
of the name's origin was detailed under the
surname Kou 勾.

See also Kou¹ 勾, Feng¹ 風, Hsü¹ 須.

## 252. K'ou⁴ 寇

The surname K'ou 寇 initially derived from the name of the official post, ssu-k'ou 司寇, the Minister of Justice in the Chou 周 dynasty. According to Yüan ho hsing tsuan 元何姓纂, Su Fen-sheng 蘇忿生 was a ssu-k'ou in the Chou dynasty and his descendants adopted his title as their common surname. Hsing shih k'ao lüeh 姓氏考略 attributes the founding of the surname to Wei K'ang-shu 衛康叔 who also held the position of ssu-k'ou in the Chou dynasty.

See also Ssu¹-k'ou⁴ 司寇, Su¹ 蘇, Wei⁴ 衛.

## 253. Ku¹ 辜

The character "Ku 辜" means crime, guilt, or sin. According to Yüan ho hsing tsuan 元和姓纂, the origin of the surname Ku 辜 was related to its literary meaning and Ku was originally adopted as a common surname by those who had committed crimes or were guilty in their past. The Ku families settled primarily in Chüan-chou 泉州, Fu-chien 福建 province.

## 254. Ku³ 古

The surname Ku 古 originated from two sources. 1. According to Feng shu t'ung 風俗通, it branched from the surname Chi 姬 of the ancestral line of Huang-ti 黃帝 and the founder of the surname was Ku kung Tan-fu 古公亶父, who was the grand father of Chou Wen-wang 周文王. And 2. Ch'ien fu lun 潛夫論 says: The surname Ku branched from either the surname Ku-ch'eng 古成 or T'u-hsi 吐奚. Both multiple surnames were originally adopted by a group of the Hu 胡 People. They were later subdued by the Han 漢 People and changed their surnames to Ku 古 after they settled in Han territories. The Ku families initially settled in T'ai Commandery (T'ai chün 代郡), which is the present T'ai hsien 代縣 in Shan-hsi 山西 province. In antiquity, T'ai chün 代郡 was called Hsin-an

chün 新安郡 so that the Ku families adopted
Hsin-an 新安 as their ancestral hall name (t'ang
ming 堂名) in commemoration.

255. Ku³ 谷

The surname Ku 谷 originated from two sources.
1. Hsing shih k'ao lüeh 姓氏考略 describes the
origin of the surname as follows: The surname Ku
谷 branched from the surname Ying 嬴.   The
founder of the family name was Po I 伯益 who was
a descendant of Chuan Hsü 顓頊 and was
graciously given the surname Ying 嬴 by the
Great Yü (Ta Yü 大禹) because of his
contribution in training birds and taming
animals.  Several generations later, Ch'in Fei-
tzu 秦非子 , a descendant of Po I, was bestowed
with the feudal territory Ch'in-ku 秦谷, and his
descendants, some adopted Ying 嬴 and others
adopted Ku 谷 as their common surnames.  The Ku
family originally settled in Shen-hsi 陝西
province.   2. According to Wei shu kuan shih
chih 魏書官氏志, the surname Ku branched from
the surname Ku-hui 谷會.  Ku-hui was originally
adopted by a group of Hu 胡 People who invaded
China during the Southern and Northern dynasties
(Nan pei ch'ao 南北朝).   The Group was later
subdued by the Han 漢 People and they changed
their surname to Ku after their settlement in
Han territories.

See also Ku³-hui⁴ 谷會 , Ying¹ 嬴.

256. Ku³-hui⁴ 谷會

According to Wei shu kuan shih chih 魏書官氏志,
the surname Ku-hui 谷會 was adopted by a group
of the Hu 胡 People who invaded China during the
Southern and Northern dynasties (Nan pei ch'ao
南北朝).  They were later subdued by the Han 漢
People and changed their surname to Ku 谷 after
their settlement in Han territories.

See also Ku³ 谷.

257. Ku³-liang² 穀梁

The origin of the surname Ku-liang 穀梁 was traced in <u>Hsing shih hsün yüan</u> 姓氏尋源, <u>Yüan ho hsing tsuan</u> 元何姓纂, and <u>T'ung chih Shih tsu lüeh</u> 通志氏族略. According to these documents, the surname Ku-liang follows the ancestral line of Ku-liang Ts'u 穀梁赤 from Shan-tung 山東 province during the Spring and Autumn (Ch'un ch'iu 春秋) Period. After the T'ang 唐 dynasty, the family relocated to Hsia-p'ei 下邳 which is located in the present Hsü-chou 徐州, Chiang-su 江蘇 province.

258. Ku⁴ 顧

According to <u>Ming hsien shih tsu yen hsing lei kao</u> 名賢氏族言行類稿, the surname Ku 顧 was traced to the lineage of Kou Chien 勾踐 who was the leader of the State of Yüeh (Yüeh kuo 越國) during the Warring States (Chan kuo 戰國) Period. One of his descendants was enfeoffed at the vassal state of Ku 顧 and was entitled as the Marquise Ku-yü (Ku-yü hou 顧余侯) during the Western Han (Hsi Han 西漢) period and Ku was adopted as a common surname by his descendants. The family originally settled in Kuei-chi 會稽, Che-chiang 浙江 and later migrated to Chiang-su 江蘇 province.

259. K'uai³ 蒯

According to <u>Ku chin hsing shih shu pien cheng</u> 古今姓氏書辨證, the surname K'uai 蒯 originated from the name of a vassal state, the District of K'uai (K'uai i 蒯邑), and the founder of the surname, K'uai Te 蒯得, was the Grand master (ta-fu 大夫) of the State of Chin (Chin kuo 晉國) during the Spring and Autumn (Ch'un ch'iu 春秋) Period. The K'uai family initially settled in Lo-yang 洛陽, Ho-nan 河南 and later expanded to Hsiang-yang 襄陽, Hu-pei 湖北 province. Hsiang-yang 襄陽 was adopted as the family's ancestral hall name (t'ang ming 堂名) in memory of its ancestry.

260. Kuan¹ 關

The surname Kuan 關 originated from two sources.

1. <u>Hsing yüan yün p'u</u> 姓源韻譜 says: It originated from the ancestral line of Kuan Lung-feng 關龍逢 who was a Grand Minister (ta-ch'en 大臣) in the Hsia 夏 dynasty. The family originally settled in Ann-i 安邑, located in the present Hsia hsien 夏縣, Shan-hsi 山西 province and later prospered in Kan-su 甘肅 province. 2. <u>Feng shu t'ung</u> 風俗通 traces the surname Kuan to the title of the official post, kuan-ling 關令, Director of the Pass in the Sui 隋 and T'ang 唐 dynasties. Kuan-ling was the official guard at a strategic point on the border for protection against intruders. Kuan was later adopted as the common surname by the descendants of the family who held the post. This branch of the Kuan family settled primarily in Shan-tung 山東 and Chiang-su 江蘇 provinces.

261. Kuan³ 管

<u>Yüan ho hsing tsuan</u> 元何姓纂 describes the origin of the surname Kuan 管 as follows: The surname Kuan originated from the name of a feudal territory located in Kuang-ch'eng 管城, in the present Cheng-chou hsien 鄭州縣, Ho-nan 河南 province. The feudal territory was bestowed on Kuan Shu-hsien 管叔鮮, the third son of Chou Wen-wang 周文王, and later Kuan was adopted as the common surname by his descendants. The family settled primarily in Ho-nan 河南 province near the area where the surname originated.

262. Kuang³ 廣

<u>Feng shu t'ung</u> 風俗通 and <u>Hsing shih k'ao lüeh</u> 姓氏考略 trace the surname Kuang 廣 to the ancestral line of Kuang Ch'eng-tzu 廣成子 during the regin of Huang-ti 黃帝. The family originally settled in Tan-yang hsien 丹陽縣, Chiang-su 江蘇 province and later expanded to An-hui 安徽 province.

263. K'uang¹ 匡

<u>Feng shu t'ung</u> 風俗通 traces the origin of the surname K'uang 匡 to the name of a vassal state,

the District of K'uang (K'uang i 匡邑), in the
State of Lu (Lu kuo 魯國). K'uang was adopted
as a common surname by the residents of the
District and they settled in Shan-tung 山東
province.

264. K'uang⁴ 況

Hsing shih k'ao lüeh 姓氏考略 traces the origin
of the surname K'uang 況 to the following two
sources: 1. The surname follows the lineage of
K'uang Ch'ang-ning 況長寧 of the Shu Kingdom
(蜀國, A.D. 221-263) during the period of Three
Kingdoms (Shan kuo 三國, A.D. 220-280). The
family initially settled in Ssu-ch'uan 四川 and
later expanded to Chiang-hsi 江西 provinces. 2.
Huang Chung 黃鐘 in the Ming 明 dynasty changed
his name to K'uang Chung 況鐘 and his
descendants subsequently adopted K'uang as their
common surname. This branch of the family
prospered in Shan-hsi 山西 and other areas in
southern China.

See also Huang² 黃.

265. Kuei¹ 歸

According to T'ung chih Shih tsu lüeh
通志氏族略, the surname Kuei 歸 derived from the
name of the ancient state, the State of Hu-tzu
(Hu-tzu kuo 胡子國). Kuei 歸 was adopted as the
common surname in the Spring and Autumn Period
(Ch'un ch'iu 春秋) after the State of Hu-tzu was
defeated by the State of Ch'u (Ch'u kuo 楚國)
and the State of Hu-tzu became the State of Kuei
(Kuei kuo 歸國).

266. Kuei⁴ 桂

According to Hsing shih k'ao lüeh 姓氏考略, the
surname Kuei 桂 branched from the surname Chi 季
of the ancestral line of Huang-ti 黃帝. Chi Sun
季孫 was the feudal prince of the State of Ch'i
(Ch'i kuo 齊國) in the Spring and Autumn (Ch'un
ch'iu 春秋) Period. When his descendant Chi Chen
季楨 was murdered, Chi Chen's brother Chi Mu
季睦 escaped from his homeland and changed the

surname of his family into Kuei 桂.
Subsequently, Kuei was adopted as the common
surname and the family settled in Yu-chou 幽州,
located in parts of the present Ho-pei 河北 and
Liao-ning 遼寧 provinces.

See also Chi⁴ 季.

## 267. K'uei² 夔

Hsing shih k'ao lüeh 姓氏考略 traces the
ancestral line of the surname K'uei 夔 to the
Great Yü (Ta Yü 大禹) and the name was adopted
from an ancient state name located in the State
of Yüeh (Yüeh kuo 越國) of the Spring and Autumn
(Ch'un ch'iu 春秋) Period.

## 268. Kung¹ 龔

According to Yüan ho hsing tsuan 元和姓纂, Ku
chin hsing shih shu pien cheng 古今姓氏書辨證
and Wan hsing t'ung p'u 萬姓統譜, the surname
Kung 龔 can be traced to the multiple surname
Kung-kung 共公 in the Legendary Period. Kung-
kung 共公氏 was a Grand Minister (ta-ch'en 大臣)
to Huang-ti 黃帝. Following his death, his son
Lung 龍 succeeded to the post and later his
descendants adopted Kung 龔, the combined form
of the surnames Kung 共 and Lung 龍, as the
common surname. The family initially settled in
Wu-ling 武陵, Hu-nan 湖南 province.

See also Hung² 洪, Lung² 龍.

## 269. Kung¹ 弓

The origin of the surname Kung 弓 can be traced
to the following two sources: 1. According to
Hsing shih k'ao lüeh 姓氏考略, Hui 揮, the fifth
son of Huang-ti 黃帝, invented the bow (kung 弓)
and was enfeoffed at the feudal territory Chang
張. Chang and Kung were both adopted as
surnames by his descendants. The initial
settlement of the Kung family was located in
T'ai-yüan hsien 太原縣, Shan-hsi 山西 province.
2. Wan hsing t'ung p'u 萬姓統譜 traces the

surname's origin to its founder, Shu Kung 叔弓, a grand master (ta-fu 大夫) of the State of Lu (Lu kuo 魯國) in Shan-tung 山東 province. This Kung family prospered in T'ai-yüan hsien 太原縣, Shan-hsi 山西 province. By the Southern and Northern Dynasties (Nan pei ch'ao 南北朝), a large number of the Kung 弓 descendants changed their surname to Chang 張 because of political uncertainty in their homeland.

See also Chang[1] 張.

270. Kung[1] 公

According to T'ung chih Shih tsu lüeh 通志氏族略, the surname Kung 公 branched from the surname Chi 姬 of the ancestral line of Huang-ti 黃帝 and followed by the lineage of the Duke of Chou (Chou kung 周公) from the State of Lu (Lu kuo 魯國) in the Spring and Autumn (Ch'un ch'iu 春秋) Period. The Kung family settled primarily in Meng-yin 蒙陰, Shan-tung 山東 province.

See also Chi[1] 姬.

271. Kung[1] 宮

According to Ku chin hsing shih shu pien cheng 古今姓氏書辨證, the surname Kung 宮 materialized from the position, Official Guard in the Chou 周 palace (kung 宮). The first person to adopt this family name was Kung Chih-ch'i 宮之奇 who was the Grand Master (ta-fu 大夫) of the State of Yü (Yü kuo 虞國) during the Spring and Autumn (Ch'un ch'iu 春秋) Period. The early activities of the Kung family were primarily concentrated in Shan-hsi 山西 province where the State of Yü was located.

272. Kung[3] 鞏

According to Hsing shih k'ao lüeh 姓氏考略 and Ming hsien shih tsu yen hsing lei kao 名賢氏族言行類稿, the surname Kung 鞏 derived from the place name Kung hsien 鞏縣 located in Ho-nan 河南 province. It was originally the site of the feudal state Kung-po kuo 鞏伯國 which was bestowed by the Duke of Hui (Hui kung 惠公) on his son in the Chou 周 dynasty. Kung was later adopted as the common surname by his descendants and the family settled in Shan-yang 山陽, Ho-nan 河南 province.

273. Kung⁴ 貢

According to <u>Yüan ho hsing tsuan</u> 元何姓纂 and <u>Hsing shih chi chiu p'ien</u> 姓氏急就篇, the surname Kung 貢 branched from the surname Tuan-mu 端木 and the founder of the surname was Tuan-mu ssu 端木賜. He was a disciple of Confucius and was commonly known by his social name Tze-kung 子貢. Tze-kung came from the State of Wei (Wei kuo 衛國) during the Spring and Autumn (Ch'un ch'iu 春秋) Period. Kung was later adopted as the common surname by his descendants. The State of Wei, where the Kung family originally settled, was located in the present areas of the Ho-pei 河北 and Ho-nan 河南 provinces.

See also Mu⁴ 木, Tuan¹ 端, Tuan¹-mu⁴ 端木.

274. Kung⁴ 共

See Kung¹ 龔.

275. K'ung¹ 空

According to <u>Wan hsing t'ung p'u</u> 萬姓統譜, the surname K'ung 空 was a popular surname in Yün-nan 雲南 province and it was adopted predominantly by minority groups living in that region.

276. K'ung³ 孔

The Kung 孔 surname belongs to the lineage of Huang-ti 黃帝. <u>Kuang yün</u> 廣韻 states the origin of the surname as follows: The surname K'ung branched from the surname Tzu 子 which initially adopted by a son of Ti K'u 帝嚳. By the Shang 商 dynasty, Ch'eng-t'ang (成湯, 1766-

1753 B.C.), a descendant of Ti K'u, assumed the appellatic title of T'ai-i 太乙 and subsequently his descendants adopted K'ung 孔 (formed by combining the word Tzu 子 with I 乙) as their common surname. The first person to adopt the surname was K'ung Fu-chia 孔夫嘉 of the State of Sung (Sung kuo 宋國). After he was murdered, his sons escaped to the State of Lu (Lu kuo 魯國) and the K'ung families settled in Ch'ü-fu 曲阜, Shang-tung 山東 province. Shih chi K'ung-tze shih chia 史記孔子世家 traces the family tree of Confucius (K'ung-tze 孔子) as well as detailing the origin of the surname K'ung.

277. Kung¹-hsi¹ 公西

The origin of the surname Kung-hsi 公西 was traced in Hsing shih hsün yüan 姓氏尋源. According to the book, the surname follows the lineage of Chou Wen-wang 周文王 and branched from the surname Chi-sun 季孫 of the State of Lu (Lu kuo 魯國) in the Spring and Autumn (Ch'un ch'iu 春秋) Period. A member of this family was Kung-hsi Ch'ih 公西赤 who was a disciple of Confucius.

See also Chi⁴-sun¹ 季孫.

278. Kung¹-liang² 公良

According to Hsing shih k'ao lüeh 姓氏考略, the surname Kung-liang 公良 derived from the Feudal Prince (kung-tzu 公子) Liang 良 who was known as Kung-tzu Liang 公子良 of the State of Ch'en (Ch'en kuo 陳國) in the Chou 周 dynasty. Kung-liang was adopted as a common surname by his descendants. A member of this family was Kung-liang Ju 公良儒 who was a disciple of Confucius in the Spring and Autumn (Ch'un ch'iu 春秋) Period.

279. Kung¹-sun¹ 公孫

The origin of the surname Kung-sun 公孫 was detailed in Shih chi 史記, T'ung chih Shih tsu lüeh 通志氏族略 and Shang yu lu 尚友錄. According to these books, the founder of the surname was Huang-ti 黃帝. His surname, Kung-sun 公孫 was given by his father Shao-tien 少典 who also named him Chi 姬 which was inspired by the name of the river Chi shui 姬水 located in the vicinity of his residence. Huang-ti was also known as Hsüan-yüan shih 軒轅氏, it was named after his birthplace. Another of his name was Yu-hsiung shih 有熊氏 which was adopted from the name of his initial founding territories.

See also Chi[1] 姬, Hsüan[1]-yüan[2] 軒轅, Kung[1]-yang[2] 公羊.

280.  Kung[1]-yang[2] 公羊

The origin of the surname Kung-yang 公羊 was traced in both T'ung chih Shih tsu lüeh 通志氏族略 and Shang yu lu 尚友錄. According to these books, the surname Kung-yang branched from the surname Chi 姬 of the ancestry of Chou Wen-wang 周文王 and the founder of the surname was Kung-sun Yang-ju 公孫羊孺. His descendants, some adopted Kung-sun 公孫 while others adopted Kung-yang 公羊 as their common surnames. The Kung-yang family settled primaily in Tun-ch'iu 頓丘, located in the present Ch'ing-feng hsien 清豐縣, Ho-pei 河北 province.

See also Chi[1] 姬, Kung[1]-sun[1] 公孫.

281.  Kung[1]-yeh[3] 公冶

The surname Kung-yeh 公冶 branched from the surname Chi 姬 and the founder of the surname was Chi Yeh 季冶 of the State of Lu (Lu kuo 魯國). He was known by his social name as Kung-yeh 公冶. The name was used by his descendants and was adopted as the common surname. The family settled primarily in Shan-tung 山東 province. A representative of the family was Kung-yeh Ch'ang 公冶長, who was a disciple and son-in-law of Confucius, his deeds were documented by Confucius in his book Lun yü Kung-yeh p'ien 論語公冶篇.

See also Chi[4] 季.

**282. Kuo[1] 郭**

The surname Kuo 郭 derived from two sources: 1. Hsing shih k'ao lüeh 姓氏考略 traces the origin of the surname as follows: The surname Kuo appeared early in the Hsia 夏 dynasty. It initially referred to the residential area of a walled compound (kuo 郭) of a town and was eventually adopted by the people who lived there. 2. Yüan ho hsing tsuan 元何姓纂 traces the origin of the surname Kuo differently: The surname Kuo branched from the surname Chi 姬 of the ancestral line of Huang-ti 黄帝. The fourth brother of Chou Wen-wang 周文王 was bestowed with the feudal territory Kuo 虢 and was nicknamed Kuo shu 虢叔. He changed his surname into Kuo 郭, a simplified version of Kuo 虢 and his descendants adopted it as their common surname. The initial settlement of the family was in T'ai-yüan 太原, Shan-hsi 山西 province where the feudal territory Kuo 虢 was located.

**283. Kuo[1] 過**

The origin of the surname Kuo 過 was cited in Wan hsing t'ung p'u 萬姓統譜, T'ung chih Shih tsu lüeh 通志氏族略, and Ming hsien shih tsu yen hsing lei kao 名賢氏族言行類稿. According to these books, it derived from the name of the feudal state Kuo 過 in the Hsia 夏 dynasty. The State of Kuo 過 was later defeated by the Hsia king Shao-k'ang 少康 and its citizens subsequently adopted Kuo as their common surname in commemoration of their origin.

**284. Kuo[2] 國**

The surname Kuo 國 originated from three sources. 1. According to Yüan ho hsing tsuan 元何姓纂 and Hsing shih k'ao lüeh 姓氏考略, the surname Kuo branched from the ancestral line of Chiang T'ai-kung 姜太公, the founder of the State of Ch'i (Ch'i kuo 齊國) during the Spring and Autumn (Ch'un ch'iu 春秋) Period. 2. Yüan ho hsing tsuan 元何姓纂 says: The founder of the surname Kuo was the Grand Master (ta-fu 大夫) Kuo Ch'iao 國僑 of the State of Cheng (Cheng kuo

鄭國). This branch of the Kuo family originally settled in Ho-nan 河南 province where the State of Cheng was located. 3. According to <u>Hsing shih k'ao lüeh</u> 姓氏考略, the surname Kuo came from the State of Wei (Wei kuo 衛國), located in the areas of the present Ho-pei 河北 and Ho-nan 河南 provinces. The ancient State of Pai-chi (Pai-chi kuo 百濟國), which was a part of the Ch'ao-hsien 朝鮮 territory during the Eastern Han (Tung Han 東漢) and T'ang 唐 period, contained a population of Kuo families as well.

### 285. Lai⁴ 賴

<u>Hsing shih k'ao lüeh</u> 姓氏考略 traces the origin of the surname Lai 賴 as follows: The surname Lai originated from the name of a feudal territory, the State of Lai (Lai kuo 賴國), in the Spring and Autumn (Ch'un ch'iu 春秋) Period. The family initially settled in Ying-ch'uan 穎川, Ho-nan 河南 province.

### 286. Lan² 藍

According to <u>Shang yu lu</u> 尚友錄 and <u>Wan hsing t'ung p'u</u> 萬姓統譜, the surname Lan 藍 derived from the place name Lan-t'ien 藍田 located in Kuang-tung 廣東 province and was adopted as the common surname by its residents. The family settled primarily in Tung-wan 東莞, Kuang-tung 廣東 province.

### 287. Lan² 蘭

The surname Lan 蘭 originated from the following two sources: 1. According to <u>Wei shu kuan shih chih</u> 魏書官氏志, the surname Lan came from Wu-lo-lan shih 烏落蘭氏 of the nomadic group of Hsiung-nu 匈奴 during the reign of Hsiao Wen-ti 孝文帝 in the Northern Wei (Pei Wei 北魏) period. 2. The surname derived from the forename Lan 蘭 of the Duke of Mu (Mu kung 穆公) from the State of Cheng (Cheng kuo 鄭國) in the Spring and Autumn (Ch'un ch'iu 春秋) Period and was adopted as the common surname by his grandson.

288. Lang² 郎

The Fei 費 and the Lang 郎 families came from the same origin nearly three thousand years ago. According to Yüan ho hsing tsuan 元何姓纂, the surname Lang 郎 belongs to the ancestral line of the Duke of Chou (Chou kung 周公) and branched from the surname Fei 費 of the State of Lu (Lu kuo 魯國) during the Spring and Autumn (Ch'un ch'iu 春秋) Period. The founder of the surname Lang was the Earl of Fei (Fei po 費伯) from the State of Lu 魯. He changed his surname into Lang after he was bestowed with the vassal state in Lang Ch'eng 郎城.

See also Fei⁴ 費.

289. Lao² 勞

Yüan ho hsing tsuan 元何姓纂 and Ming hsien shih tsu yen hsing lei kao 名賢氏族言行類稿 describe the origin of the surname Lao 勞 as follows: The surname Lao originated from the name of a mountain, the Mountain of Lao (Lao shan 勞山), located in Shan-tung 山東 province. The Lao family initially settled in Po-hai 渤海 in the area of the present border provinces between Shan-tung 山東 and Ho-pei 河北.

290. Le⁴ 樂

Yüan ho hsing tsuan 元何姓纂 traces the origin of the surname Le 樂 as follows: The surname Le first appeared in the State of Sung (Sung kuo 宋國) of the Spring and Autumn (Ch'un ch'iu 春秋) Period and the founder of the surname was Sung Wei-tzu 宋微子. It was adopted as a common surname since the time of the Prince of Yen 衎, who was a descendant of Sung Wei-tzu and a son of the Duke of Tai (Tai kung 戴公), had the social name (tzu 字) Le Fu 樂父. The family initially settled in Nan-yang 南陽, Ho-nan 河南 province.

See also Yüeh⁴-cheng⁴ 樂正.

291. Lei² 雷

Yüan ho hsing tsuan 元何姓纂 traces the origin
of the surname Lei 雷 as follows: The surname
Lei follows the family tree of Fang Lei shih
方雷氏, whose daughter was a concubine (fei 妃)
of Huang-ti 黄帝. The initial settlement of the
Lei family was in two places, one in Feng-i 馮翊
(located in the present Ta-li hsien 大荔縣,
Shen-hsi 陝西 province) and the other one in Yü-
chang 豫章 (located in the present Nan-ch'ang
hsien 南昌縣, Chiang-hsi 江西 province).

292. Leng³ 冷

The surname Leng 冷 originated from two sources.
1. Shan t'ang ssu k'ao 山堂肆考 traces the
founder of surname Leng to Leng Lun 冷倫 who was
the Master Musician (ling-kuan 伶官) to Huang-ti
黄帝. 2. According to Lu shih 路史, the origin
of the surname can be traced to the ancestral
line of K'ang Shu 康叔 who was a brother of the
Chou 周 king Wu-wang 武王.

See also Ling² 伶.

293. Li² 黎

The surname Li 黎 originated from three sources.
1. According to Feng shu t'ung 風俗通, the
commonly called "Chiu-li 九黎" was a team of
nine Ministers who served during the reign of
Shao Hao (少昊, 2597-2513 B.C.). Some of the
descendants of these Ministers later adopted Li
黎 as their common surname. 2. Yüan ho hsing
tsuan 元何姓纂 and Lu shih 路史 traces the
origin of the surname Li to the name of the
feudal state, the State of Li (Li kuo 黎國), in
the Shang 商 dynasty. After Shang was defeated,
the State of Li emerged under the Chou 周 royal
domain. It was bestowed on a descendant of
T'ang Ti-yao 唐帝堯 who was named the Marquise
of Li (Li hou 黎侯) and Li 黎 was subsequently
adopted as the common surname by his
descendants. The family ininitally settled in
Ch'ang-chih hsien 常治縣, Shan-tung 山東
province where the State of Li was located. 3.
Wei shu 魏書 cites the third source of the
name's orgin as follows: The surname Li appeared

during the Southern and Northern Dynasties (Nan-pei ch'ao 南北朝). Su-li Shih 素黎氏, who belongs to the nomadic group of Hsien-pei 鮮卑 of the Hu 胡 People, was the origin of the surname Su-li 素黎, and Su-li was later changed into Li 黎 and it was adopted as the common surname after the family settled in Han 漢 territories.

294. Li³ 李

According to <u>Yüan ho hsing tsuan</u> 元何姓纂, the surname Li 李 branched from the surname Li 理 and both belong to the ancestral line of Chuan Hsü 顓頊. Chiu-yao 咎繇, a grandson of Chuan Hsü, who was the Regulatory Official for Law Enforcement (li-kuan 理官) to T'ang Ti-yao 唐帝堯, adopted the name of his official post as his surname. The surname Li 理 was changed to the surname Li 李 in the Shang 商 dynasty when Li Cheng 理徵 offended the dominant Shang king Chou-hsin 紂辛 and was expelled from his country. His son, Li Li-tsen 理利貞, survived by eating the fruits of the plant called mu-tzu 木子 and in gratitude of this deliverance, he changed his surname to Li 李 (which is the combination of the words "mu 木" on the top and "tzu 子" on the bottom). The descendants of the Li 李 family originally settled in Kan-su 甘肅 and Ho-pei 河北 provinces.

See also Li³ 理, Li⁴ 利, Li⁴ 屬, Tuan⁴-kan¹ 段干.

295. Li³ 理

According to <u>Yüan ho hsing tsuan</u> 元何姓纂, the surname Li 理 belongs to the ancestral line of Chuan Hsü 顓頊. Chiu-yao 咎繇, a grandson of Chuan Hsü, who was the Regulatory Official for Law Enforcement (li-kuan 理官) to T'ang Ti-yao 唐帝堯, adopted the name of his official post as his surname. The Li family initially settled in Kan-su 甘肅 and Ho-pei 河北 provinces.

See also Li³ 李, Li⁴ 利.

296. Li⁴ 酈

According to Yüan ho hsing tsuan 元何姓纂, the surname Li 酈 originated from the ancient place name Li hsiang 酈鄉, located in the present Nei-hsiang hsien 內鄉縣, Ho-nan 河南 province. The initial settlement of the Li family was Hsin-ts'ai hsien 新蔡縣 in Ho-nan 河南 province.

297. Li⁴ 厲

The surname Li 厲 branched from the surname Chiang 姜 of the lineage of Yen-ti 炎帝 and it originated from the following sources: 1. According to Feng shu t'ung 風俗通, the surname Li followed the ancestral line of the Duke of Li (Li kung 厲公) from the State of Ch'i (Ch'i kuo 齊國) in the Spring and Autumn (Ch'un ch'iu 春秋) Period. 2. Ku chin hsing shih shu pien cheng 古今姓氏書辨證 traces the surname to the ancient State of Li (Li kuo 厲國), located in Li hsiang 厲鄉, Hu-pei 湖北 province. 3. San kuo chih Wu chih 三國志吳志 says: The evolution of the surname Li 厲 from the surname Sun 孫 was circumstantial; in the Chou 周 dynasty, Sun Hao 孫皓 changed his surname to Li because his father Sun Hsiu 孫秀 escaped to the State of Wei (Wei kuo 魏國) to elude his enemies. 4. Wan hsing t'ung p'u 萬姓統譜 points out: The surname Li 厲 was adopted by the change of surname from Li 李. In the T'ang 唐 dynasty, Li Chin 李晉 changed his surname to Li 厲 in order to escape from his enemies.

See also Li³ 李, Sun¹ 孫.

298. Li⁴ 利

According to Yüan ho hsing tsuan 元何姓纂, the surnames Li 理, Li 利 and Li 李 came from the same origin, the ancestral line of Chuan Hsü 顓頊. Chiu-yao 咎繇, a grandson of Chuan Hsü, who was the Regulatory Official for Law Enforcement (li-kuan 理官) to T'ang Ti-yao 唐帝堯, adopted the name of his official post as his surname. The surname Li 理 was changed to the surname Li 李 in the Shang 商 dynasty when

Li Cheng 理徵 offended the dominant Shang king Chou-hsin 紂辛 and was expelled from his country. His son, Li Li-tsen 理利貞, survived by eating the fruits of the plant called mu-tzu 木子 and in gratitude of this deliverance, he changed his surname to Li 李 (which is the combination of the words "mu 木" on the top and "tzu 子" on the bottom). The descendants of the Li 李 family settled primarily in Kan-su 甘肅 and Ho-pei 河北 provinces. Lu shih 路史 traces the origin of the surname Li 利 in details as follows: Lao-tzu 老子 , the Taoist sage and the reputed author of Tao te ching 道德經, whose real name was Li Erh 李耳, traced his ancestry to Li Li-tsen 李利貞 (formerly Li Li-tsen 理利貞). Li 利 was later adopted as a common surname by the descendats of Lao-tzu. The Li 利 family primarily settled in Ho-nan 河南 province.

See also Li³ 理, Li³ 李.

299. Liang² 梁

According to Hsü Wen hsien t'ung k'ao 續文獻通考 and Ming hsien shih tsu yen hsing lei kao 名賢氏族言行類稿, the surname Liang 梁 derived from two sources: 1. It branched from the surname Ying 嬴 of the lineage of Shao Hao 少昊 and originated from his descendant Ch'in Chung 秦仲 of the ancestral line of Po I 伯益. Ching Chung's son was bestowed in Hsia-yang 夏陽 and was named the Earl of Liang (Liang po 梁伯). After his territory was defeated by the State of Ch'in (Ch'in kuo 秦國), Liang was adopted as the common surname by his descendants. 2. During the reign of Hsiao Wen-ti 孝文帝 in the Northern Wei (Pei Wei 北魏, A.D. 386-534) period, a drastic reform program which touched upon nearly every aspect of state and social functions took place; the change of innate surnames into Chinese surnames was commonplace. Under such ethos, the surname Pa-lieh-lan 拔列蘭 was changed to the surname Liang 梁 and the family settled in Han 漢 territories.

See also Pa²-lieh⁴-lan² 拔列蘭.

## 300. Liang²-ch'iu¹ 梁丘

According to <u>Shang yu lu</u> 尚友錄, the surname
Liang-ch'iu originated from the name of a vassal
state, the Liang-ch'iu District (Liang-ch'iu i
梁丘邑) in the State of Ch'i (Ch'i kuo 齊國),
where a grand master (ta-fu 大夫) was bestowed,
was later adopted as a common surname by its
residents. The family initially settled in
Ch'eng-wu hsien 城武縣, Shan-tung 山東 province
where the Liang-ch'iu District and the nearby
Liang-ch'iu Mountain (Liang-ch'iu shan 梁丘山)
were located.

## 301. Liao⁴ 廖

The surname Liao 廖 is one of the most popular
surnames in sourthern China, particularly in Fu-
chien 福建 and Kuang-tung 廣東 provinces. It
originally came from areas near the Yellow River
and was gradually adopted by the people living
in the southern provinces. The origin of the
surname can be traced to the following sources:
1. According to <u>Feng shu t'ung</u> 風俗通, the
founder of the surname was Liao Shu-an 廖叔安 in
the Legendary Period. 2. <u>Liao shih tsu p'u</u>
廖氏族譜 points out that the surname Liao came
from the change of taboo names Miao 繆 and Yen
顏 to Liao 廖. 3. <u>Hsing shih k'ao lüeh</u> 姓氏考略
traces the origin of the surname to Chou Wen-
wang's 周文王 son Po-liao 伯廖 and its ancestral
home to Chü-lu 鉅鹿, Ho-pei 河北 province.

See also Miao⁴ 繆, Yen² 顏.

## 302. Lieh⁴ 列

<u>Feng shu t'ung</u> 風俗通 traces the surname Lieh 列
to the following two sources: 1. The surname
Lieh follows the ancestral line of Lieh-shan
shih 列山氏 who was the chieftain of a tribe
during the reign of Shen-nung shih 神農氏.
Because Lieh-shan 列山 was recognized as Lieh-
shan 烈山 in ancient times, the names Lieh 列,
Lieh 烈, Lieh-shan 列山 and lieh-shan 烈山 were
later adopted as common surnames from the same
blood line. 2. The surname Lieh originated from

Lieh-tsung shih 列宗氏 of the State of Ch'u (Ch'u kuo 楚國) in the Chou 周 dynasty.

303. Lieh⁴ 烈

See Lieh⁴ 列.

304. Lieh⁴-shan¹ 列山.

See Lieh⁴ 列.

305. Lieh⁴-shan¹ 烈 山.

See Lieh⁴ 列.

306. Lien² 廉

Yüan ho hsing tsuan 元何姓纂 traces the origin of the surname Lien 廉 to the ancestral line of Huang-ti 黃帝 and the founder of the name was Ta-lien 大廉, who was a grandson of Chuan Hsü 顓頊. The Lien family initially settled on the east side of the Yellow river, commonly known as He-tung 河東.

307. Lien² 連

The surname Lien 連 originated from four sources. 1. Tso chuan 左傳 and Ming hsien shih tsu yen hsing lei kao 名賢氏族言行類稿 state that the surname derived from the Grand Master (ta-fu 大夫) Lien Ch'eng 連稱 of the State of Ch'i (Ch'i kuo 齊國). This branch of the Lien family initially settled in Shan-tung 山東 province. 2. Hsing shih k'ao lüeh 姓氏考略 says the surname belongs to the lineage of Chuan Hsü 顓頊 and originated from his descendant Hui Lien 惠連. 3. Hsing shih k'ao lüeh 姓氏考略 also traces the origin of the surname Lien to the title of the official post, lien-chang 連長 or lien-yin 連尹, Aggregation Head, in the Chou 周 dynasty. According to Kuo yü 國語, four Villages (li 里) constituted an Aggregation (lien 連) and two hundred of its fighting men constituted a Company (tsu 組) led by the Aggregation Head (lien-chang 連長). The founder of the surname Lien who held the position of Aggregation Head was from the State of Ch'u (Ch'u kuo 楚國). This branch of the Lien family originally settled in Shang-tang 上黨, Shan-hsi 山西 province. 4. The surname Lien originated from the nomadic Hsien-pei 鮮卑 Group of Yu-lien shih 有連氏. The surname Yu-lien 有連 was changed into the surname Lien 連 and subsequently was adopted by the family after its settlement in Han 漢 territories.

## 308. Lien⁴ 練

The surname Lien 練 derived from two sources. 1. Hsing yüan 姓苑 traces the surname to the place name, the Village of Lien (Lien hsiang 練鄉) in Fu-chien 福建 province. The Lien family settled primarily in Chien-an 建安, Chi-lin 吉林 province. 2. Lien shih p'u 練氏譜 says the surname Lien branched from the surname Tung 東 and its founder was Lien Ho 練何. He was the Administrative Supervisor (lu-shih ts'an-chün 錄事參軍) to the T'ang 唐 Emperor T'ai-tsung 太宗) and was in charge of supervising and drilling military troops ("lien chün 練軍"). In recognition of his meritorious services to the T'ang dynasty, he was given the honorary surname Lien 練 (to drill, to train) and was enfeoffed at Ch'i-shan 歧山 as the Marquise of Ch'i-shan (Ch'i-shan hou 歧山侯). Lien was subsequently adopted as the common surname by his descendants. The book further elaborates that the surname Hou 侯 was evolved in the Ming 明 dynasty when a descendant of the Lien family, Lien Tzu-ming 練子寧 changed his surname into Hou 侯 to elude his enemies.

See also Tung¹ 東, Hou² 侯.

## 309. Lin² 林

According to Lu shih 路史 and Yüan ho hsing tsuan 元何姓纂, the surname Lin 林 branched from the surname Tzu 子 of the ancestral line of Ch'eng-t'ang 成湯. The founder of the family name was Pi-kan 比干 who was a son of the Shang 商 king T'ai-ting (太丁, 1194-1191 B.C.). Pi-

kan was brutally murdered by the Shang king
Chou-hsin 紂辛 out of his anger with Pi-kan's
candid advice against his will. Following Pi-
kan's death, his son took refuge in the forest
(lin 林). He was bestowed with the vassal state
in Po-ling 博陵, located in the present An-p'ing
hsien 安平縣, Ho-pei 河北 province and
subsequently was attributed the surname Lin 林
by Chou Wu-wang 周武王. The family initially
settled in An-p'ing hsien 安平縣, Ho-pei 河北
and later expanded to Shan-tung 山東 and Ho-nan
河南 provinces.

See also Ch'u³ 楚.

## 310. Lin⁴ 藺

T'ung chih Shih tsu lüeh 通志氏族略 and Yüan ho
hsing tsuan 元何姓纂 both traces the origin of
the surname Lin 藺 as follows: The surname Lin
branched from the surname Han 韓 of the
ancestral line of Chou Wen-wang 周文王 and its
founder was Han K'ang 韓康. Lin originated from
the name of a vassal state, the District of Lin
(Lin i 藺邑), bestowed on Han K'ang during the
Warring States (Chan kuo 戰國) Period. His
descendants later adopted Lin as their common
surname and they initially settled in Ho-pei
河北 and Ssu-ch'uan 四川 provinces and later
expanded to other parts of China.

## 311. Ling² 凌

The surname Ling 凌 branched from the surname
Chi 姬 of the ancestral line of Huang-ti 黃帝.
T'ung chih Shih tsu lüeh 通志氏族略 and Yüan ho
hsing tsuan 元何姓纂 describe the origin of the
surname as follows: The surname Ling came from
the name of the official post, ling-jen 凌人,
Royal Iceman, who was a member of the Ministry
of State (t'ien-kuan 天官) responsible for
gathering, cutting, storing, and issuing ice for
use by the king and the court in the Chou 周
dynasty. A son of Kang-shu 康叔, who was the
youngest brother of Chou Wu-wang 周武王, held
the position of ling-jen and Ling was
subsequently adopted as the common surname by

Kang-shu's descendants. The native place of the family was in Ho-nan 河南 province.

See also Ling[2] 淩.

## 312. Ling[2] 淩

According to Hsing shih k'ao lüeh 姓氏考略, the surname Ling 淩 appeared first and later branched to the surname Ling 淩 due to an error transcribed in Kuang yün 廣韻. The name's origin was detailed under the surname Ling 淩.

See also Ling[2] 淩.

## 313. Ling[2] 泠

See Ling[2] 伶.

## 314. Ling[2] 伶

The surname Ling 伶 derived from the title of the official post, ling-kuan 伶官, the Master of Musical Entertainments. According to the chapter of Ta yüeh 大樂 in Lü shih ch'un ch'iu 呂氏春秋, the founder of the surname Lin was Ling Lun 伶倫, he was the Master Musician (ling-kuan 伶官) to Huang-ti 黃帝. Other ancient sources cite the surname Ling in different forms. In Feng shu t'ung 風俗通 and Hsing shih k'ao lüeh 姓氏考略, Ling Lun 伶倫 was cited as Ling Lun 泠倫; in Ming hsien shih tsu yen hsing lei kao 名賢氏族言行類稿, it was listed as Leng Lun 冷倫. As a result, all of the above surnames Ling 伶, Ling 泠 and Leng 冷 derived from the same origin and were traced to the common ancestor Ling Lun.

See also Leng[3] 冷, Lun[2] 倫.

## 315. Ling[4] 令

The surname Ling 令 came from the following two sources: 1. According to Feng shu t'ung 風俗通, the surname Ling 令 derived from the title of the official post, ling-yin 令尹, a District

Magistrate or Prime Minister of a Feudal State. The founder of the surname was Ling-yin Tzu Wen 令尹子文 from the State of Ch'u (Ch'u kuo 楚國) in the Chou 周 dynasty. 2. The surname Ling branched from the surname Ling-hu 令狐 due to the change of name which took place in the T'ang 唐 dynasty.

See also Ling⁴-hu² 令狐.

316. Ling⁴-hu² 令狐

According to T'ang shu tsai hsiang shih hsi piao 唐書宰相世系表, the surname Ling-hu 令狐 branched from the surname Chi 姬 of the ancetral line of Chou Wen-wang 周文王. Wen-wang's son Pi Kung-kao 畢公高 had a grandson, Pi Wan 畢萬 who was the Grand Master (ta-fu 大夫) of the State of Chin (Chin kuo 晉國). In the Spring and Autumn (Ch'un ch'iu 春秋) Period, Pi Wan's great grandson Wei-k'e 魏顆 won the battle against the State of Ch'in (Ch'in kuo 秦國) and was bestowed with the vassal state in Ling-hu 令狐, located in the present Lin-i hsien 臨猗縣, Shan-hsi 山西 province. Ling-hu was subsequently adopted as a common surname by his descendants. The family settled primarily in T'ai-yüan 太原, Shan-hsi 山西 province.

See also Ling⁴ 令.

317. Liu² 劉

The surname Liu 劉 belongs to the ancestral line of Huang-ti 黃帝 and came from the following sources: 1. According to T'ung chih Shih tsu lüeh 通志氏族略, a descendant of T'ang Ti-yao 唐帝堯 was bestowed with the feudal territory Liu which was located in T'ang hsien 唐縣, Ho-pei 河北 province. 2. Ming hsien shih tsu yen hsing lei kao 名賢氏族言行類稿 traces the origin of the surname as follows: The surname Liu originated from the name of a vassal state, the District of Liu (Liu i 劉邑), bestowed on a descendant of Chou Wen-wang 周文王 who was a grand master (ta-fu 大夫) in the Chou dynasty. The family settled primarily in Yen-shih hsien

偃師縣, Ho-nan 河南 province where the District of Liu was located. 3. The surname Liu was evolved from the change of surnames from Lou 婁 and Hsiang 項 surnames. 4. The surname Liu was adopted by Hsiung-nus 匈奴 after they emigrated and settled in China during the Northern Wei (Pei Wei 北魏) Period.

See also Hsiang⁴ 項, Lou² 婁, Tsung¹-cheng⁴ 宗正, Yün⁴ 員.

318. Liu³ 柳

Yüan ho hsing tsuan 元何姓纂 describes the origin of the surname Liu 柳 as follows: The founder of the family name was Liu-hsia Hui 柳下惠, the assumed name (hao 號) of Chang Chin 展禽, who was a great grandson of the Duke of Chou (Chou kung 周公). The surname Liu was evolved from the name of the vassal state Liu-hsia 柳下 bestowed on Chang Chin 展禽. In order to express his appreciation (hui 惠) for the natural environment, especially for the vassal state Liu-hsia 柳下, he adopted Liu-hsia Hui 柳下惠 as his assumed name. Liu was later adopted as a common surname by his descendants and the family settled in Shan-hsi 山西 province.

319. Lo² 羅

Ming hsien shih tsu yen hsing lei kao 名賢氏族言行類稿 and Hsing shih k'ao lüeh 姓氏考略 trace the origin of the surname Lo 羅 as follows: The surname Lo can be traced to Chu-jung shih 祝融氏, who was a son of Chuan Hsü 顓頊. Lo originated from the name of a feudal territory, I-ch'eng 宜城, of the State of Lo (Lo kuo 羅國), bestowed on a descendant of Chu-jung shih 祝融氏 in the Chou 周 dynasty. The family initially settled in Hsiang-yang hsien 襄陽縣, Hu-pei 湖北 province where the State of Lo was located, and later prospered in Chang-sha 長沙, Hu-nan 湖南 and Nan-chang 南昌, Chiang-hsi 江西 provinces.

320. Lo⁴ 駱

According to Yüan ho hsing tsuan 元何姓纂, the
surname Lo 駱 branched from the surname Chiang
姜. The founder of the family name was Chiang
Lo 姜駱 who was a son of the Grand Duke of Ch'i
(Ch'i t'ai-kung 齊太公), the honorary name of
Chiang Tzu-ya 姜子牙 from the Spring and Autumn
(Ch'un ch'iu 春秋) Period. The descendants of
the Lo family settled in Kuei-chi hsien 會稽縣,
Che-chiang 浙江 province.

321. Lou² 婁

According to Feng shu t'ung 風俗通, the surname
Lou 婁 belongs to the lineage of Chuan Hsü 顓頊
and originated from the name of a feudal
territory, the ancient State of Chu-lou (Chu-lou
kuo 邾婁國) in the Chou 周 dynasty. The State
of Chu-lou was located in Chou hsien 鄒縣, Shan-
tung 山東 province.

See also Chu¹ 朱, Liu² 劉.

322. Lu² 盧

Yüan ho hsing tsuan 元何姓纂 and T'ung chih Shih
tsu lüeh 通志氏族略 trace the origin of the
surname Lu 盧 as follows: The name branched
from the surname Chiang 姜 of the ancestral line
of the Grand Duke of Ch'i (Ch'i T'ai-kung
齊太公), the honorary name of Chiang Tzu-ya
姜子牙. Chiang Hsi 姜傒, a great grandson of
Chiang Tzu-ya, was enfeoffed at the vassal state
in Lu hsien 盧縣 and his descendants
subsequently adopted Lu as their common surname.
The initial settlement of the Lu family was
located in Shan-tung 山東 province.

See also Chiang¹ 姜.

323. Lu³ 魯

According to Yüan ho hsing tsuan 元何姓纂, the
surname Lu 魯 originated from the name of the
feudal territory, the State of Lu (Lu kuo 魯國),
which was bestowed on Po Ch'in 伯禽, who was a
son of the Duke of Chou (Chou kung 周公) in the

Chou 周 dynasty. The Lu family initially settled in Shan-tung 山東 and later expanded to Chiang-su 江蘇 and An-hui 安徽 provinces.

324. Lu⁴ 路

Yüan ho hsing tsuan 元何姓纂 traces the origin of the surname Lu 路 as follows: Huang-ti 黃帝 bestowed one of his son on the vassal state of Lu 潞 which is located near the Lu River (Lu shui 潞水) in Shan-hsi 山西 province. His descendants adopted the simplified character Lu 路 as their common surname and settled in Shan-hsi province. The family later expanded to the south, in places such as Yang-p'ing 陽平 and An-ting 安定 in Shen-hsi 陝西 and Hsiang-ch'eng 襄城 and Ch'en-liu 陳留 in Ho-nan 河南 provinces.

325. Lu⁴ 陸

According to T'ang shu tsai hsiang shih hsi piao 唐書宰相世系表, the surname Lu 陸 belongs to the ancestral line of Yü Ti-shun 虞帝舜. T'ung 通, the youngest son of Ch'i Hsüan-wang 齊宣王, was bestowed with the vassal state in Lu hsiang 陸鄉 of P'ing-yüan 平原, Pan hsien 般縣, and Lu was adopted as the common surname since that time. The family initially settled in Yüng-chi hsien 永濟縣, Shan-hsi 山西 province.

326. Lu⁴ 逯

Feng shu t'ung 風俗通 traces the origin of the surname Lu 逯 as follows: The surname originated from the name of a vassal state, the District of Lu (Lu i 逯邑), in the State of Ch'in (Ch'in kuo 秦國) of the Warring States (Chan kuo 戰國) Period and it was adopted as the common surname by its residents. The family initially settled in Kan-su 甘肅 and Shen-hsi 陝西 provinces and later prospered in Kuang-p'ing 廣平, Ho-pei 河北 province.

327. Lu⁴ 祿

The surname Lu 祿 originated from two sources.

1. According to Feng shu t'ung 風俗通, the surname derived from the social name Lu-fu 祿父 of the Shang 商 King Wu-keng 武庚. He was a son of Chou-hsin (紂辛, 1154-1122 B.C.), the last king of the Shang dynasty. 2. Wan hsing t'ung p'u 萬姓統譜 documented that Lu also came from the title of the official post, ssu-lu 司祿, Record Keeper. According to Chou-li 周禮, ssu-lu was a member of the Ministry of Education (ti-kuan 地官) who kept accounts councerning issuance of funds and supplies to various government agencies in the Chou 周 dynasty. This branch of the Lu family originally settled in Fu-feng 扶風, Shen-hsi 陝西 province.

328. Lu⁴ 鹿

The surname Lu 鹿 originated from two sources. 1. According to Feng shu t'ung 風俗通, Lu derived from the name of the vassal state in Wu-lu 五鹿, located in the present P'u-yang hsien 濮陽縣, Ho-nan 河南 province. The place was bestowed on a grand master (ta-fu 大夫) of the State of Wei (Wei kuo 衛國) and later adopted as a common surname by his descendants. 2. According to Wei shu kuan shih chih 魏書官氏志, the surname branched from A-lu-hüan shih 阿鹿桓氏 of the nomadic group of Hsiung-nu 匈奴 during the reign of Hsiao Wen-ti 孝文帝 in the Northern Wei (Pei Wei 北魏) Period.

329. Lü³ 呂

According to Shuo wen chieh tzu 說文解字, the founder of the family name Lü 呂 was Ta-yüeh 大嶽. He was the Grand Minister (ta-ch'en 大臣) to Yü Ti-shun 虞帝舜 and was bestowed as the Marquise of Lü (Lü hou 呂侯) by Yü Ti-shun. His descendants adopted Lü as their common surname and setttled in Nan-yang hsien 南陽縣, Ho-nan 河南 province.

330. Lü² 閭

According to Kuang yün 廣韻, the surname Lü 閭 originated from the following sources: 1. It branched from the surname Lü-ch'iu 閭丘 and follows the ancestral line of Lü-ch'iu Ying 閭丘嬰 who was the Grand Master (ta-fu 大夫) of the State of Ch'i (Ch'i kuo 齊國) in the Spring and Autumn (Ch'un ch'iu 春秋) Period. 2. The surname derived from the name of the official post, lü-shih 閭師, Supervisor of Villages, who was a member of the Ministry of Education (ti-kuan 地官) and was responsible for assigning people of the royal capital and the six Districts (hsiang 鄉) of the royal domain to state-requisitioned services, supervising the census, and collecting taxes in the Chou 周 dynasty. 3. The surname came from the social name Tzu-Lü 子閭 of a son of Ch'u P'ing-wang 楚平王 in the Chou 周 dynasty.

See also Lü²-ch'iu¹ 閭丘.

### 331. Lü²-ch'iu¹ 閭丘

The surname Lü-ch'iu 閭丘 came from the following two sources: 1. According to Shang yu lu 尚友錄, Lü-ch'iu 閭丘 originated from the name of a vassal state, the Lü-ch'iu District (Lü-ch'iu i 閭丘邑), in the State of Chu (Chu kuo 邾國) of the Spring and Autumn (Ch'un ch'iu 春秋) Period. It was later adopted as a common surname by its residents and the family settled in Shan-tung 山東 province. 2. Kuang yün 廣韻 traces the founder of the surname to Lü-ch'iu Ying 閭丘嬰 who was the Grand Master (ta-fu 大夫) of the State of Ch'i (Ch'i kuo 齊國) in the Spring and Autumn (Ch'un ch'iu 春秋) Period.

See also Chu¹ 朱, Tsou¹ 鄒, Lü² 閭.

### 332. Luan² 欒

Yüan ho hsing tsuan 元何姓纂 and Hsing shih k'ao lüeh 姓氏考略 trace the origin of the surname Luan 欒 as follows: The surname belongs to the ancestral line of T'ang Shu-yü 唐叔虞, who was the youngest brother of Chou Ch'eng-wang (周成王, 1115-1078 B.C.). Luan originated from the name of a vassal state, the District of Luan (Luan i 欒邑), bestowed on Pin 賓, who was a grandson of the Marquise of Ching (Ching hou 靖侯) from the State of Chin 晉 in the Spring and Autumn (Ch'un ch'iu 春秋) Period. The initial settlement of the family was Luan-ch'eng hsien 欒城縣, Ho-pei 河北 province where the vassal state was located.

333.  Lun² 倫

According to the chapter of Ta yüeh 大樂 in Lü shih ch'un ch'iu 呂氏春秋, the founder of the surname Lun 倫 was Ling Lun 伶倫 who was the Master of Musical Entertainments (ling-kuan 伶官) to Huang-ti 黃帝. Some of his descendants adopted Lin 伶 and others adopted Lun 倫 as their common surname.

See also Lin² 伶.

334.  Lung² 隆

The surname Lung 隆 can be traced to the following two sources: 1. According to Hsing shih k'ao lüeh 姓氏考略, it derived from a place name located in the State of Lu (Lu kuo 魯國) during the Spring and Autumn (Ch'un ch'iu 春秋) Period. This branch of the family prospered in Nan-yang 南陽, Shan-tung 山東 province. 2. Shih chi 史記 says:  Hsiung-nu 匈奴, a nomadic group of the Hu 胡 People, adopted Lung as the common surname after they settled in Han 漢 territories.

335.  Lung² 龍

Ming hsien shih tsu yen hsing lei kao 名賢氏族言行類稿 and Hsing shih k'ao lüeh 姓氏考略 trace the origin of the surname Lung 龍 to the Grand Minister (ta-ch'en 大臣) to Yü Ti-shun 虞帝舜 whose forename was Lung 龍. He held the post of na-yen 納言 who made advisory comments to the emperor. Lung was later adopted as a common surname by his descendants. The original settlement of the family was Wu-ling 武陵 and T'ien-shui 天水 in Kan-su 甘肅 province.

See also Kung[1] 龔.

336. Ma[2] 麻

The surname Ma 麻 originated from two different
sources and both of them appeared during the
Spring and Autumn (Ch'un ch'iu 春秋) Period. 1.
According to Feng shu t'ung 風俗通, the surname
was adopted from Ma Ying 麻嬰, a grand master
(ta-fu 大夫) of the State of Ch'i (Ch'i kuo
齊國); and the Ma family initially settled in
Ch'ü-fu 曲阜, Shan-tung 山東 province. 2. Hsing
shih k'ao lüeh 姓氏考略 says:    Ma originated
from the name of a vassal state, the District of
Ma (Ma i 麻邑), bestowed on a grand master of
the State of Ch'u (Ch'u kuo 楚國) and Ch'u was
adopted as a common surname by his descendants.
This branch of the Ma family originally settled
in Ma-ch'eng hsien 麻城縣, Hu-pei 湖北 province
where the District of Ma was located.

337. Ma[3] 馬

Ma 馬 is one of the most popular surnames among
Chinese Muslims.    According to Yüan ho hsing
tsuan 元何姓纂, the surname Ma 馬 branched from
the surname Ying 嬴 of the ancestral line of
Chuan Hsü 顓頊.  Its founder, the feudal prince
Chao She 趙奢, was bestowed with the honorary
name Ma Fu-chün 馬服君 (Tamer of Horses) due to
his directorship for the cavalry during the
Warring States (Chan kuo 戰國) Period, and his
descendants adopted the surname Ma as their
common surname. The Ma family initially settled
in Fu-feng 扶風, Shen-hsi 陝西  province.

338. Mai[4] 麥

Shang yu lu 尙友錄 and Ku chin hsing shih shu
pien cheng 古今姓氏書辨證 cite scantily the
origin of the surname Mai 麥.    The books
documented the name's past prominence in Kao-yao
高要 and Shih-hsing 始興 in Kuang-tung 廣東 and
later in Ju-nan 汝南, Ho-nan 河南 provinces. An
outstanding representative of the family was the
General-in-Chief (ta-chiang-chün   大將軍) Mai
T'ieh-chang 麥鐵杖 in the Sui (隋, A.D. 581-618)

dynasty who originated from Kao-yao 高要, Kuang-tung 廣東 province.

### 339. Man³ 滿

According to <u>Hsing shih k'ao lüeh</u> 姓氏考略, the surname Man 滿 came from the lineage of Yü Ti-shun 虞帝舜 and was adopted posthumously by the descendants of Hu Kung-man 胡公滿, who was bestowed with the State of Ch'en (Ch'en kuo 陳國) by Wu-wang 武王 during his reign in the Chou 周 dynasty. The Man family originally settled in Ho-nan 河南 province where the State of Ch'en was located.

See also Ch'en² 陳, Hu² 胡, T'ien² 田, Yao² 姚.

### 340. Man⁴ 曼

The surname Man 曼 originated from the following three sources: 1. Chuan Hsü 顓頊 gave the honorary surname Man 曼 to Shao Hao's 少昊 son and Man was adopted as a common surname by his descendants. 2. According to <u>Lu shih</u> 路史, the surname Man derived from the ancestral line of the Marquise of Man (Man hou 曼侯) who was an uncle of the Shang 商 king Wu-ting 武丁. 3. Man 曼 and Man 蔓 were used interchangeably in antiquity and both names were later adopted as common surnames.

See also Teng⁴ 鄧, Man⁴ 蔓.

### 341. Man⁴ 蔓

See Man⁴ 曼.

### 342. Mao² 毛

According to <u>Yüan ho hsing tsuan</u> 元何姓纂 and <u>Wan hsing t'ung p'u</u> 萬姓統譜, the surname Mao 毛 derived from the name of a vassal state, the District of Mao (Mao i 毛邑), bestowed on Mao Po-tan 毛伯聃 who was the ninth son of Chou Wen-wang 周文王. Mao was later adopted as the common surname by his descendants and they settled in Jung-yang 榮陽, Ho-pei 河北 province.

343.  Mao² 茅

According to <u>Wan hsing t'ung p'u</u> 萬姓統譜 and <u>Ku chin hsing shih shu pien cheng</u> 古今姓氏書辨證, the surname Mao 茅 derived from the surname Chi 姬 of the ancestral line of the Duke of Chou (Chou kung 周公) and originated from the name of the feudal territory, the State of Mao (Mao kuo 茅國), bestowed on his third son Mao Shu 茅叔. Mao was later adopted as the common surname by Mao Shu's descendants and the family settled in Ch'en-liu 陳留, Ho-nan 河南 province.

344.  Mei² 梅

According to <u>T'ang shu tsai hsiang shih hsi piao</u> 唐書宰相世系表, the surname Mei 梅 branched from the surname Tzu 子 and its founder was the Earl of Mei (Mei po 梅伯).  He was a brother of T'ai-ting (太丁, 1194-1191 B.C.) and was bestowed with the feudal territory Mei by his brother during the Shang 商 dynasty; Mei was adopted as the common surname by his descendants.  <u>Hsing shih k'ao lüeh</u> 姓氏考略 points out that the family initially settled in Ju-nan hsien 汝南縣, Ho-nan 河南 province.

345.  Meng² 蒙

According to <u>Lu shih Shu chuan chi</u> 路史疏傳記 and <u>Hsing shih k'ao lüeh</u> 姓氏考略, the surname Meng 蒙 follows the ancestral line of Chuan Hsü 顓頊 and derived from the place name Meng-shuang 蒙雙.  Meng was originally adopted as a common surname by a citizen of Meng-shuang who was a descendant of Chuan Hsü and the family initially settled in An-ting 安定, Ho-pei 河北 province.

346.  Meng⁴ 孟

<u>Yüan ho hsing tsuan</u> 元何姓纂 and <u>T'ung chih Shih tsu lüeh</u> 通志氏族略 trace the origin of the surname as follows: The surname Meng 孟 branched from the surname Meng-sun 孟孫.  The name was

traced to the lineage of Chou Wen-wang 周文王 and its founder, Meng-sun 孟孫, was a feudal lord from the State of Lu (Lu kuo 魯國) in the Spring and Autumn (Ch'un ch'iu 春秋) Period. Both Meng 孟 and Meng-sun 孟孫 were later adopted as common surnames by his descendants. The ancestral region of the family was Shan-tung 山東 and Ho-nan 河南 provinces.

See also Chung⁴ 仲, Chung⁴-sun¹ 仲孫, Meng⁴-sun¹ 孟孫.

347. Meng⁴-sun¹ 孟孫

According to Yüan ho hsing tsuan 元何姓纂 and T'ung chih Shih tsu lüeh 通志氏族略, the surnames Meng 孟 and Meng-sun 孟孫 came from the same blood line and belongs to the lineage of Chou Wen-wang 周文王. The founder of the surname, Meng-sun 孟孫, was a descendant of Chou Wen-wang and a feudal lord of the State of Lu (Lu kuo 魯國) in the Spring and Autumn (Ch'un ch'iu 春秋) Period. Both Meng and Meng-sun were later adopted as common surnames by his descendants and the family originally settled in Shan-tung 山東 and Ho-nan 河南 provinces.

See also Chung⁴ 仲, Chung⁴-sun¹ 仲孫, Meng⁴ 孟.

348. Mi² 麋

Yüan ho hsing tsuan 元何姓纂, T'ung chih Shih tsu lüeh 通志氏族略 and Hsing shih k'ao lüeh 姓氏考略 trace the genealogy of the surname Mi 麋 as follows: A grand master (ta-fu 大夫) of the State of Ch'u (Ch'u kuo 楚國) was enfeoffed at the South Commandery (Nan chün 南郡) of the road station Mi ting 麋亭 in the Spring and Autumn (Ch'un ch'iu 春秋) Period, and from this his descendants adopted Mi as their common surname. The family's place of origin was located in Tung-hai hsien 東海縣, Chiang-su 江蘇 province.

349. Mi³ 米

According to <u>Yüan ho hsing tsuan</u> 元何姓纂 and <u>Ming hsien shih tsu yen hsing lei kao</u> 名賢氏族言行類稿, the surname Mi 米 originated from the place name, the State of Mi (Mi kuo 米國), located in Western Territories (Hsi-yü 西域) which was the residence of the Hu 胡 People, and was adopted as a common surname in the T'ang 唐 dynasty after their settlement in Han 漢 territories. The Mi family initially settled in Kao-p'ing 高平, of western Kan-su 甘肅 province, which was commonly called Lung-hsi 隴西.

350. Mi³ 芈

According to <u>Shih pen</u> 世本, the origin of the surname Mi 芈 came from the following two sources: 1. The surname follows the lineage of Chuan Hsü 顓頊 and derived from the honorary surname Mi 芈 which was given to Chuan Hsü's descendant Lu Chung 陸終 of his sixth son Chi Lien 季連. The Mi family later settled in the State of Ch'u (Ch'u kuo 楚國) during the Spring and Autumn (Ch'un ch'iu 春秋) Period. 2. Another branch of the Mi 芈 family came from the ancestral line of Chu-jung shih 祝融氏.

See also Shang⁴-kuan¹ 上官, Ch'u³ 楚, Yün⁴ 惲.

351. Mi⁴ 密

See Hsü¹ 須.

352. Mi⁴-hsü¹ 密須

According to <u>Shih pen</u> 世本, the surname Mi-hsü 密須 was traced to the ancient State of Mi-hsü (Mi-hsü 密須國) in the Shang 商 dynasty. Mi-hsü was adopted as a common surname by the residents of that state. The surname later branched to the surnames Mi 密 and Hsü 須 in the Chou 周 dynasty. The Mi-hsü family initially settled in Kan-su 甘肅 province.

See also Hsü¹ 須.

## 353. Miao[2] 苗

According to <u>T'ung chih Shih tsu lüeh</u> 通志氏族略 and <u>Feng shu t'ung</u> 風俗通, the surname Miao 苗 originated from the State of Ch'u (Ch'u kuo 楚國) in the Spring and Autumn (Ch'un ch'iu 春秋) Period. Its founder, Pen Huang 賁皇, who was a feudal prince of the State of Ch'u, was bestowed with the vassal state of Miao and his descendants later adopted Miao as their common surname. The family initially settled in Chi-yüan hsien 濟源縣, Ho-nan 河南 province.

## 354. Miao[4] 繆

According to <u>Yüan ho hsing tsuan</u> 元何姓纂 and <u>T'ung chih Shih tsu lüeh</u> 通志氏族略, the surname Miao 繆 belongs to the ancestral line of Chuan Hsü 顓頊 and derived posthumously from the Duke of Miao (Miao kung 繆公) of the State of Ch'in (Ch'in kuo 秦國) in the Spring and Autumn (Ch'un ch'iu 春秋) Period. The place of origin was located in Lan-ling 蘭陵, Shan-tung 山東 province.

See also Liao[4] 廖.

## 355. Min[3] 閔

The origin of the surname Min 閔 was cited in <u>Wan hsing t'ung p'u</u> 萬姓統譜, <u>T'ung chih Shih tsu lüeh</u> 通志氏族略, <u>Shang yu lu</u> 尚友錄, and <u>Ku chin hsing shih shu pien cheng</u> 古今姓氏書辨證. According to these books, Min was adopted posthumously as the common surname by people whose ancestors died young (the meaning of "min 閔"). A representative of the family was Min Sun 閔損 whose surname came from his ancestor died of an early death. Min Sun was one of the prominent disciples of Confucius and he originally came from T'ai-yüan 太原, Shan-hsi 山西 province.

## 356. Ming[2] 明

According to <u>Yüan ho hsing tsuan</u> 元何姓纂 and

Wan hsing t'ung p'u 萬姓統譜, the founder of
the surname Ming 明 was Meng Ming-shih 孟明視,
who was a son of the Earl of Ching (Ching po
井伯) named Pai Li-hsi 百里奚 and a descendant
of Yü Chung 虞仲. Meng Ming-shih was a Grand
Councilor (tsai-hsiang 宰相) to Duke Ch'in Mu-
kung 秦穆公 and was commemorated by his
descendants through the adoption of his social
name (tzu 字) Ming as their common surname. The
family initially settled in P'ing-yüan 平原,
Shen-hsi 陝西 province.

## 357. Mo⁴ 莫

The surname Mo 莫 derived from three different
sources. 1. Hsing shih k'ao lüeh 姓氏考略
traces the genealogy of the surname as follows:
Mo originated from the place name, the Town of
Mo (Mo cheng 鄭城), which was built by Chuan Hsü
顓頊. For the purpose of simplifiction, the
radical was dropped and Mo 莫 was adopted as the
common surname by its residents. The family
settled in Jen-ch'iu hsien 任丘縣, Ho-pei 河北
province where the Town of Mo was located. 2.
The surname Mo originated from the title of the
official post, mo-ao 莫敖, and the founder of
the surname was Ch'ü Yüan 屈原 from the State
of Ch'u (Ch'u kuo 楚國), who held the post in
the Spring and Autumn (Ch'un ch'iu 春秋) Period.
3. According to T'ung chih Shih tsu lüeh
通志士族略, the surname Mo 莫 derived from the
lineage of Yü Ti-shun 虞帝舜 and branched from
the surname Mo 幕 as the result of a change in
form for the name by his descendants. This
branch of the Mo family prospered in Chü-lu
鉅鹿, Ho-pei 河北 and Chiang-ling 江陵, Hu-pei
湖北 provinces.

See also Mo⁴ 幕.

## 358. Mo⁴ 墨

According to Hsing shih k'ao lüeh 姓氏考略 and
T'ung chih Shih tsu lüeh 通志氏族略, the surname
Mo 墨 branched from the surname Mo-t'ai 墨台,
which was changed to the single character form
by dropping "t'ai 台" by the Chou 周 ruler whose

royal domain was the ancient State of Ku-chu (Ku-chu kuo 孤竹國), located in the area between Ho-pei 河北 and Je-ho 熱河 provinces. The ruler of Ku-chu (commonly known as Ku-chu chün 孤竹君) changed his surname from Mo-t'ai to Mo and this marked the first generation of the Mo family. The Mo families settled primarily in Shen-hsi 陝西 and Ssu-ch'uan 四川 provinces and they adopted the ancestral hall name (t'ang ming 堂名) Liang kuo 梁國.

See also Mo⁴-t'ai² 墨台.

359. Mo⁴ 幕

See Mo⁴ 莫.

360. Mo⁴-ch'i² 万俟

The origin of the multiple surname Mo-ch'i 万俟 was listed in <u>Wei shu kuan shih chih</u> 魏書官氏志 and <u>Shang yu lu</u> 尚友錄. According to these documents, Mo-chi was initially a branch of T'o-pa shih 拓跋氏 in the Northern Wei (Pei Wei 北魏) dynasty, part of the Hsien-pei 鮮卑 group. The Hsien-pei group was later subdued and stayed in Han 漢 territories and adopted Mo-chi as their common surname. The family settled primarily in Shan-hsi 山西 province.

361. Mo⁴-t'ai² 墨台

The origin of the surname Mo-t'ai 墨台 was documented in <u>Ku chin hsing shih shu pien cheng</u> 古今姓氏書辨證, <u>Shang yu lu</u> 尚友錄, and <u>T'ung chih Shih tsu lüeh</u> 通志氏族略. According to these books, the surname Mo-t'ai belongs to the lineage of the Shang 商 King Ch'eng-t'ang 成湯 and follows the ancestral line of the feudal prince Ch'eng Mo-t'ai 成墨台 from the State of Sung (Sung kuo 宋國).

See also Mo⁴ 墨.

362. Mou² 牟

Feng shu t'ung 風俗通 traces the surname Mou 牟 from the lineage of Huang-ti 黃帝 to the ancestral line of Chu-jung shih 祝融氏. According to the source, Mou was initially the name of an ancient state which was under the territorial administration of Chou 周 dynasty's viscounts (the feudal lords with the status of tzu 子) who were descendants of Chu-jung shih and Mou was later adopted as a common surname by the descendants of the family and they settled in Shan-tung 山東 province.

363. Mu⁴ 牧

Feng shu t'ung 風俗通 and Ming hsien shih tsu yen hsing lei kao 名賢氏族言行類稿 trace the origin of the surname Mu 牧 as follows: The founder of the surname Mu was Li Mu 力牧, who was a grand minister (ta-ch'en 大臣) to Huang-ti 黃帝. Mu was later adopted as a common surname by his descendants and the family initially settled in Shan-tung 山東 and later prospered in Ho-nan 河南 and Shen-hsi 陝西 provinces during the reign of Wu-wang 武王 in the Chou 周 dynasty.

364. Mu⁴ 木

According to Ch'ien fu lun 潛夫論, the surname Mu 木 branched from the surname Tuan-mu 端木 of Tuan-mu Ssu 端木賜 who was a disciple of Confucius from the State of Wei (Wei kuo 衛國) in the Spring and Autumn (Ch'un ch'iu 春秋) Period and was commonly known by his social name (tze 字) Tze-kung 子貢. Some of his descendants adopted Tuan-mu 端木 and others adopted the single character of Tuan 端 or Mu 木 as their common surname.

See Tuan¹-mu⁴ 端木.

365. Mu⁴ 穆

According to Yüan ho hsing tsuan 元何姓纂, the surname Mu 穆 belongs to the ancestral line of Ch'eng-t'ang 成湯 and originated from the posthumous title of the Duke of Mu (Mu kung

穆公) from the State of Sung (Sung kuo 宋國) in the Spring and Autumn (Ch'un ch'iu 春秋) Period. It was adopted posthumously as the common surname by his descendant, Mu Sheng 穆生 in the Western Han (Hsi Han 西漢) dynasty and the family initially settled in Ho-nan 河南 province.

366. Mu⁴ 慕

According to <u>Ku chin hsing shih shu pien cheng</u> 古今姓氏書辨證, the surname Mu 慕 branched from the surname Mu-jung 慕容 and originally came from the ancestral line of Ti K'u 帝嚳 (Kao-hsin shih 高辛氏). The Mu family settled primarily in K'ai-feng 開封, Ho-nan 河南 province.

See also Mu⁴-jung² 慕容.

367. Mu⁴-jung² 慕容

The surname Mu-jung 慕容 belongs to the ancestral line of Ti K'u 帝嚳 (Kao-hsin shih 高辛氏). According to the documents, <u>San kuo chih Hsien-pei chuan</u> 三國志鮮卑傳, <u>Chin shu</u> 晉書, and <u>T'ung chih Shih tsu lüeh</u> 通志氏族略, Ti K'u's youngest son conquered northern China and stationed his military in that region. In the Ch'in 秦 and Han 漢 periods, the troops were defeated by the nomadic group of Hsiung-nu 匈奴 and withdrew to the Mountain of Hsien-pei (Hsien-pei shan 鮮卑山). They renamed themselves as the Group of Hsien-pei 鮮卑 and adopted the surname Mu-jung; inspired by the phonetic similarities of their unique hair decorations. The Mu-jung family settled primarily in the northeastern region of China. <u>Ku chin hsing shih shu pien cheng</u> 古今姓氏書辨證 states: The surname Mu 慕 branched from the surname Mu-jung 慕容 and was adopted widely; this caused the decline of the Mu-jung families.

See also Tou⁴ 豆, Tou⁴-lu² 豆盧, Mu⁴ 慕.

368. Na⁴ 那

The surname Na 那 derived from three different

sources. 1. <u>Wan hsing t'ung p'u</u> 萬姓統譜 states that the name follows the ancestral line of the Shang 商 King Wu-ting 武丁 and branched from the surname Ch'uan 權 of the State of Ch'uan 權 (Ch'üan kuo 權國). In the Chou 周 dynasty, the State of Ch'uan was defeated by Wu-wang 武王 of the State of Ch'u 楚 and he relocated the State of Ch'uan to Na 邢, which was later adopted as the common surname by the descendants of Wu-ting who lived in Na and they later settled in Tan-yang 丹陽 and T'ien-shui 天水 in Hu-pei 湖北 province. 2. <u>Hsing shih k'ao lüeh</u> 姓氏考略 describes the name's orgin as follows: The surname Na was traced to the change of names by the Hu 胡 People, including the Groups of Hsien-pei 鮮卑, Chiang 羌, and Yih 夷. These groups later settled their families in Han 漢 territories and changed their surnames to Na.

See also Ch'üan² 權.

369. Nai⁴ 能

<u>Ming hsien shih tsu yen hsing lei kao</u> 名賢氏族言行類稿 traces the origin of the surname Nai 能 as follows: The founder of surname was Hsiung Chih 熊摯 who belongs to the royal family of the State of Ch'u (Ch'u kuo 楚國) in the Spring and Autumn (Ch'un ch'iu 春秋) Period. When Ch'u kuo was defeated and became unstable, Hsiung Chih escaped from his homeland and changed his surname to Nai 能 by removing the radical from his original surname Hsiung 熊. The family settled primarily in T'ai-yüan 太原 and Hua-yin 華陰 in Shan-hsi 山西 province.

See also Hsiung² 熊.

370. Nan² 南

The surname Nan 南 originated from the following four sources. 1. According to <u>Shih chih</u> 史記, the surname Nan follows the ancestral line of the Great Yü (Ta Yü 大禹) in the Hsia 夏 dynasty. 2. <u>T'ung chih Shih tsu lüeh</u> 通志氏族略 says: The surname came from the place name of

the Village of Nan (Nan hsiang 南鄉) where a man
from the State of Chin (Chin kuo 晉國) lived in
seclusion after his retirement and Nan was
adopted as a common surname by his descendants.
3. The surname Nan branched from the surname
Tzu-nan 子南 of Tzu-nan shih 子南氏 who came
from the State of Ch'u (Ch'u kuo 楚國) in the
Chou 周 dynasty.  4. The surname Nan derived
from the social name Tzu-nan 子南 of the feudal
prince Ying 郢 from the State of Wei (Wei kuo
衛國) in the Spring and Autumn (Ch'un ch'iu
春秋) Period.  Nan was adopted as a common
surname by his descendants.

371.  Nan²-kung¹ 南宮

The surname Nan-kung 南宮 derived from two
sources.  1. According to Shang yu lu 尚友錄,
the name branched from the surname Chi 姬 of the
ancestral line of Chou Wen-wang 周文王 and its
founder was Wen-wang's descendant Nan-kung Kua
南宮括.  He was a capable and intelligent
minister for Chou Wen-wang.  He adopted Nan-kung
南宮 as his common surname because of his
residence, which was located in Nan-kung 南宮.
2. Shih chi Chung-ni ti tzu lieh chuan
史記仲尼弟子列傳 states the origin of the
surname as follows:  Chung-sun Yüeh 仲孫閱, a
feudal prince from the State of Lu (Lu kuo 魯國)
in the Spring and Autumn (Ch'un ch'iu 春秋)
Period, changed his surname to Nan-kung because
of his residence in Nan-kung 南宮.  He was one
of the prominent disciples of Confucius.

See also Chung⁴-sun¹ 仲孫.

372.  Nan²-kuo¹ 南郭

See Tung¹-kuo¹ 東郭.

373.  Nan²-men² 南門

According to Ch'ing 清 scholar Chang Shu 張澍
who states in his book Hsing shih wu shu
姓氏五書, ancient Chinese cities were commonly
surrounded with walls.  Nan-men 南門, meaning
the south gate of a city,  was adopted as a

common surname by people living in the locale. It was said that the Nan-men family populated Ho-nan 河南 province.

See also Tung¹-men² 東門, Hsi¹-men² 西門, Pei²-men² 北門.

## 374. Ni² 倪

Yüan ho hsing tsuan 元何姓纂 and Hsing shih k'ao lüeh 姓氏考略 trace the genealogy of the surname Ni 倪 as follows: The surname branched from the surname Ni 郳 and originated from the name of the fedual territory Ni 郳, bestowed on a son of the Duke of Wu (Wu kung 武公) from the State of Chu (Chu kuo 邾國) in the Spring and Autumn (Ch'un ch'iu 春秋) Period. Ni 郳 was adopted as the common surname since that time. Several generations later, the descendants of the Ni family changed their surname to Ni 倪 to avoid revenge from rivals. The Ni family originally settled in Shan-tung 山東 province.

See also Ni² 郳.

## 375. Ni² 郳

According to Yüan ho hsing tsuan 元何姓纂, the surname Ni 郳 originated from the name of the fedual territory Ni 郳, bestowed on a son of the Duke of Wu (Wu kung 武公) from the State of Chu (Chu kuo 邾國) in the Spring and Autumn (Ch'un ch'iu 春秋) Period. Ni 郳 was adopted as the common surname since that time. The Ni family originally settled in Shan-tung 山東 province.

See also Ni² 倪.

## 376. Nieh⁴ 聶

The origin of the surname Nieh 聶 appeared in Yüan ho hsing tsuan 元何姓纂, Hsing shih k'ao lüeh 姓氏考略 and T'ung chih Shih tsu lüeh 通志氏族略. These sources indicate that the surname Nieh originated from the name of the feudal state Nieh Ch'eng 聶城, bestowed on a son of the Duke Ch'i-ting (Ch'i-ting kung 齊丁公) as a dependant state of the State of Ch'i (Ch'i kuo 齊國) in the Spring and Autumn (Ch'un ch'iu 春秋) Period. Nieh was later adopted as a common surname by his descendants after the State of Ch'i was defeated by the State of Wei (Wei kuo 衛國). The family initially settled in the area of Ho-nan 河南 and Ho-pei 河北 provinces where the State of Wei was located and later pervaded Shan-hsi 山西 and An-hui 安徽 provinces during the Ch'in 秦 and Han 漢 periods.

377. Nieh⁴ 乜

According to <u>Wan hsing t'ung p'u</u> 萬姓統譜 and <u>Ku chin hsing shih shu pien cheng</u> 古今姓氏書辨證, the surname Nieh 乜 was of foreign origin, which derived from one of the surnames adopted by the people living in Western Territories (Hsi-yü 西域). The Nieh families currently populated Kan-su 甘肅 province.

378. Nien² 年

The surname Nien 年 came from two sources. 1. According to <u>Lu shih</u> 路史, the surname belongs to the lineage of Yen-ti 炎帝 and branched from the surname Chiang 姜 of the ancestral line of Chiang Tzu-ya 姜子牙 who was the Grand Duke of Ch'i (Ch'i T'ai-kung 齊太公) in the Chou 周 dynasty. 2. <u>Ming shih</u> 明史 further points out that the surname branched from the surname Yen 嚴 (which branched from the surname Chuang 莊) of the ancestral line of Chuang-wang (莊王, 696-681 B.C.) from the State of Ch'u (Ch'u kuo 楚國) in the Spring and Autumn (Ch'un ch'iu 春秋) Period. Nien was probably mistakenly adopted by some descendants of the Yen families due to the phonetic similarities in sound of these two characters.

See also Chung¹ 莊, Yen² 嚴.

379. Ning² 甯

According to <u>Shih chi</u> 史記, the surnames Ning 甯

and Ning 寧 were used interchangeably and both derived from the same blood line. <u>Hsing shih k'ao lüeh</u> 姓氏考略 traces the genealogy of the surnames as follows: The surname Ning 甯 derived from the name of a vassal state, the District of Ning (Ning i 甯邑), bestowed on a son of the Duke of Ch'eng (Cheng kung 成公) who was a descendant of K'ang Shu 康叔 from the State of Wei (Wei kuo 衛國) in the Spring and Autumn (Ch'un ch'iu 春秋) Period. The Ning families initially settled in Ho-pei 河北 and Ho-nan 河南 provinces.

See also Ning[2] 寧.

380. Ning[2] 寧

According to <u>Shih chi</u> 史記, the surnames Ning 寧 and Ning 甯 were used interchangeably and both derived from the same blood line. The description of the surname's origin was detailed under the surname Ning 甯.

See also Ning[2] 甯.

381. Niu[2] 牛

<u>T'ang shu tsai hsiang shih hsi piao</u> 唐書宰相世系表 and <u>Yüan ho hsing tsuan</u> 元何姓纂 describe the origin the surname Niu 牛 as follows: The surname came from the ancestral line of Sung Wei-tzu 宋微子, the eldest brother of the Shang 商 King Chou-hsin (紂辛, 1154-1122 B.C.) and originated from the social name of a descendant of Sung Wei-tzu called Niu-wen 牛文. Niu was later adopted as the common surname by his descendants and the family settled primarily in Lung-hsi 隴西, Kan-su 甘肅 province.

382. Niu[3] 鈕

<u>Ming hsien shih tsu yen hsing lei kao</u> 名賢氏族言行類稿 and <u>T'ung chih Shih tsu lüeh</u> 通志氏族略 cite several persons who apparently adopted the surname Niu 鈕 in the Eastern Chin (Tung Chin 東晉, 317-420 A.D.) dynasty and document their original settlement in Chiang-su

江蘇 province.  Currently, Chiang-su contains the largest population of Niu families in China.

383.  Nung[2] 農

According to <u>Wan hsing t'ung p'u</u> 萬姓統譜, the surname Nung 農 derived from Shen-nung shih 神農氏, the Divine Farmer.  He was an emperor who taught his people how to farm but did not issued decrees, rewards or punishments.  During his reign between the third and second centuries B.C., the period reflected political idealism and peasant Utopianism.

384.  Ou[1] 歐

<u>Lu shih</u> 路史 and <u>T'ang shu tsai hsiang shih hsi piao</u> 唐書宰相世系表 describe the genealogy of the surname Ou 歐 as follows:  The surname Ou branched from the surname Chi 姬 and follows the ancestral line of Kou Chien 勾踐, the ruler of the State of Yüeh (Yüeh kuo 越國) in the Spring and Autumn (Ch'un ch'iu 春秋) Period.  The name's founder, Wu-chiang 無疆, was a seventh generation descendant of Kou Chien.  He was bestowed with a feudal territory near the Mountain Ou-yü (Ou-yü shan 歐餘山) and some of his descendants adopted Ou as their common surname and settled in P'ing-yang 平陽, Shen-hsi 陝西 province.  Others adopted Ou-yang 歐陽, meaning the rising of the sun (t'ai yang 太陽) from Mountain Ou-yü as their surname.  The Mountain was located in the present Wu-hsing hsien 吳興縣, Che-chiang 浙江 province where the Ou-yang families initially settled and later expanded to Chiang-su 江蘇 and Shan-tung 山東 provinces.

385.  Ou[1]-yang[2] 歐陽

See Ou[1] 歐.

386.  Pa[1] 巴

<u>Yüan ho hsing tsuan</u> 元何姓纂 and <u>T'ung chih Shih tsu lüeh</u> 通志氏族略 trace the genealogy of the

surname Pa 巴 as follows: The surname derived from the name of the feudal territory, the State of Pa (Pa kuo 巴國), located in Pa hsien 巴縣, Ssu-ch'uan 四川 province in the Chou 周 dynasty. It was later adopted as a common surname and the family initially settled in Pa hsien 巴縣, Ssu-ch'uan 四川 province and later prospered in Po-hai 渤海, Shan-tung 山東 province in the Han 漢 dynasty.

387. Pa²-lieh⁴-lan² 拔列蘭

According to <u>Wei shu kuan shih chih</u> 魏書官氏志, Pa-lieh-lan shih 拔列蘭氏 originally came from the nomadic group of Hsien-pei 鮮卑 and later changed his surname to Liang 梁 after the Hsien-pei Group settled in Han 漢 territories during the Northern Wei (Pei Wei 北魏) period.

See also Liang² 梁.

388. Pai² 白

<u>Yüan ho hsing tsuan</u> 元何姓纂 describes the origin of the surname Pai 白 as follows: The surname belongs to the lineage of Huang-ti 黃帝 and its founder was Pai Kung-sheng 白公勝 of the State of Ch'u (Ch'u kuo 楚國) during the Spring and Autumn (Ch'un ch'iu 春秋) Period. After the fall of the State, his descendants adopted Pai as their common surname and the family settled in the area of the present Shan-hsi 山西 and Shen-hsi 陝西 provinces.

389. Pai³ 柏

<u>Hsing shih k'ao lüeh</u> 姓氏考略 traces the genealogy of the surname Pai 柏 to the name of the feudal territory, the State of Po (Po kuo 柏國), in the Spring and Autumn (Ch'un ch'iu 春秋) Period. The State of Po was later defeated by the State of Ch'u (Ch'u kuo 楚國) and Pai 柏 was adopted as the common surname by its residents. The family initially settled in Ho-nan 河南 and later prospered in Shan-tung 山東 provinces.

390. Pai³-li³ 百里

Feng shu t'ung 風俗通 and T'ung chih Shih tsu lüeh 通志氏族略 trace the origin of the surname Pai-li 百里 as follows: The surname originated from Pai-li Hsi 百里奚 who was the Grand Councilor (tsai-hsiang 宰相), the paramount executive official to Duke Ch'in Mu (Ch'in Mu kung 秦穆公) in the Spring and Autumn (Ch'un ch'iu 春秋) Period. Pai-li Hsi changed his surname by adopting the name of his residence located in Pai-li 百里 and it later became the common surname of his clan. The family originally settled in Hsin-ts'ai 新蔡, Ho-nan 河南 province.

391. Pan¹ 班

Feng shu t'ung 風俗通 and Ming hsien shih tsu yen hsing lei kao 名賢氏族言行類稿 trace the origin of the surname Pan 班 to its founder Tou Pan 鬥班 of the State of Ch'u (Ch'u kuo 楚國) in the Spring and Autumn (Ch'un ch'iu 春秋) Period. Pan was adopted as the common surname by his descendants and the family settled primarily in Hu-nan 湖南, Hu-pei 湖北, and Shan-hsi 山西 provinces during the late Ch'in 秦 period.

392. P'an¹ 潘

According to Yüan ho hsing tsuan 元何姓纂, the surname P'an 潘 belongs to the ancestral line of Chou Wen-wang 周文王 and derived from the name of a vassal state, the District of P'an (P'an i 潘邑), bestowed on Chi Sun 季孫 who was a great grandson of Chou Wen-wang 周文王. P'an was later adopted as the common surname by the descendants of Chi Sun and the family initially settled in Shen-hsi 陝西 province and later expanded to An-hui 安徽, Chaing-su 江蘇, and Che-chiang 浙江 provinces.

393. P'ang² 龐

According to Shang yu lu 尚友錄 and T'ung chih Shih tsu lüeh 通志氏族略, the surname P'ang 龐 branched from the surname Chi 姬 of the

ancestral line of Chou Wen-wang 周文王 and
originated from the name of a villiage, the
Village of P'ang (P'ang hsiang 龐鄉), bestowed
on a descendant of Wen-wang's son Pi Kung-kao
畢公高. P'ang was subsequently adopted as the
common surname and the family initially setled
in Ch'iao-kuo 譙國, Ho-pei 河北 province.

394. Pao¹ 包

Yüan ho hsing tsuan 元何姓纂 traces the
genealogy of the surnames Pao 包 as follows: The
founder of the surname was Sheng Pao-hsü 申包胥
who was a grand master (ta-fu 大夫) of the State
of Ch'u (Ch'u kuo 楚國) in the Spring and Autumn
(Ch'un ch'iu 春秋) Period. Pao was adopted as
the common surname by his descendants and the
family initially settled in Sheng i 申邑 of the
present Nang-yang hsien 南陽縣, Ho-nan 河南
province.

395. Pao¹ 鮑

According to Yüan ho hsing tsuan 元何姓纂 and Ku
chin hsing shih shu pien cheng 古今姓氏書辨證,
the surname Pao 鮑 belongs to the lineage of the
Great Yü (Ta Yü 大禹) and originated from the
name of the feudal territory Pao 鮑, bestowed on
his descendant Pao Ching-shu 鮑敬叔. Pao was
adopted as a common surname by the descendants
of Pao Ching-shu and the family settled in Shan-
tung 山東 province.

396. Pao³ 保

Hsing P'u 姓譜 and T'ung chih Shih tsu lüeh
通志氏族略 state that the surname Pao 保
originated from the name of the official post,
pao-chang 保章, Royal Astrologer, in the Chou 周
dynasty. According to Chou li 周禮, pao-chang
was charged with keeping records of the
movements of the sun, moon, planets, and stars
for the prepartion of the state-issued annual
calendar and reporting any celestial
irreglarities that might be considered omens.
Pao 保 was adopted as a common surname by the
descendants whose family members were appointed

to the post.

**397. Pao⁴ 暴**

> According to Feng shu t'ung 風俗通, the founder
> of the surname Pao 暴 was the Duke Pao-hsin
> (Pai-hsin kung 暴辛公) in the Shang 商 dynasty.
> Due to the literary meaning of the character
> "pao 暴", meaning violence, the surname Pao was
> not widely adopted. Many of the Duke's
> descendants later changed their surname which
> resulted in the decline of the population of Pao
> families.

**398. Pei⁴ 貝**

> The surname Pei 貝 originated from the place
> name, Pei ch'iu 貝丘, located in Ch'ing-ho hsien
> 清河縣, Ho-pei 河北 province. The Pei family
> settled primarily in Chiang-su 江蘇 and Che-
> chiang 浙江 provinces.

**399. Pei¹-kuo¹ 北郭**

> See Tung¹-kuo¹ 東郭.

**400. Pei¹-men² 北門**

> The origin of the surname Pei-men 北門 was cited
> in T'ung chih Shih tsu lüeh 通志氏族略.
> According to the book, Pei-men, meaning the
> north gate of a city, was adopted as the common
> surname by people living in the locale.

> See also Tung1-men2 東門, Hsi¹-men² 西門, Nan²-
> men² 南門.

**401. P'ei² 邳**

> Hsing shih k'ao lüeh 姓氏考略 describe the
> genealogy of the surname P'ei 邳 as follows: The
> surname P'ei 邳 branched from the surname Hsüeh
> 薛 and derived from the name of a feudal
> territory located in P'ei hsien 邳縣, Chiang-su
> 江蘇 province. The founder of the surname was
> Hsi Chung 奚仲 who was a descendant of the Jen

任 family from the lineage of Huang-ti 黃帝. Hsi Chung was a grand minister (ta-ch'en 大臣) to the Great Yü (Ta Yü 大禹). He was initially enfeoffed at the feudal territory of the State of Hsüeh (Hsüeh kuo 薛國) and later re-enfeoffed at P'ei 邳. P'ei was adopted as a common surname by his descendants and the family settled primarily in Shan-hsi 山西, An-hui 安徽, and Ho-nan 河南 provinces.

See also Jen² 任, Hsüeh¹ 薛.

402. P'ei² 裴

T'ung chih Shih tsu lüeh 通志氏族略 traces the genealogy of the surname P'ei 裴 to the name of a village, the Village of P'ei (P'ei hsiang 裴鄉). It was bestowed on Po I 伯益 during the regin of the Great Yü (Ta Yü 大禹) and Pei was adopted as the common surname by the descendants of Po I. The family initially settled in the area east of the Yellow River which was commonly called He-tung 河東.

403. Pen¹ 賁

According to Ming hsien shih tsu yen hsing lei kao 名賢氏族言行類稿, the founder of the surname Pen 賁 was Pen P'u 賁浦 from the State of Ch'i (Ch'i kuo 齊國) in the Spring and Autumn (Ch'un ch'iu 春秋) Period.

404. P'eng² 彭

According to Yüan ho hsing tsuan 元何姓纂, the surname P'eng 彭 belongs to the lineage of Chuan Hsü 顓頊 and its founder was P'eng Tsu 彭祖. P'eng originated from the name of the feudal territory Ta-p'eng 大彭, bestowed on P'eng Tsu in the Shang 商 dynasty and was later adopted as the common surname by his descendants. The family settled in T'ung-ch'eng hsien 銅城縣, Chiang-su 江蘇 province where the feudal territory Ta-p'eng was located.

See also Wei² 韋.

## 405.  Pi⁴ 畢

According to <u>Shu ching</u> 書經, the surname Pi 畢 derived from Pi Kung-kao 畢公高. He was the the fifteenth son of Chou Wen-wang 周文王 and was bestowed with the feudal territory of the State of Pi (Pi kuo 畢國) and later adopted Pi as his surname. The State of Pi, where the Pi family initially settled, was located in the present Shen-hsi 陝西 province.

## 406.  Pi⁴ 費

The surname "費" materialized from three sources according to its phonetic variations. <u>Hsing shih k'ao lüeh</u> 姓氏考略 traces the surname Pi 費 to Pi hsien 費縣 which was the feudal territory bestowed on Hsiao-yu 孝友, who was a son of the Duke Ch'i Huan (Ch'i Huan kung 齊桓公), in the Spring and Autumn (Ch'un ch'iu 春秋) Period. The descendants of Hsiao-yu settled in Pi hsien 費縣, Shan-tung 山東 province.

See also Fei³ 費, Fei⁴ 費.

## 407.  P'i² 皮

According to <u>Yüan ho hsing tsuan</u> 元何姓纂, the surname Pi 皮 originated from Fan Chung-pi 樊仲皮 who was a son of Chou Wen-wang 周文王 and was enfeoffed at the vassal state of Yang-fan 陽樊 and eventually adopted Fan 樊 as his surname. The Fan family settled in Nan-yang hsien 南陽縣, Ho-nan 河南 province where the feudal territory Yang-fan was located. Several generations later, Pi 皮 was adopted as a common surname by some of the descendants from the Fan 樊 family. The Pi family initially settled in Shan-hsi 山西 and later expanded to Ho-nan 河南 province.

See also Fan² 樊.

## 408.  Pieh² 別

<u>Hsing shih k'ao lüeh</u> 姓氏考略 mentions scantily

the origin of the surname 別 as follows: The surname Pieh came from Ching-chao 京兆 and the original settlement of the family was T'ien-shui 天水 in Kan-su 甘肅 province.

## 409. Pien¹ 邊

The surname Pien 邊 can be traced to the lineage of Ch'eng T'ang 成湯, the first king of the Shang 商 dynasty. According to <u>Yüan ho hsing tsuan</u> 元何姓纂 and <u>T'ung chih Shih tsu lüeh</u> 通志氏族略, Pien derived from the social name Tze-pien 子邊 of the King's descendant Ch'eng 城 who was a feudal prince of the State of Sung (Sung kuo 宋國) in the Chou 周 dynasty. It was later adopted as a common surname by Ch'eng's descendants and the family settled in Ho-nan 河南 province.

## 410. Pien⁴ 卞

According to <u>Yüan ho hsing tsuan</u> 元何姓纂, the surname Pien 卞 belongs to the ancestral line of Chen To 振鐸 who was the thirteenth son of Chou Wen-wang 周文王. Pien originated from the name of the feudal territory, Pien 卞, bestowed on a son of Chen To, and later adopted as the common surname by his descendants. The family initially settled in Ting-tao hsien 定陶縣, Shan-tung 山東 province.

See also Ts'ao² 曹.

## 411. Ping³ 邴

The suranme Ping 邴 derived from a place name located in the State of Ch'i (Ch'i kuo 齊國) of the Spring and Autumn (Ch'un ch'iu 春秋) Period. Currently, the Ping families reside primarily in Shan-tung 山東 province where the State of Ch'i was located.

## 412. P'ing² 平

The surname P'ing 平 derived from two sources. 1. <u>Hsing shih k'ao lüeh</u> 姓氏考略 traces its genealogy as follows: The surname P'ing was adopted posthumously from Yen P'ing-chung 晏平仲 who was a grand councilor (tsai-hsiang 宰相) from the State of Ch'i (Ch'i kuo 齊國) in the Chou 周 dynasty. The family initially settled in Shan-tung 山東 province where the State of Ch'i was located. 2. According to Yüan ho hsing tsuan 元何姓纂, P'ing originated from the name of a vassal state, the District of P'ing (P'ing i 平邑), bestowed on a son of the Marquise Han-ai (Han-ai hou 韓哀侯) and later adopted as a common surname by his descendants. The family settled primarily in Ho-nan 河南 province.

413.  Po² 薄

According to Hsing shih k'ao lüeh 姓氏考略, the surname Po 薄 belongs to the lineage of the Shang 商 King Ch'eng-t'ang 成湯 and its founder was Po-ku shih 薄姑氏. The surname originated from the name of a vassal state in Po-ch'eng 薄城, bestowed on a grand master (ta-fu 大夫) of the State of Sung (Sung kuo 宋國) in the Spring and Autumn (Ch'un ch'iu 春秋) Period. Po was later adopted as the common surname by his descendants.

414.  Po² 伯

The surname Po 伯 derived from two sources. 1. Feng shu t'ung 風俗通 traces the founder of the surname to Po I 伯益. He was the animal tamer as well as bird trainer during the reign of Yü Ti-shun 虞帝舜 and was honored with the surname Ying 嬴 by the king. The majority of Po I's descendants adopted the surname Ying 嬴 and others kept their ancestor's surname Po 伯 as their common surnames. 2. Ku chin hsing shih shu pien cheng 古今姓氏書辨證 describes the origin of the surname Po as follows: The surname Po branched from the surname Chiang 姜 of the ancestral line of Yen-ti 炎帝 (Shen-nung shih 神農氏) and the founder of the surname was Po I 伯夷 in the Chou 周 dynasty.

See also Chiang¹ 姜, Chi² 籍, Ying¹ 嬴.

415. Pu³ 卜

According to <u>Yüan ho hsing tsuan</u> 元何姓纂, the surname Pu 卜 originated from the name of the official post, pu-shih kuan 卜筮官, Diviner, who was in charge of imperial divination in the Court of Imperial Sacrifices in the Chou 周 dynasty. Pu was adopted as a common surname by the descendants whose family member was appointed to Pu-shih kuan and the family prospered in northern China during the Ch'in 秦 and Han 漢 periods.

416. Pu⁴ 步

According to <u>Yüan ho hsing tsuan</u> 元何姓纂, the origin of the surname Pu 步 came from two sources. 1. It originated from the name of a vassal state in the State of Chin (Chin kuo 晉國) which was bestowed on the Grand Master (ta-fu 大夫) Ch'üeh Pu-yang 卻步陽 in the Spring and Autumn (Ch'un ch'iu 春秋) Period. This branch of the Pu family originally settled in Shan-tung 山東 and later expanded to Chiang-su 江蘇 and other southern provinces. 2. The second origin was evolved from the change of surname from Ch'üeh 卻 to Pu 步.

See also Ch'üeh⁴ 卻.

417. P'u² 濮

The surname P'u 濮 derived from two sources. 1. According to <u>Hsing yüan</u> 姓苑 and <u>Ming hsien shih tsu yen hsing lei kao</u> 名賢氏族言行類稿, the surname originated from the name of the vassal state in P'u hsien 濮縣, Shan-tung 山東 province, bestowed on a grand master (ta-fu 大夫) of the State of Ch'i (Ch'i kuo 齊國) in the Spring and Autumn (Ch'un ch'iu 春秋) Period. 2. According to <u>Lu shih</u> 路史, the P'u families settled primarily in P'u-yang 濮陽 and Hua hien 滑縣 in Ho-nan 河南 province came from two origins. One originated from the ancestral line of Yü Ti-shun 虞帝舜 and the other from the minority of Pai-p'u 百濮. The families later pervaded Hu-pei 湖北 and Ssu-ch'uan 四川

provinces.

### 418. P'u² 蒲

The origin of the surname P'u 蒲 was closely related to the tufted marsh plants called rushes. According to <u>Lu shih</u> 路史, the surname was traced to Yu-hu shih 有扈氏 of the lineage of Huang-ti 黃帝. His descendants adopted the surname P'u inspired by the full growth of rushes (p'u 蒲) in the ponds of their family gardens. The family settled primarily in the area east of the Yellow River which was commonly called He-tung 河東.

### 419. P'u³ 浦

<u>Hsing shih k'ao lüeh</u> 姓氏考略 points out that the surname P'u 浦 branched from the surname Chiang 姜 of the ancestral line of Lü Shang 呂尚, who was the Grand Duke Chiang T'ai (Chiang T'ai kung 姜太公) during the regin of Chou Wu-wang 周武王 and his residence was near the P'u River. The surname originated from the name of the P'u River (P'u chiang 浦江), which passes through Shan-tung 山東 and P'u was eventually adopted as the common surname by the decendants of Lü Shang. The family initially settled in Shan-tung and later crossed the river into Chiang-su 江蘇 and Che-chiang 浙江 provinces.

### 420. P'u²-yang² 濮陽

The multiple surname P'u-yang 濮陽 originated from the place name P'u-yang hsien 濮陽縣 located in Ho-nan 河南 province. It is the place where Emperor Chuan Hsü 顓頊 was buried. P'u-yang was later adopted as the common surname by his descendants who guarded his mausoleum.

### 421. Sang¹ 桑

The surname Sang 桑 derived from three sources. 1. According to <u>Wan hsing t'ung p'u</u> 萬姓統譜, it originated from Shao Hao 少昊 (Chin-t'ien shih 金天氏). He was enthroned in Ch'iung-sang 窮桑 located in the present Ch'ü-fu 曲阜, Shang-tung

山東 province.  Sang was later adopted as a common surname by his descendants and the family settled in Shang-tung province. 2. <u>Hsing shih k'ao lüeh</u> 姓氏考略 states that the surname derived from the ancestral line of Yen-ti 炎帝 (Shen-nung shih 神農氏) who was also called Sang-shui shih 桑水氏 and Sang was later adopted as a common surname by his descendants. 3. According to <u>Hsing yüan</u> 姓苑,  the surname Sang belongs to the ancestral line of Chuan Hsü 顓頊 (Kao-yang shih 高陽氏) and derived from the social name of the feudal prince Tzu-sang 子桑 of the State of Ch'in (Ch'in kuo 秦國) in the Chou 周 dynasty.  Sang was later adopted as the common surname by his descendants and the family settled primarily in Ho-nan 河南 province.

## 422.  Sha¹ 沙

The surname Sha 沙 derived from several sources. Some are foreign and others are domestic sources.  1. <u>Wang hsing t'ung p'u</u> 萬姓統譜 traces the name to its usage by the minorities of the Yih 夷  people from the State of Pai-chi (Pai-chi kuo 百濟國), an ancient state in Ch'ao-hsien 朝鮮 during the T'ang 唐 dynasty.  The Yih people later settled in Han 漢 territories and continued to use their surname Sha after they were subdued by the T'ang 唐 dynasty. 2. <u>T'ung chih Shih tsu lüeh</u> 通志氏族略 says: At the end of the T'ang dynasty,  the nomadic groups of the Hu 胡 People such as Hsien-pei 鮮卑 and T'u-chüeh 突厥 were assimilated by the Han 漢 People; they adopted the surname Sha and settled in Han territories.  3. <u>Hsing shih k'ao lüeh</u> 姓氏考略 describes the name's origin as follows: The surname Sha follows the ancestral line of Yen-ti 炎帝 (Shen-nung shih 神農氏) and was descended from Su-sha shih 夙沙氏 of Ju-nan 汝南.  4. According to <u>Pai chia hsing kao lüeh</u> 百家姓考略,  the surname derived from Sha-sui shih 沙隨氏 and was adopted as a common surname by his descendants in the Han 漢 dynasty.

## 423.  Shan¹ 山

The origin of the surname Shan 山 (mountain) is

related to the word's meaning. According to <u>Ming hsien shih tsu yen hsing lei kao</u> 名賢氏族言行類稿 and <u>T'ung chih Shih tsu lüeh</u> 通志氏族略, it originated from the name of the official post, shan-shih 山師, Mountain Tax Master, in the Chou 周 dynasty. The person was a member of the Ministry of War (hsia-kuan 夏官) responsible for the supervision of noted mountains and lakes, excluded from fiefs, granted to the feudal lords and for the collection of royal taxes on timber, game, and fish taken from them. Shan was later adopted as the common surname by the descendants of the family who held the post.

424. Shan⁴ 單

According to <u>Yüan ho hsing tsuan</u> 元何姓纂, the surname Shan 單 originated from the name of the feudal territory, the Shan Commandery (Shan-i 單邑), bestowed on Chen 臻 by his father Chou Chen-wang (周成王, 1115-1078 B.C.). It was adopted as a common surname by his descendants and the family settled primarily in Ho-nan 河南 province.

425. Shang¹ 商

The surname Shang 商 derived from the name of the dynastic appelation of the Shang 商 dynasty. It was traced originally to the ancestral line of Ti K'u 帝嚳 (Kao-hsin shih 高辛氏) and followed by T'ang Ti Yao 唐帝堯. Fourteen generations later, Ch'eng T'ang 成湯 was enthroned and became the first king of the Shang 商 dynasty. According to <u>Yüan ho hsing tsuan</u> 元何姓纂 and <u>T'ung chih Shih tsu lüeh</u> 通志氏族略, Shang was adopted as the common surname after the Shang dynasty was overthrown by the Chou 周 dynasty. The family initially settled in Shen-hsi 陝西 and later expanded to southern provinces.

426. Shang³ 賞

The surname Shang 賞 derived from two sources.
1. <u>Ming hsien shih tsu yen hsing lei kao</u>

名賢氏族言行類稿 says: Shang was one of the eight major surnames that populated the Wu Kingdom (Wu kuo 吳國, A.d. 222-280) during the Period of Three Kingdoms (Wei 魏, Shu 蜀, and Wu 吳 collectively called Shan kuo 三國, A.D. 220-280) and the surname was widely adopted in Chiang-nan 江南 including Che-chiang 浙江 and Chiang-su 江蘇 provinces.  2. According to Wan hsing t'ung p'u 萬姓統譜, the surname was also adopted by the people of the State of Western Hsia (Hsi-hsia kuo 西夏國) and they originally came from the nomadic group of Hsien-pei 鮮卑 from the House of To-pa 拓跋. They invaded China during the Sung 宋 period and occupied Sung territories for nearly 200 years until they were subdued by Mongolian forces.   Subsequently, these people settled in China and adopted the surname Shang 賞 as their common surname.

427.  Shang⁴ 尚

According to Yüan ho hsing tsuan 元何姓纂, the surname Shang 尚 branched from the surname Chiang 姜 of the ancestral line of Yen-ti 炎帝 and its founder was Lh Shang 呂尚 who was the Grand Duke of Chiang T'ai (Chiang T'ai-kung 姜太公) during the reign of Chou Wu-wang 周武王. Shang was adopted as the common surname by his descendants and the family settled primarily in Ching-ho 清河, Ho-pei 河北 and Shang-tang 上黨, Shan-hsi 山西 provinces.

428.  Shang⁴-kuan¹ 上官

According to T'ang shu tsai hsiang shih hsi piao 唐書宰相世系表, the multiple surname Shang-kuan 上官 branched from the surname Mi 芈 and originally was the name of a district (i 邑). Its founder was the feudal prince Lan 蘭; he was the Grand Master (ta-fu 大夫) of Shang-kuan District (Shang-kuan i 上官邑) bestowed by his father, Ch'u Chuang-wang 楚莊王 during the Spring and Autumn (Ch'un ch'iu 春秋) Period. Shang-kuan was adopted as the common surname by his descendants and the family originally settled in T'ien-shui 天水, Kan-su 甘肅 and later expanded to Ho-nan 河南 province.

See alos Mi³ 芈.

## 429. Shao² 韶

The surname Shao 韶 originated from two sources.
1. According to <u>T'ung chih Shih tsu lüeh</u>
通志氏族略, it derived from the place name Shao
chou 韶州 in the Kuang-tung 廣東 province. The
following six Districts (hsiens 縣) were
territories of Shao chou in the Sui 隋 dynasty:
Ch'ü-chiang 曲江, Yüeh-ch'ang 樂昌, Jen-hua
仁化, Ju-yüan 乳源, Weng-yüan 翁源 and Ying-te
英德. These places were the original settlement
of Shao families. 2. <u>Hsin yüan</u> 姓苑 and <u>Wang
hsing t'ung p'u</u> 萬姓統譜 memtions that the Shao
families also populated K'ai-feng 開封, Ho-nan
河南 province and they originally came from
T'ai-yüen 太原, Shan-hsi 山西 province.

## 430. Shao⁴ 邵

According to <u>T'ung chih Shih tsu lüeh</u>
通志氏族略, the surname Shao 邵 branched from
the surname Chao 召 and the adoption of the
surname was initiated by the Duke Chao-kung Shih
召公奭 who added the radical to his surname.
The Shao 邵 family settled primarily in An-yang
安陽 and Ju-nan 汝南 of Ho-nan 河南 province.

See also Chao⁴ 召.

## 431. She¹ 佘

See Yü² 余.

## 432. She⁴ 庫

The surnames She 庫 and She 厍 derived from the
same origin and later branched into two names
either by human error or for symplification
purposes.

See also She⁴ 庫.

## 433. She⁴ 庫

According to Hsing shih k'ao lüeh 姓氏考略, the character "庫" when pronounced as "she" refers to a surname, differs from "k'u", a noun. Feng shu t'ung 風俗通 and T'ung chih Shih tsu lüeh 通志氏族略 trace the name's origin to the title of the official post, k'u-shih 庫使, Storehouse Commissioner, who was in charge of a government storehouse at any level, such as arms and supplies in the Ministry of War. It was adopted as the common surname in the Han 漢 dynasty by the descendants of the family who held the position. The surname She 庫 branched from the surname She 庫 either by error in writing or for symplification purposes. Both of the She 庫 and She 庫 families originally settled in the area of the Mountains T'ien-t'ai 天臺 and K'uo-ts'ang 括蒼 in Che-chiang 浙江 province.

See also She[4] 庫.

434. She[4]-nan[2] 社南

The surname She-nan 社南 originated from a place name. Feng shu t'ung 風俗通 traces the surname's origin to the State of Ch'i (Ch'i kuo 齊國) in the Spring and Autumn (Ch'un ch'iu 春秋) Period. Many citizens of the State of Ch'i moved to She-nan 社南, Shan-tung 山東 province and adopted the place name as their common surname.

See also She[4]-pei[3] 社北.

435. She[4]-pei[3] 社北

Similar to the surname She-nan 社南, Feng shu t'ung 風俗通 cites that the surname was adopted from a place name by the citizens of the State of Ch'i (Ch'i kuo 齊國) who moved to She-pei 社北, Shan-tung 山東 province.

See also She[4]-nan[2] 社南.

436. Shen[1] 申

The surname Shen 申 originated from two sources.

1. According to <u>Yüan ho hsing tsuan</u> 元何姓纂, it branched from the surname Chiang 姜 of the ancestral line of Yen-ti 炎帝 and its founder was Shen Lü 申呂, who was bestowed with the feudal territory Shen and became the Earl of Shen (Shen po 申伯). Shen was later adopted as the common surname by his descendants. 2. <u>Hsing shih k'ao lüeh</u> 姓氏考略 describes the origin of the surname as follows: The surname Shen 申 branched from the surname Shen-shu 申叔 and follows the ancestral line of Po I 伯夷. Its founder, Shen-shu Shih 申叔時, was a grand master (ta-fu 大夫) of the State of Ch'u (Ch'u kuo 楚國) in the Chou 周 dynasty. Shen originated from the name of a vassal state, the District of Shen (Shen i 申邑), bestowed on Shen-shu Shih by Chou Wu-wang 周武王 and was adopted as the common surname by his descendants. The name Shih 時 was also adopted by a descendant of Shen-shu Shih 申叔時 and later became a common surname.

See also Shih² 時, Shen¹-shu² 申叔.

437. Shen³ 沈

According to <u>Yüan ho hsing tsuan</u> 元何姓纂, the surname Shen 沈 originated from the name of the feudal territory Shen 沈 bestowed on P'u Chi 晡季 who was the tenth son of Chou Wen-wang 周文王. It was later adopted as a common surname and the family settled primarily in Ho-nan 河南 and An-hui 安徽 provinces.

See also Yeh⁴ 葉, Yu² 尤.

438. Shen⁴ 慎

According to <u>Hsing shih k'ao lüeh</u> 姓氏考略, the origin of the surname Shen 慎 came from two sources. 1. It was adopted from the social name Shen-tzu 慎子 of Ch'in Hua-li 禽滑釐, who was an educator and a Mohist, a practitioner of Mo-tzu's 墨子 doctrines, from the State of Wei (Wei kuo 魏國) during the Warring States (Chan kuo 戰國) Period. 2. The surname derived from the place name Shen hsien 慎縣, located in the State of Ch'u (Ch'u kuo 楚國) in the Spring and Autumn (Ch'un ch'iu 春秋) Period and the ancestral home of the family was located in T'ien-shui 天水, Kan-su 甘肅 province.

439. Shen[1]-shu[2] 申叔

According to <u>Hsing shih k'ao lüeh</u> 姓氏考略, the founder of the surname was Shen-shu Shih 申叔時, who was a grand master (ta-fu 大夫) of the State of Ch'u (Ch'u kuo 楚國) in the Chou 周 dynasty. The evolution of the surname was detailed under the surname Shen 申.

See also Shen[1] 申.

440. Shen[1]-t'u[2] 申徒

<u>Feng shu t'ung</u> 風俗通 describes the connection of the names Shen-t'u 申徒 and Shen-t'u 申屠 as follows: The surname Shen-t'u 申徒 originated as a result of the change of surname from Shen-t'u 申屠. Many people believed that the word "t'u 屠", meaning "to slaughter, butcher, or massacre" will bring misfortune to their families so they changed the word to its homonymous form "t'u 徒" and adopted Shen-t'u 申徒 instead.

See also Shen[1]-t'u[2] 申屠.

441. Shen[1]-t'u[2] 申屠

According to <u>Shang yu lu</u> 尚友錄, the origin of the surname Shen-t'u 申屠 is the culmination of two events. Chou Wu-wang 周武王 bestowed a descendant of Po I 伯夷 as the Marquise of Shen (Shen hou 申侯) in the feudal State of Shen (Shen kuo 申國), located in the present Nan-yang hsien 南陽縣, Ho-nan 河南 province. At the end of the Western Chou (Hsi Chou 西周) dynasty, some of the descendants of Shen hou relocated from their old settlement in Ho-nan to T'u-yüan 屠原 in Kan-su 甘肅 province. They eventually adopted the combined Shen and T'u (Shen-t'u 申屠) as their common surname and formally settled in Kan-su 甘肅 province.

See also Shen[1]-t'u[2] 申徒.

442. Sheng[4] 盛

According to <u>Ming hsien shih tsu yen hsing lei kao</u> 名賢氏族言行類稿, the surname Sheng 盛 branched from the surname Chi 姬 of the lineage of Huang-ti 黃帝 and originated from the name of the feudal territory, the State of Sheng (Sheng kuo 盛國), during the reign of Chou Mu-wang (周穆王, 1001-946 B.C.). The descendants of the Sheng family initially settled in Ho-nan 河南 and Ssu-ch'uan 四川. provinces.

443. Shih[1] 施

<u>Yüan ho hsing tsuan</u> 元何姓纂 states the genealogy of the surname Shih 施 as follows: The surname Shih belongs to the ancestral line of Duke Lu Hui (Lu Hui kung 魯惠公) and originated from Shih Fu 施父 who was a grand master (ta-fu 大夫) of the State of Lu (Lu kuo 魯國) and a son of Lu Hui kung. Shih was adopted as the common surname by the fifth generation descednats of Hui kung in the Chou 周 dynasty and the family initially settled in Shan-tung 山東 province.

444. Shih[1] 師

According to <u>Yüan ho hsing tsuan</u> 元何姓纂, the surname Shih 師 derived from the title of the official post, shih-yin 師尹, Master, which was a generic reference to the Palace Mentor with teaching resposibilities in the Chou 周 dynasty. Shih was adopted as the common surname by the descendants of the family who held the position and they settled primarily in T'ai-yüan 太原, Shan-hsi 山西 and Lang-yeh 瑯琊, Shan-tung 山東 provinces.

See also Shuai[4] 帥.

445. Shih[2] 石

The surname Shih 石 derived from the following two sources: 1. According to <u>Wei shu kuan shih</u>

chih 魏書官氏志, the surname Shih branched from Wu-shih-lan shih 烏石蘭氏 of the nomadic group of Hsiung-nu 匈奴 during the reign of Hsiao Wen-ti 孝文帝 in the Northern Wei (Pei Wei 北魏) period. 2. Yüan ho hsing tsuan 元和姓纂 traces the founder of the surname Shih 石 to Shih T'ai-chung 石䲷仲 whose father was the Grand Master (ta-fu 大夫) Shih La 石腊 from the State of Wei (Wei kuo 衛國) in the Spring and Autumn (Ch'un ch'iu 春秋) Period.

### 446. Shih² 時

Hsing shih k'ao lüeh 姓氏考略 traces the genealogy of the surname Shih 時 as follows: The surname Shih 時 branched from the surname Shen 申 of the ancestral line of Po I 伯夷. and its founder was Shen-shu Shih 申叔時 who was a grand master (ta-fu 大夫) of the State of Ch'u (Ch'u kuo 楚國) in the Chou 周 dynasty. When Shen was adopted as a common surname by the descendants of Shen-shu Shih 申叔時, some of his descendants adopted Shih as their common surname instead. The Shih family initially settled in Ho-nan 河南 province.

See also Shen¹ 申.

### 447. Shih³ 史

The surname Shih 史 originated from the name of the official post, shih 史, Scribe, which was a title commonly incorporated into compound titles such as t'ai-shih 太史, yü-shih 御史, or identified by a prefixed agency name. According to Lu shih 路史, Ch'ang-chieh 倉頡 was appointed to Shih-kuan 史官, Historian, during the reign of Huang-ti 黃帝 and shih was subsequently adopted as the common surname by his descendants and they settled in Hsüan-ch'eng hsien 宣城縣, An-hui 安徽 province. 2. Yüan ho hsing tsuan 元何姓纂 traces the genealogy of the surname to I 佚 who held the post of T'ai-shih 太史, Grand Scribe, in the Chou 周 dynasty. His descendants adopted Shih as their common surname and they settled in Wu-chang 武昌, Hu-pei 湖北 province.

## 448.  Shih⁴ 士

The surname Shih 士 derived from the name of the
official post, shih-shih 士師, Serviceman. T'ung
chih Shih tsu lüeh 通志氏族略 traces the surname
Shih to Hsi Shu 隰叔 who was a son of the Earl
of Tu (Tu po 杜伯).  After the State of Tu (Tu
kuo 杜國) was defeated by Chou Hsüan-wang
周宣王, Hsi Shu escaped to the State of Chin
(Chin kuo 晉國) and was appointed to shih-shih
士師, Serviceman, and Shih was subsequently
adopted as a common surname by his descendants.

See also Fan⁴ 范.

## 449.  Shou⁴ 壽

According to Feng shu t'ung 風俗通, the surname
Shou 壽 was traced to Shou Meng 壽夢, who was a
descendant of Chou Wen-wang 周文王 and the ruler
of the State of Sung (Sung kuo 宋國) in the
Spring and Autumn (Ch'un ch'iu 春秋) Period.

## 450.  Shu¹ 殳

The surname Shu 殳 derived from two sources.  1.
Hsing shih k'ao lüeh 姓氏考略 and Ming hsien
shih tsu yen hsing lei kao  名賢氏族言行類稿
traces the surname to its founder Shu Chiang
殳斨 who was the Grand Minister (ta-ch'en 大臣)
of Yü Ti-shun 虞帝舜.  2.  Hsing shih k'ao lüeh
姓氏考略 also traces the name's origin to the
noun "Shu 殳", the bamboo spear which was a
weapon in antiquity.  Shu was later adopted as a
common surname by the descendants of the family
that produced shu in ancient times.  The Shu
family primarily settled in Wu-kung hsien
武功縣, Shan-tung 山東 province.  They adopted
Wu-kung as their ancestral hall name (t'ang ming
堂名) in memory of their ancestors.

## 451.  Shu¹ 舒

According to Feng shu t'ung 風俗通, T'ung chih
Shih tsu lüeh 通志氏族略, and Shang yu lu
尚友錄, the surname Shu 舒 derived from the name
of the feudal territory, the State of Shu (Shu

kuo 舒國), bestowed on Shu Chiu-tzu 舒鳩子 during the Spring and Autumn (Ch'un ch'iu 春秋) Period. After The State of Shu was defeated by the State of Ch'u (Ch'u kuo 楚國), its descendants adopted Shu as their common surname and they settled in Chü-lu 鉅鹿, Ho-pei 河北 province.

452. Shu[1] 疏

See Shu[4] 束.

453. Shu[4] 束

Wan hsing t'ung p'u 萬姓統譜 traces the genealogy of the surname Shu 束 as follows: The surname Shu 束 branched from the surname Shu 疏 and its founder was Shu Meng-ta 疏夢達. Due to the political instability at the end of the Western Han (Hsi Han 西漢) dynasty, Shu Meng-ta relocated his family and relatives from Shan-tung 山東 and Chiang-su 江蘇 provinces to Nan-yang 南陽, Ho-nan 河南 province and subsequently changed his surname into Shu 束. The family later prospered in Nan-yang 南陽, Ho-nan 河南 province.

454. Shuai[4] 帥

Kuang yün 廣韻 and Ming hsien shih tsu yen hsing lei kao 名賢氏族言行類稿 trace the origin of the name Shuai 帥 to the surname Shih 師, founded by Shih Yü 師禹 who was the Imperial Secretary (shang-shu 尚書) in the State of Chin (Chin kuo 晉國) during the Spring and Autumn (Ch'un ch'iu 春秋) Period. He changed his surname to Shuai Yü 帥禹 to avoid the taboo name Shih 師 of the Duke of Ching (Ching kung 景公) in the State of Chin and later his descendants adopted Shuai as their common surname.

See also Shih[1] 師.

455. Shuang[1] 雙

According to <u>T'ung chih Shih tsu lüeh</u>
通志氏族略, the surname Shuang 雙 belongs to the
ancestral line of Chuan Hsü 顓頊 and derived
from the name of a feudal territory located in
the Town of Shuang-meng (Shuang-meng ch'eng
雙蒙城); it was bestowed on a descendant of
Chuan Hsü and later adopted as a common surname
by the family. Members of the family settled
primarily in T'ien-shui 天水, Kan-su 甘肅
province.

456.  Shui³ 水

The origin of the surname Shui 水 (water) was
traced in <u>Hsing shih wu shu</u> 姓氏五書, written by
the Ch'ing 清 scholar Chang Shu 張澍.  The book
says: the surname Shui was adopted by the people
who lived by the water and it was initially
adopted by the people living in the communities
of Yin hsien 鄞縣, Che-chiang 浙江 and Wu-hsing
吳興, Chiang-su 江蘇 provinces.  Presently,
anyone who has the surname Shui can trace back
to these two places.

457.  So³ 索

<u>Yüan ho hsing tsuan</u> 元何姓纂 mentions scantily
the genealogy of the surname So 索 as follows:
The So clan was one of the largest family units
in the Shang 商 period and the family originally
settled in Tun-huang 敦煌, Wu-wei 武威 of the
Kan-su 甘肅 province.

458.  Ssu¹ 司

According to <u>Hsing shih k'ao lüeh</u> 姓氏考略, the
surname Ssu 司 was originated from the name of
a district (i 邑) located in the State of Wei
(Wei kuo 衛國) during the Spring and Autumn
(Ch'un ch'iu 春秋) Period.  The family settled
initially in Chün hsien 濬縣, Ho-nan 河南
province where the State of Wei was located.
There are several double character surnames
which begin with Ssu, such as Ssu-ma 司馬, Ssu-
t'u 司徒, Ssu-k'ou 司寇, and Ssu-ch'eng 司城.
They all derived from official titles in the
Chou 周 dynasty.

See also Ssu¹-ma³ 司馬, Ssu¹-t'u² 司徒, Ssu¹-k'ou⁴ 司寇, and Ssu¹-ch'eng² 司城.

459. Ssu⁴ 姒

According to <u>Hsing shih k'ao lüeh</u> 姓氏考略, the surname Ssu 姒 derived from Pao Ssu 褒姒 who was the favorite concubine of the Chou 周 king Yu-wang 幽王 (781-770 B.C.).

460. Ssu¹-ch'eng² 司城

According to <u>T'ung chih Shih tsu lüeh</u> 通志氏族略, the Duke Wu (Wu kung 武公) from the State of Sung (Sung kuo 宋國) was the Ssu-k'ung 司空, the Minister of Works (tung-kuan 冬官), in the Chou 周 dynasty. The official title was later changed into Ssu-ch'eng 司城 and the new name was subsequently adopted as a common surname.

See also Ssu¹-k'ung¹ 司空.

461. Ssu¹-k'ou⁴ 司寇

The surname Ssu-k'ou 司寇 initially derived from the name of the official title, Ssu-k'ou 司寇, the Minister of Justice, in the Chou 周 dynasty. According to <u>T'ung chih Shih tsu lüeh</u> 通志氏族略, the surname Ssu-k'ou 司寇 was traced to the ancestral line of the Duke Ling (Ling kung 靈公) from the State of Wei (Wei kuo 衛國), whose son was the Ssu-k'ou, the Minister of Justice (ch'iu-kuan 秋官) at the royal court to the Chou 周 king.

See also Ssu¹ 司, K'ou⁴ 寇.

462. Ssu¹-k'ung¹ 司空

The surname Ssu-k'ung 司空 initially derived from the name of the official title, Ssu-k'ung 司空, the Minister of Works (tung-kuan 冬官), in the Chou 周 dynasty. According to <u>T'ung chih Shih tsu lüeh</u> 通志氏族略, the surname was traced to the ancestral line of the Great Yü (Ta Yü

大禹), a descendant of his was the Ssu-k'ung during the Chou Period. As one of the six great Ministers (ch'ing 卿) in the Chou 周 government, Ssu-k'ung supervised all governmental construction and provisioning through many subordinate agencies and agents. The evolution of the surname was detailed under the surname Ssu-ch'eng 司城.

See also Ssu¹-ch'eng² 司城.

463.   Ssu¹-ma³ 司馬

Shang yu lu 尚友錄 describes the origin of the surname Ssu-ma 司馬 as follows: The surname Ssu-ma derived from the ancestral line of Ch'eng Po-hsiu 程伯休 whose father held the post of Ssu-ma 司馬, the Minister of War (hsia-kuan 夏官), in the Chou 周 dynasty.   Some of his descendants adopted the official title Ssu-ma and others adopted Ch'eng 程 as their common surnames.

See also Ssu¹ 司, Ch'eng² 程.

464.   Ssu¹-t'u² 司徒

The surname Ssu-t'u 司徒 initially derived from the name of the official title, Ssu-t'u 司徒, the Minister of Education (ti-kuan 地官), in the Chou 周 dynasty.   According to T'ung chih Shih tsu lüeh 通志氏族略, the surname was traced to the ancestral line of Yü Ti-shun 虞帝舜, a descendant of his was the Ssu-t'u in the Chou Period.   As one of the six great Ministers (ch'ing 卿) in the Chou 周 government, Ssu-t'u was in charge of training in and the enforcement of proper moral and political values among the people, with specific responsibility of overseeing commercial activities through a large staff of subbordinates.

See also Ssu¹ 司.

465.   Su¹ 蘇

According to Yüan ho hsing tsuan 元何姓纂, the surname Su 蘇 belongs to the ancestral line of Chuan Hsü 顓頊 and originated from the place name, Su ch'eng 蘇城, bestowed on K'un Wu 昆吾 in the Hsia 夏 dynasty. The Su family initially settled in Ling-chang hsien 臨漳縣, Ho-nan 河南 province and later relocated to Ho-nei 河內, Kan-su 甘肅 province in the Chou 周 period.

See also K'ou⁴ 寇, Ch'ih¹ 郗.

## 466. Su⁴ 宿

The surname Su 宿 derived from three sources. 1. According to Yüan ho hsing tsuan 元何姓纂, it originated from the name of an ancient state, the State of Su-ku (Su-ku kuo 宿固國). during the reign of T'ai Hao 太昊 (Fu-shi shih 伏羲氏). Su was later adopted as a common surname by the citizens of Su-ku. The following two sources came after the Southern and Northern Dynasties (Nan-pei ch'ao 南北朝). 2. According to Pei shih 北史, Jo Tou-ken 若豆根 was given the honorary surname Su 宿 by a king and it was later adopted as a common surname by his descendants in the Southern and Northern Dynasties (Nan-pei ch'ao 南北朝). 3. Wei shu 魏書 says that Liu Tzu-wen 劉子文 was also given the honorary surname Su 宿 by a king and it was later adopted as a common surname by his descendants in the Southern and Northern Dynasties (Nan-pei ch'ao 南北朝).

## 467. Su⁴ 粟

According to Yüan ho hsing tsuan 元和姓纂, the surname Su 粟 originated from the title of the official post, chih-su tu-wei 治粟都尉, Commandant-in-Chief of the Granaries. The person was principally in charge of the capital granaries; a position that was held in the Western Han (Hsi Han 西漢) dynasty. Han Hsin 韓信 was appointed to the post during the reign of the Han 漢 Emperor Kao-tsu 高祖, Liu Pang 劉邦 and Su 粟 was subsequently adopted as a common surname by his descendants.

468.  Sui² 隨

According to <u>Ch'ien fu lun</u> 潛夫論 and <u>Lu shih</u> 路史, the surname Sui 隨 derived from the name of the feudal territory, the State of Sui (Sui kuo 隨國), bestowed on Shih Hui 士會 by a Chou 周 king. The State of Sui was later defeated by the State of Ch'u (Ch'u kuo 楚國) and Sui was adopted as a common surname by the descendants of Shih Hui. The family settled primarily in Shi-chou 隨州, Hu-pei 湖北 province where the State of Sui was located.

See also Sui² 隋.

469.  Sui² 隋

<u>Hsing shih hsün yüan</u> 姓氏尋源 and <u>Hsing shih k'ao lüeh</u> 姓氏考略 describe the origin of the surname as follows: The surname Sui 隋 branched from the surname 隨 and the founder of the name was the Sui 隋 emperor, Wen-ti 文帝 (A.D. 589-605). He removed the name's radical and adopted Sui 隋 as his dynastic appellation. Sui was later adopted as a common surname in memory of Sui Wen-ti.

See also Sui² 隨.

470.  Sun¹ 孫

According to <u>Yüan ho hsing tsuan</u> 元何姓纂, the surname Sun 孫 belongs to the ancestral line of Chou Wen-wang 周文王 and originated from Hui Sun 惠孫 of the State of Wei (Wei kuo 衛國) in the Chou 周 dynasty. Sun was adopted as a common surname by his descendants and they settled in T'ai-yüan 太原, Shan-hsi 山西 province.

See also Li⁴ 厲.

471.  Sung¹ 松

According to <u>Ming hsien shih tsu yen hsing lei kao</u> 名賢氏族言行類稿, Ch'in She-huang (秦始皇, 221-209 B.C.) was caught in a sudden downpour on his way back to the palace after a routine ceremony to pay tribute to his ancestors. With his procession hiding under a gigantic pine tree (sung shu 松樹), he later honored the tree with commentaries engraved in a stone and Sung was subsequently adopted as a common surname by the local residents. The Sung family initially settled in I-shui hsien 沂水縣, Shan-tung 山東 province.

472. Sung⁴ 宋

Wan hsing t'ung p'u 萬姓統譜 and T'ang shu tsai hsiang shih hsi piao 唐書宰相世系表 trace the origin of the surname Sung 宋 as follows: The surname branched from the surname Tzu 子 and originated from the name of the feudal territory, the State of Sung (Sung kuo 宋國), bestowed on Wei Tzu-ch'i 微子啓 (the eldest son the the Shang 商 king Ti-i 帝乙) by Chou Wu-wang 周武王. After the State of Sung was defeated by the State of Ch'u 楚, citizens of the State of Sung formally adopted Sung as their common surname and settled in Ho-nan 河南 province.

See also Tsou¹ 鄒.

473. Ta² 笪

The surname Ta 笪 derived from the Chien-chou Commandery (Chien-chou chün 建州郡) in the T'ang 唐 dynasty and later the place name was changed to Chien-an 建安. It is located in Chien-ou hsien 建甌縣, Fu-chien 福建 province. According to Hsing shih k'ao lüeh 姓氏考略 and T'ung chih Shih tsu lüeh 通志氏族略, the Ta families later prospered in Kou-jung hsien 句容縣, Chiang-su 江蘇 province.

474. Tai⁴ 戴

The surname Tai 戴 came from two sources. 1. According to Wan hsing t'ung p'u 萬姓統譜 and Shang yu lu 尚友錄, the surname derived posthumously from the Duke of Tai (Tai kung 戴公) in the State of Sung (Sung kuo 宋國) during the Spring and Autumn (Ch'un ch'iu 春秋)

Period. 2. <u>T'ung chih Shih tsu lüeh</u> 通志氏族略 traces its origin to the name of the feudal territory of the State of Tai (Tai kuo 戴國) located in K'ai-feng 開封, Ho-nan 河南 province. After Tai kuo was defeated by the State of Cheng (Cheng kuo 鄭國), residents from Tai kuo adopted Tai as their common surname and settled in Tai-ch'eng 戴城 where the site of Tai kuo was originally located.

475. T'ai² 邰

    <u>Shuo wen chieh tzu</u> 說文解字 describes the origin of the surname T'ai 邰 as follows: The surname originated from the name of the feudal territory T'ai 邰 bestowed on Hou Chi 后稷 who was the Minister of Agriculture to T'ang Ti-yao 唐帝堯. T'ai was adopted as the common surname by the descendants of Hou-chi, who initially settled in Wu-kung hsein 武功縣, Shen-hsi 陝西 province where the feudal territory was located, and the family later prospered in P'ing-lu hsien 平廬縣, Shan-tung 山東 province.

476. T'ai² 臺

    According to <u>Yüan ho hsing tsuan</u> 元何姓纂, the founder of the surname T'ai 臺 was T'ai t'ai 臺駘 who was the Minister of Water Resources to Chuan Hsü 顓頊. The family settled primarily in P'ing-lu hsien 平廬縣, Shan-tung 山東 province.

477. T'ai⁴-shu² 太叔

    <u>Hsing shih hsün yüan</u> 姓氏尋源 describes the origin of the surname T'ai-shu 太叔 as follows: The surname branched from the surname Chi 姬 of the ancestral line of Huang-ti 黃帝 and its founder was T'ai-shu I 太叔儀 who was a feudal prince of the State of Wei (Wei kuo 衛國) which was ruled by Wu-wang's 武王 brother K'ang Shu 康叔 in the Chou 周 dynasty. T'ai-shu was later adopted as a common surname and the family initially settled in Ho-nan 河南 and Ho-pei 河北 areas and later prospered in Tung-p'ing 東平, Shan-tung 山東 province.

478. T'an² 譚

The surname T'an 譚 came from two sources: 1. Yüan ho hsing tsuan 元何姓纂 traces the origin of the surname T'an 譚 as follows: the surname derivd from the name of the feudal territory, the State of T'an (T'an kuo 譚國) in the Spring and Autumn (Ch'un ch'iu 春秋) Period. After the State of T'an was defeated by the State of Chü (Chü kuo 莒國), its descendants formally adopted T'an as their common surname. The family initially settled in Shan-tung 山東 and later prospered in Hu-nan 湖南 provinces. 2. The surname T'an 譚 branched from the surname T'an 談 due to a change of character for the name to avoid revenge of the family by the rivals.

See also T'an² 談.

479. T'an² 談

The surname T'an 談 derived from the following two sources: 1. According to Ch'ien chia hsing 千家姓, the eldest son of the Shang 商 king Ti-i 帝乙 whose name was Wei Tzu-ch'i 微子啓 was bestowed with the feudal territory of the State of Sung (Sung kuo 宋國) by Chou Wu-wang 周武王. Thirty-six generations later, the State of Sung was ruled by T'an Chün 談君 after he defeated the State of Ch'u (Ch'u kuo 楚國) and T'an was adopted as a common surname by his descendants. 2. The surname T'an follows the ancestral line of Chi T'an 籍談 who was a grand master (ta-fu 大夫) in the Chou 周 dynasty. His descendants initially adopted the surname T'an 談 but later changed to T'an 譚 after the family escaped from the homeland to avoid revenge by the rivals.

See also Chi² 籍, T'an² 譚.

480. T'an²-t'ai² 澹臺

The multiple surname T'an-t'ai 澹臺 originated from the name of a lake, Lake T'an-t'ai (T'an-t'ai hu 澹臺湖), in Chiang-su 江蘇 province. For generations, Chiang-su and Che-chiang 浙江 are populated with T'an-t'ai families, and lately, many settled in T'ai-yüan 太原, Shan-hsi 山西 adopting T'ai-yüen as their ancestral hall name (t'ang ming 堂名).

481. Tang³ 黨

According to <u>Hsing shih k'ao lüeh</u> 姓氏考略, the surname Tang 黨 came from the ancestral line of the Chou Wen-wamg 周文王 and its founder, Tang shih 黨氏, was a grand master (ta-fu 大夫) from the State of Lu (Lu kuo 魯國) in the Spring and Autumn (Ch'un ch'iu 春秋) Period. The Tang family originally settled in Feng-i 馮翊, Shan-tung 山東 province.

See also Chang³ 仉.

482. T'ang¹ 湯

<u>Ming hsien shih tsu yen hsing lei kao</u> 名賢氏族言行類稿 traces the origin of the surname T'ang 湯 as follows: The surname derived from Ch'eng-t'ang (成湯, 1766-1753 B.C.), the first king of the Shang 商 dynasty. T'ang was adopted posthumously by his descendants and they settled in Chung-shan 中山 and Fan-yang 范陽 in Ho-pei 河北 province.

483. T'ang² 唐

The surname T'ang derived from two different sources. 1. According to <u>Yüan ho hsing tsuan</u> 元何姓纂, Ti-yao (帝堯, 2356-2255 B.C.) was initially enfeoffed at Tao 陶 and later relocated in T'ang 唐 and adopted T'ang as his dynastic appellation. Subsequently, T'ang was adopted as the common surname by his descendants. The family initially settled in T'ang hsien 唐縣, Ho-pei 河北 province. 2. <u>Hsing shih k'ao lüeh</u> 姓氏考略 traces the genealogy of the surname to Shu-yü 叔虞 who was enfeoffed in the feudal territory of the State of T'ang (T'ang kuo 唐國) during the reign of Chou Ch'eng-wang 周成王 and his descendants also adopted T'ang as their common surname. This branch of the T'ang family initially settled in I-ch'eng hsien 翼城縣, Shan-hsi 山西 province.

See also Tao[2] 陶, Chin[4] 晉.

### 484. T'ao[2] 陶

The surname Tao 陶 came from two different sources, as cited in <u>Yüan ho hsing tsuan</u> 元何姓纂: 1. Ti-yao 帝堯, also called T'ao-t'ang shih 陶唐氏, was initially enfeoffed at T'ao 陶, located in the present Ting-t'ao hsien 定陶縣, Shan-tung 山東 province and later relocated to T'ang 唐, located in the present T'ang hsien 唐縣, Ho-pei 河北 province. Some of his descendants adopted T'ao and others adopted T'ang as their common surnames. 2. The surname T'ao also derived from the name of the official post, t'ao-cheng 陶正, Potter, who headed Government Pottery Works in the Chou 周 Palace. Yü E 虞閼 who was a descendant of Ti-yao was appointed to t'ai-cheng in the Chou dynasty. His descendants adopted T'ao as their common surname and the family initially settled in Ho-nan 河南 and later populate Chiang-su 江蘇 and Chiang-hsi 江西 provinces.

See also T'ang[2] 唐.

### 485. Teng[4] 鄧

According to <u>Yüan ho hsing tsuan</u> 元何姓纂, the surname Teng 鄧 branched from the surname Man 曼 and derived from the name of a feudal territory, the state of Teng (Teng kuo 鄧國), bestowed on a descendant of Chin-t'ien shih 金天氏 in the late Shang 商 dynasty. Teng was subsequently adopted as a common surname by the family and they settled in Teng hsien 鄧縣, Ho-nan 河南 province where the State of Teng was located.

See also Man[4] 曼.

### 486. T'eng[2] 滕

The origin of the surname T'eng 滕 was cited in <u>Wan hsing t'ung p'u</u> 萬姓統譜 as follows: The surname T'eng originated from the name of a feudal territory, the State of T'eng (T'eng kuo 滕國), bestowed on Ch'o Shu-hsiu 錯叔繡 who was a son of Chou Wen-wang 周文王. T'eng was adopted as the common surname by his descendants and the family settled in T'eng hsien 滕縣, Shan-tung 山東 province where the State of T'eng was located.

487. Ti² 狄

Wan hsing t'ung p'u 萬姓統譜 and T'ang shu tsai hsiang shih hsi piao 唐書宰相世系表 trace the origin of the surname Ti 狄 as follows: The surname Ti branched from the surname Chi 姬 and derived from the name of the vassal state Ti-ch'eng 狄城, bestowed on the youngest son of Chou Ch'eng-wang 周成王. Ti was later adopted as a common surname by the the family's descendants and they settled in T'ai-yüan 太原, Shan-hsi 山西 and T'ien-shui 天水, Shen-hsi 陝西 provinces. An outstanding representative of the family was Ti Jen-chieh 狄仁傑 who was the Grand Councilor (tsai-hsiang 宰相) to T'ang T'ai-chung 唐太宗.

488. Tiao¹ 刁

Yüan ho hsing tsuan 元何姓纂 and Feng shu t'ung 風俗通 trace the genealogy of the surname Tiao 刁 to its founder, Shu-tiao 豎刁, who was the Grand Master (ta-fu 大夫) of the State of Ch'i (Ch'i kuo 齊國) in the Spring and Autumn (Ch'un ch'iu 春秋) Period. Tiao was adopted as a common surname by his descendants and the family settled in Shan-tung 山東 province where the State of Ch'i was located.

489. T'iao² 調

According to Hsing yüan 姓苑, the surname T'iao 調 derived from the name of the official post, t'iao-jen 調人, Arbitrator, in the Chou 周 dynasty. T'iao-jen was a member of the Ministry of Education (ti-kuan 地官) responsible for mediating quarrels among commoners and determining appropriate action when someone was accidentally injured or killed.

490. Tien³ 典

The surname Tien 典 originated from two sources. 1. <u>Hsing shih k'ao lüeh</u> 姓氏考略 says: Fu-hsi shih 伏羲氏 married Shao-tien shih 少典氏 and Tien was adopted as a common surname by the family. 2. <u>Ming hsien shih tsu yen hsing lei kao</u> 名賢氏族言行類稿 traces the origin of the surname to the name of the official post, tien-chi 典籍, Manager of the Library. Tien 典 and Chi 籍 were both adopted as common surnames.

See also Chi$^2$ 籍.

## 491. T'ien$^2$ 田

According to <u>Yüan ho hsing tsuan</u> 元何姓纂 and <u>T'ung chih Shih tsu lüeh</u> 通志氏族略: The surname T'ien 田 branched from the surname Ch'en 陳 in the Hsia 夏 dynasty. This came about when Prince Ch'en Wan 陳完 eluded his enemies and escaped to the State of Ch'i (Ch'i kuo 齊國) where he was bestowed with the vassal state of the District of T'ien (T'ien i 田邑) and subsequently changed his surname to T'ien 田. The original settlement of the T'ien family was located in Pei-p'ing hsien 北平縣, Ho-pei 河北 province.

See also Ch'en$^2$ 陳, Fa$^3$ 法, Hu$^2$ 胡, Yao$^2$ 姚.

## 492. Ting$^1$ 丁

Ting 丁 is a popular Chinese surname and it came from at least five different sources. 1. <u>Hsing shih k'ao lüeh</u> 姓氏考略 traces the genealogy of the surname as follows: The surname Ting first came into existence from the Duke of Ting (Ting hou 丁侯) during the reign of Chou Wu-wang 周武王. However, there is no mention of the ancestor of the Duke in any historical documents. 2. <u>Wan hsing t'ung p'u</u> 萬姓統譜, <u>Yüan ho hsing tsuan</u> 元何姓纂 and <u>T'ung chih Shih tsu lüeh</u> 通志氏族略 cite the genealogy of surname Ting as follows: The surname Ting branched from the surname Chiang 姜 of the ancestral line of Huang-ti 黃帝 and it was adopted posthumously during the Chou 周 dynasty by the grandsons of Ting Chi 丁伋, who was a descendant of Huang-ti. The family initially settled in Shang-tung 山東 province. 3. According to <u>Chiang piao chih</u> 江表志, the surname Ting came from the change of surname by Sun Ku'ang 孫匡 who was a grandson of Sun Ch'üan 孫權. Sun Ku'ang vandalized military weapons during the Eastern Han (Tung Han 東漢) dynasty and subsequently the family changed its surname to Ting 丁 to avoid persecution by the royal court. 4. <u>Feng ch'uang hsiao tu</u> 楓窗小牘 cites the origin of the surname Ting as follows: The surname Ting came from the change of surname by Yü Ching 于慶 in the Sung 宋 dynasty. Due to his inappropriate public behavior, he was asked by his family members to change his last name. 5. According to Yang Shih-ch'i's 楊士奇 <u>Tung li wen chi</u> 東里文集, some of the people who adopted the surname Ting originally was from the northwestern part of China known as the Western Territories (Hsi-yü 西域). After their emigration from the Western Territories, Ting was adopted as their surname as they settled in less remote parts of China.

493. T'o³ 庹

According to <u>Hsing yüan</u> 姓苑, the surname T'o 庹 derived from the following two sources: 1. It came from the ancestral line of T'o Wu-ch'ang 庹五常 in the Ming 明 dynasty. 2. The surname T'o 庹 branched from the surname Tu 度 due to a transcription error by a descendant of the T'o family.

See also Tu⁴ 度.

494. T'o⁴-pa² 拓跋

The T'o-pa 拓跋 family founded the Northern Wei (Pei Wei 北魏, 386-534 A.D.) dynasty. The surname belongs to the ancestral line of the Hsien-pei 鮮卑 Group and its origin was documented in <u>Wei shu kuan shih chih</u> 魏書官氏志 as follows: Huang-ti 黃帝 had a son named Ch'ang I 昌意 whose son was ordered to guard Northern Territories against foreign intruders. T'o-pa was later adopted as a common surname which was inspired by the Hu meaning of the words; "T'o 拓" means "territorial expansion" and "Pa 跋" means "ruler". T'o-pa was later changed to Yüan 元 by Hsiao Wen-ti 孝文帝 in the Northern Wei (Pei Wei 北魏) dynasty; thus, the name was transformed from a Hu 胡 surname into a Han 漢 surname.

See also Yüan² 元.

495. Tou³ 斗

According to <u>Hsing shih k'ao lüeh</u> 姓氏考略, the surname Tou 斗 branched from the surname Chiang 姜 and originally was a surname used by the tribal group of the I 夷 people living in eastern China. Lately, the Tou family populates Lin-hai 臨海, Che-chiang 浙江 province.

496. Tou³ 斜

According to <u>Hsing yüan</u> 姓苑, the surnames Tou 斜 and Tou 斗 were used interchangeably in antiquity and both came from the same blood line.

See also Tou³ 斗.

497. Tou⁴ 竇

<u>Ming hsien shih tsu yen hsing lei kao</u> 名賢氏族言行類稿 states the origin of the surname Tou 竇 as follows: The surname tou 竇 was traced to the ancestral line of Chuan Hsü 顓頊. In the Hsia 夏 dynasty, the Prince Shao-k'ang 少康 was born in a hollow (tou 竇) due to the disturbances of the country by rivals. In order to hide the identity of the Prince, he was reared as a commoner. After Shao-k'ang grew up, he defeated enemies, strengthened the political status of the Hsia dynasty, and eventually re-united his country. In memory of his deed to the Hsia dynasty, his son adopted Tou as his common surname and the family settled in Chi-ning 濟寧, Shan-tung 山東 province.

## 498. Tou⁴ 豆

The surname Tou 豆 derived from the following
two sources: 1. <u>Lu shih</u> 路史 traces the
ancestral line of the surname to the State of
Ch'u (Ch'u kuo 楚國) in the Spring and Autumn
(Ch'un ch'iu 春秋) Period. A representative of
the family was To Ju-i 豆如意 from the Western
Han (Hsi Han 西漢) dynasty. 2. The surname To
豆 branched from the surname To-lu 豆盧.
According to <u>Wei shu kuan shih chih</u> 魏書官氏志,
To-lu derived from the tribal group of Hsien-pei
鮮卑, Mu-jung shih 慕容氏. When the Chieftain
Mu-jung Ch'ang 慕容萇 was sbudued by Hsiao Wen-
ti 孝文帝 of the Northern Wei (Pei Wei 北魏)
dynasty, he was given the family name To-lu 豆盧
by the emperor. Subsequently, the tribe
immigrated in Han 漢 territories and adopted the
single character To 豆 as their common surname.

See also Mu⁴-jung² 慕容, Tou⁴-lu² 豆盧.

## 499. Tou⁴-lu² 豆盧

The origin of the surname To-lu 豆盧 was
described in <u>Wei shu kuan shih chih</u> 魏書官氏志.
According to the book, the surname To-lu derived
from the tribal group of Hsien-pei 鮮卑, Mu-jung
shih 慕容氏. When the Chieftain Mu-jung Ch'ang
慕容萇 was sbudued by Hsiao Wen-ti 孝文帝 of the
Northern Wei (Pei Wei 北魏) dynasty, he was
given the family name To-lu 豆盧 by the emperor.
Subsequently, the tribe immigrated in Han 漢
territories and adopted the single character To
豆 as their common surname.

See also Mu⁴-jung² 慕容, Tou⁴ 豆.

## 500. Tsai³ 宰

The surname Tsai 宰 branched from the multiple
surname Tsai-fu 宰父 and came from the following
two sources: 1. According to <u>Yüan ho hsing tsuan</u>
元何姓纂, the founder of the surname was Tsai
Kung 宰孔 who was a descendant of Chou Wen-wang
周文王. Tsai Kung was the Chief Minister (t'ai-

tsai 太宰) to a Chou king and later adopted the
title of his official post as his surname. The
family initially settled in Shan-tung 山東
province. 2. <u>Hsing chieh</u> 姓解 states the origin
of the name as follows: A Chief Minister (t'ai-
tsai 太宰) to a Chou king adopted Tsai as his
common surname and the family settled in Shan-
hsi 山西 province.

See also Tsai$^3$-fu$^4$ 宰父.

501. Ts'ai$^4$ 蔡

<u>Hsing shih k'ao lüeh</u> 姓氏考略 traces the
genealogy of the surname Ts'ai 蔡 as follows:
The surname Tsai originated from the name of a
feudal territory, the State of Ts'ai (Ts'ai kuo
蔡國), bestowed on Ts'ai Chung-hu 蔡仲胡 who
was a great grandson of Chou Wen-wang 周文王.
Ts'ai was later adopted as the common surname by
his descendants. The family initially settled
in Chi-yang hsien 濟陽縣, 河南 province and
later expanded to Feng-t'ai hsien 鳳台縣, An-hui
安徽 province.

502. Tsai$^3$-fu$^4$ 宰父

The surname Tsai-fu 宰父 derived from the name
of the official post, tsai-fu 宰夫, Assistant
Minister of State, in the Chou 周 dynasty.
Tsai-fu was a general aid, in the Ministry of
State (t'ien-kuan 天官), to the Minister (ta-
tsai 大宰, or, t'ai-tsai 太宰) and to the Vice
Ministers (hsiao-tsai 小宰) in all matters
pertaining to administrative regulations, the
conduct of officials, state ceremonies, and
fiscal affairs.

See also Tsai$^3$ 宰.

503. Tsan$^3$ 昝

According to <u>Pai chia hsing kao lüeh</u> 百家姓考略
and <u>Wei shu kuan shih chih</u> 魏書官氏志, the
surname Tsan 昝 originally came from Chiu shih
咎氏 and later changed into 昝 due to the word
meaning of Chiu 咎, meaning disaster. The name

first appeared between the Han 漢 and Chin 晉
periods. <u>Shang yu lu</u> 尚友錄 mentions that the
initial settlement of the family was T'ai-yüan
shih 太原市 in Shan-hsi 山西 province.

504. Tsang¹ 臧

The origin of the surname Tsang 臧 was cited in
<u>Yüan ho hsing tsuan</u> 元何姓纂, <u>Wan hsing t'ung</u>
<u>p'u</u> 萬姓統譜, and <u>T'ung chih Shih tsu lüeh</u>
通志氏族略. According to these sources, the
surname Tsang branched from the surname Chi 姬
and originated from the name of a vassal state,
the District of Tsang (Tsang i 臧邑), bestowed
on a son of the Duke Lu Hsiao (Lu Hsiao kung
魯孝公). It was later adopted as a common
surname by his descendants and the family
settled primarily in Ying-ch'uan 穎川, Ho-pei
河北 and T'ien-shui 天水, Shen-hsi 陝西
provinces.

505. Ts'ang¹ 蒼

<u>Ku chin hsing shih shu pien cheng</u> 古今姓氏書辨證
traces the origin of the surname Ts'ang 蒼 to a
talented man, Ts'ang Shu 蒼舒. He was one of
the eight greatest novelists during the reign of
Chuan Hsü 顓頊. The Ts'ang family initially
settled in Wu-ling 武陵, Hu-nan 湖南 province.

506. Ts'ang¹ 倉

<u>Hsing shih k'ao lüeh</u> 姓氏考略 traces the origin
of the surname Ts'ang 倉 to the title of the
official post, ts'ang-jen 倉人, Granary
Official, in the Chou 周 dynasty. According to
<u>Chou li</u> 周禮, ts'ang-jen 倉人 was a member of
the Ministry of Education (ti-uan 地官) who
oversaw granaries located throughout the royal
domain under the supervision of the Ministry's
Granary Masters. Ts'ang was later adopted as a
common surname by the descendants of the family
who held the post in the Chou period.

507. Ts'ao² 曹

According to Yüan ho hsing tsuan 元何姓纂, the origin of the surname Ts'ao 曹 was traced to the following two sources: 1. The surname Ts'ao belongs to the lineage of Chuan Hsü 顓頊 and its founder was Ts'ao Chia 曹挾, who was bestowed with a feudal territory, the State of Chu (Chu kuo 邾國) during the reign of Chou Wu-wang 周武王. After Ch'u Hsüan-wang 楚宣王 defeated the State of Ch'u, the descendants of Ts'ao Chia, some removed the radical on the right side of Chu 邾 and adopted Chu 朱 and others adopted Ts'ao 曹 as their common surname. The families settled primarily in Chou hsien 鄒縣, Shan-tung 山東 province. 2. The surname derived from the name of the feudal territory, the State of Ts'ao (Ts'ao kuo 曹國), bestowed on Chen To 振鐸 by his father Chou Wen-wang 周文王. Ts'ao was adopted as a common surname by the family and it settled in Ting-tao hsien 定陶縣, Shan-tung 山東 province.

See also Chu[1] 朱, Pien[4] 卞.

### 508. Ts'en[2] 岑

According to Lu shih ch'un ch'iu 呂氏春秋 and T'ung chih Shih tsu lüeh 通志氏族略, the surname Ts'en 岑 originated from the name of a feudal territory bestowed on Chou Ch'ü 周渠 who was a feudal prince in the Chou 周 dynasty. Ts'en was adopted as a common surname by his descendants and the family settled mainly in Han-cheng hsien 韓城縣, Shen-hsi 陝西 province.

### 509. Tseng[1] 曾

The origin of the surname Tseng 曾 was cited in Yüan ho hsing tsuan 元何姓纂, Hsing shih k'ao lüeh 姓氏考略, and Shih pen 世本. According to these sources, the surname Tseng branched from the surname Ssu 姒 of the ancestral line of the Great Yü (Ta Yü 大禹) in the Hsia 夏 dynasty. After Shao-k'ang 少康, a fifth generation descendant of the Great Yü, revived the Hsia dynasty, he bestowed his youngest son Ch'ü-lieh 曲烈 with the State of K'uai (K'uai kuo 鄶國). Subsequently, the State of K'uai was defeated by

the State of Chü (Chü kuo 莒國) and the Prince
of K'uai 鄶 fled to the State of Lu (Lu kuo
魯國) and adopted the simplified form Tseng 曾
from the State name K'uai 鄶 as his common
surname. The State of K'uai was located in the
present Yih hsien 嶧縣, Shang-tung 山東 province
where the Tseng 曾 family originally settled.
The clan gradually expanded to Chiang-shi 江西,
Fu-chien 福建 and Kuang-tung 廣東 provinces.

510. Tso³ 左

Yüan ho hsing tsuan 元何姓纂 and T'ung chih Shih
tsu lüeh 通志氏族略 cite the genealogy of the
surname Tso 左 as follows: The surname
originated from the name of the feudal Prince of
Tso (commonly called Tso kung-tze 左公子) in the
State of Ch'i (Ch'i kuo 齊國) during the Spring
and Autumn (Ch'un ch'iu 春秋) Period. The
family initially settled in Shan-tung 山東
province where the State of Ch'i was located.

511. Tso³-ch'iu¹ 左丘

According to T'ung chih Shih tsu lüeh
通志氏族略, the founder of the multiple surname
Tso-ch'iu 左丘 was Tso-ch'iu Ming 左丘明 who was
a Grand Historian (t'ai-shih 太史) in the Ming
明 dynasty.

512. Tsou¹ 鄒

The surname Tsou 鄒 generated from two sources.
1. According to Hsing shih k'ao lüeh 姓氏考略,
the surname Tsou branched from the surname Chu
朱 and originated from the name of the feudal
territory, the State of Chu (Chu kuo 邾國), in
the Spring and Autumn (Ch'un ch'iu 春秋) Period;
it was renamed the State of Chu-lou (Chu-lou kuo
邾婁國) and further changed into the State of
Tsou (Tsou kuo 鄒國) during the Warring States
(Chan kuo 戰國) Period. Tsou kuo was located
in Tsou hsien 鄒縣, Shan-tung 山東 province
where the Tsou family initially settled. 2.
Yüan ho hsing tsuan 元何姓纂 describes the
genealogy of the surname as follows: The
surname Tsou branched from the surname Sung 宋

of the State of Sung (Sung kuo 宋 國). Sung was adopted as a common surname by the descendants of the Duke of Sung in the Chou 周 dynasty. After several generations of development, the family relocated to Tsou and adopted Tsou as their common surname as well. The family initially settled in Shang-ch'iu 商丘, Ho-nan 河南 province.

See also Chu[1] 朱, Lü[2]-ch'iu[1] 閭丘, Sung[4] 宋, T'u[2] 屠.

## 513. Tsu[3] 祖

According to <u>Yüan ho hsing tsuan</u> 元何姓纂, the surname Tsu 祖 belongs to the ancestral line of Ch'eng-t'ang 成湯, the first king and founder of the Shang 商 dynasty. Tsu was adopted from the social name (tzu 字) of Shang kings including Tsu-i (祖乙, 1525-1506 B.C.), Tsu-hsin (祖辛, 1506-1490 B.C.), Tsu-ting (祖丁, 1465-1433 B.C.), Tsu-keng (祖庚, 1265-1258 B.C.), and Tsu-chia (祖甲, 1258-1225 B.C.). The Tsu family initially settled in Cho hsien 涿縣 and later expanded to Fan-yang 范陽, Ho-pei 河北 province.

## 514. Ts'ui[1] 崔

According to <u>Yüan ho hsing tsuan</u> 元何姓纂 and <u>T'ang shu tsai hsiang shih hsi piao</u> 唐書宰相世系表, the surname Ts'ui 崔 branched from the surname Chiang 姜 of the ancestral line of Chiang Tzu-ya 姜子牙 who was the Grand Duke of Ch'i (Ch'i t'ai-kung 齊太公) in the Spring and Autumn (Ch'un ch'iu 春秋) Period. Ts'ui originated from the name of the feudal territory Ts'ui 崔 bestowed on Chiang Shu-i 姜叔乙 and later adopted as a common surname by his descendants. The family initially settled in Tsui-shih cheng 崔氏城 which was located in the present Chang-ch'iu hsien 章丘縣, Shan-tung 山東 province.

## 515. Tsung[1] 宗

According to <u>Yüan ho hsing tsuan</u> 元何姓纂, the surname Tsung 宗 derived from the name of the official post, tsung-po 宗伯, the Minister of Rites, who was the senior ceremonialist of the Court of the Imperial Clan in the Chou 周 dynasty. The ancestral home of the family was the region east of the Yangtze River commonly known as He-tung 河東.

516. Ts'ung² 從

According to <u>Ming hsien shih tsu yen hsing lei kao</u> 名賢氏族言行類稿, the surname Ts'ung 從 originated from the place name of Ts'ung-yang 樅陽. Ts'ung 從, the simplified version of the word Ts'ung 樅, was later adopted as a common surname by its local residents. The family settled primarily in Tung-wan 東莞, located in Pao-an hsien 寶安縣, Kuang-tung 廣東 province.

517. Tsung¹-cheng⁴ 宗正

According to <u>T'ung chih Shih tsu lüeh</u> 通志氏族略, the surname Tsung-cheng 宗正 branched from the surname Liu 劉 and originated from the name of the official post, tsung-cheng 宗正, Chamberlain for the Imperial Clan, who was one of the Nine Chamberlains (Chiu-ch'ing 九卿) in the central government and as member of the imperial family, he maintained the genealogy of the imperial family and monitored the conduct of imperial relatives. The position was established during the reign of the Ch'in 秦 Emperor, Shih Huang-ti 始皇帝 and was initially held by a Liu 劉 family member. After Tsung-cheng was adopted as a common surname, the family remained in Chiang-su 江蘇 province where the Liu family originally settled.

See also Liu² 劉.

518. Tu¹ 都

<u>Hsing shih k'ao lüeh</u> 姓氏考略 traces the origin of the surname Tu 都 from the following two sources: 1. The surname originated from Kung-tu shih 公都氏, the feudal prince of Li-yang Commandery (Li-yang chün 黎陽郡) in the State of Ch'i (Ch'i kuo 齊國). Tu was later adopted as

the common surname by his descendants. 2. The surname originated from the social name Tzu-tu 子都 of the feudal prince Kung-sun Yen 公孫閼 from the State of Chen (Chen kuo 鄭國) during the Spring and Autumn (Ch'un ch'iu 春秋) Period. Tu was later adopted as the common surname by his descendants and the family settled in Ho-nan 河南 province.

519. Tu[1] 督

The surname Tu 督 originated from two sources. 1. According to <u>Hsing yüan</u> 姓苑 and <u>Lu shih</u> 路史, the surname Tu came from the ancestral line of the Grand Master (ta-fu 大夫) Hua Tu 華督 from the State of Sung (Sung kuo 宋國) in the Spring and Autumn (Ch'un ch'iu 春秋) Period. Some of his descendants adopted Hua 華 and others adopted Tu 督 as their common surname and the families settled primarily in Ssu-ch'uan 四川 province. 2. <u>Hsing shih k'ao lüeh</u> 姓氏考略 says: The surname Tu derived from the place name Tu-k'ang 督亢 located in Ho-pei 河北 province where the family which adopted Tu initially settled.

See also Hua[2] 華.

520. Tu[3] 堵

The origin of the surname Tu 堵 was traced in <u>Hsing shih k'ao lüeh</u> 姓氏考略 and <u>Ku chin hsing shih shu pien cheng</u> 古今姓氏書辨證. According to the sources, the surname Tu branched from the surname Chi 姬 of the ancestral line of Chou Wen-wang 周文王 and its founder was Tu shu 堵叔 who came from the State of Cheng (Cheng kuo 鄭國) in the Chou dynasty. The family initially settled in Ho-nan 河南 province where the State of Cheng was located and later pervaded Chiang-su 江蘇 and Che-chiang 浙江 provinces.

521. Tu[4] 杜

See Fan[4] 范.

522. Tu[4] 度

According to <u>Yüan ho hsing tsuan</u> 元和姓纂, the surname Tu 度 follows the ancestral line of Chuan Hsü 顓頊 and derived from the name of the official post, tu-chih 度支, Minister of Revenue, the chief of fiscal official under the Department of State Affairs (shang-shu sheng 尚書省) in the Sui 隋 dynasty. Tu was adopted as a common surname by the descendants of the family who were appointed to the post. Two outstanding representatives of the family were Tu Shang 度尚 and Tu Tsung-hsien 度宗顯 from the Yüan 元 dynasty. The surname Tu 度 was later branched to the surname T'o 庹 due to mistakes in writing.

See also T'o[3] 庹.

523. T'u[2] 涂

The T'u River (T'u he 涂河) is the name of a tributary of the Yangtze River and according to <u>Ming hsien shih tsu yen hsing lei kao</u> 名賢氏族言行類稿, the surname T'u 涂 derived from the T'u River and the family who adopted T'u originally settled in Nan-ch'ang 南昌, Chiang-hsi 江西 province.

524. T'u[2] 屠

<u>Shih i chi</u> 拾遺記 states the origin of the surname T'u 屠 as follows: Huang-ti 黃帝 defeated Ch'ih Yu 蚩尤 in Chu-lu 涿鹿 and relocated his military force to Tsou-t'u 鄒屠. Both characters Tsou 鄒 and T'u 屠 were later adopted as common surnames.

See also Tsou[1] 鄒.

525. Tuan[1] 端

See Tuan[1]-mu[4] 端木.

526. Tuan[4] 段

The surname Tuan 段 originated from three sources. 1. <u>Shih chih Wei shih chia</u> 史記魏世家

states as follows: The surname Tuan branched
from the multiple surname Tuan-kan 段干 and
originated from the name of a vassal state, the
Tuan-kan District (Tuan-kan i 段干邑), in the
State of Wei (Wei kuo 魏國) during the Warring
States (Chan kuo 戰國) Period. The founder of
the family name was Tuan-kan Mu 段干木. Both
Tuan and Tuan-kan were later adopted as common
surnames and the families settled in the area of
Shan-hsi 山西 and Ho-pei 河北 provinces where
the State of Wei 魏 was located. 2. <u>Yüan ho</u>
<u>hsing tsuan</u> 元何姓纂 traces the genealogy of
surname to Kung Shu-tuan 共叔段 who was a feudal
prince of the State of Cheng (Cheng kuo 鄭國) in
the Spring and Autumn (Ch'un ch'iu 春秋) Period.
3. The surname Tuan also originated from the
nomadic group of Hsien-pei 鮮卑 of the Hu 胡
People. They settled in Han 漢 territories
during the Later Han (Hou Han 後漢, A.D. 947-
950) period and formally adopted Tuan as a
common surname.

See also Tuan⁴-kan¹ 段干.

527. Tuan⁴-kan¹ 段干

According to <u>Shih chi</u> 史記 and <u>Wan hsing t'ung</u>
<u>p'u</u> 萬姓統譜, the surname Tuan-kan 段干 branched
from the surname Li 李 of the ancestral line of
Li Tsung 李宗 who was a descendant of Lao-tzu
老子 whose real name was Li Erh 李耳. The
surname Tuan-kan 段干 originated from the name
of a vassal state, the Tuan-kan District (Tuan-
kan i 段干邑), bestowed on Li Tsung and was
later adopted as a common surname by his
descendant named Tuan-kan Mu 段干木.

See also Li³ 李, Tuan⁴ 段.

528. Tuan¹-mu⁴ 端木

According to <u>Yüan ho hsing tsuan</u> 元何姓纂 and
<u>Hsing shih chi chiu p'ien</u> 姓氏急就篇, the
founder of the multiple surname Tuan-mu 端木 was
Tuan-mu Ssu 端木賜. He was a disciple of
Confucius from the State of Wei (Wei kuo 衛國)
in the Spring and Autumn (Ch'un ch'iu 春秋)

Period and was commonly known by his social name Tze-kung 子貢. Some of his descendants adopted Tuan-mu 端木 and others adopted the single character of Tuan 端 or Mu 木 as their common surname. The surname Tuan-mu 端木 later branched to the surname Kung 貢.

See also Tuan[1] 端, Mu[4] 木, Kung[4] 貢.

529. Tung[1] 東

According to <u>Hsing shih k'ao lüeh</u> 姓氏考略, the surname Tung 東 follows the ancestral line of T'ai Hao 太昊 (Fu-hsi shih 伏羲氏) and its founder was Tung Pu-shih 東不識, a friend of Yü Ti-shun 虞帝舜. The Tung family originally settled in P'ing-yüan 平原, Shan-tung 山東 province.

See also Lien[4] 練.

530. Tung[3] 董

According to <u>T'ang shu tsai hsiang shih hsi piao</u> 唐書宰相世系表 and <u>T'ung chih Shih tsu lüeh</u> 通志氏族略, the surname Tung 董 branched from the surname Chi 姬 of the ancestral line of Huang-ti 黃帝 and originated from Tung Fu 董父. He was given the honorary surname Tung by Yü Ti-shun 虞帝舜 and later his descendants adopted Tung as their common surname.

531. T'ung[2] 童

According to <u>Yüan ho hsing tsuan</u> 元何姓纂, the founder of the family name T'ung 童 was Lao T'ung 老童 who was a son of Chuan Hsü 顓頊. Tung was adopted as a common surname by the descendants of Lao tung and they settled initially in northern Shan-tung 山東 near Po-hai 渤海 and later moved to southern Shan-tung province. It became a popular surname in southern China during the Sung 宋 and Ming 明 dynasties.

532. T'ung[2] 佟

According to <u>Lu shih</u> 路史, the founder of the
surname T'ung 佟 was the Grand Astrologer (t'ai-
shih 太史) Chung-ku 終古 to the Shang 商 king.
During the Ming 明 period, T'ung families
settled in Liao-ning 遼寧 province near a
tributary of the Ya-lü River (Ya-lü chiang
鴨綠江) and the tribuatry was later renamed
T'ung-chia River (T'ung-chia chiang 佟家 江,
meaning the T'ung family's river). After the
Ming dynasty, Manchus gradually moved from north
to south and settled alongside the T'ung-chia
River. Following the re-settlement, they
adopted the surname T'ung as their common
surname as well. Today, the T'ung family is
primarily comprised of the above two branches,
the native Han 漢 people and the Manchus.

533. Tung¹-fang¹ 東方

According to <u>Shang yu lu</u> 尙友錄, the multiple
surname Tung-fang 東方 follows the ancestral
line of T'ai Hao 太昊 (Fu-hsi shih 伏羲氏) and
the founder of the surname was Tung-fang Shuo
東方朔. He was abandoned by his parents when he
was only three days old and was discovered at
the moment when the sun was rising from the east
(tung-fang 東方); his adoptive parent named him
Tung-fang Shuo and Tung-fang was adopted as a
common surname by his descendants.

534. Tung¹-kung¹ 東宮

According to <u>Yüan ho hsing tsuan</u> 元和姓纂 and
<u>Hsing shih chi chiu p'ien</u> 姓氏急就篇, Duke Ch'i
Chuang (Ch'i Chuang kung 齊莊公)'s son Te-ch'en
得臣 was elected as the successor of the throne
and resided at eastern ("tung 東") region of the
Chou 周 Palace ("kung 宮"), commonly known as
tung-kung 東宮. Unfortunately, Te-ch'en died
when he was young and people adopted the name of
his residence, Tung-kung 東宮, as their common
surname in memory of him.

535. Tung¹-kuo¹ 東郭

The multiple surname Tung-kuo 東郭 branched from

the surname Chiang 姜. <u>Shang yu lu</u> 尚友錄 traces its ancestral line to the Duke Ch'i Huan (Ch'i Huan kung 齊桓公) during the Spring and Autumn (Ch'un ch'iu 春秋) Period. The surname Tung-kuo was adopted by his descendants whose residence was located in eastern region ("tung 東") of the walled compound ("kuo 郭") of the Chou 周 Palace which generally called Tung-kuo 東郭. The family originally settled in Shan-tung 山東 province where the State of Ch'i 齊 was located. Other regional names such as Hsi-kuo 西郭, Nan-kuo 南郭, and Pei-kuo 北郭 also came from similar reasons.

536. Tung$^1$-men$^2$ 東門

    <u>Shang yu lu</u> 尚友錄 traces the origin of the surname Tung-men 東門 as follows: The surname Tung-men branched from the surname Chi 姬 of the ancestral line of Huang-ti 黃帝. It was initially adopted by a son of the Duke of Chuang (Chuang kung 莊公) from the State of Lu (Lu kuo 魯國) because his residence was located in Tung-men. The family settled primarily in Shan-tung 山東 province.

    See also Hsi$^1$-men$^2$ 西門, Nan$^2$-men$^2$ 南門, Pei$^3$-men$^2$ 北門.

537. Tzu$^1$ 支

    <u>Ming hsien shih tsu yen hsing lei kao</u> 名賢氏族言行類稿 states the origin of the surname Tzu 支 as follows: The surname Tzu derived from the alien State of Yüeh-tzu (Yüeh-tzu kuo 月支國). It was the largest state of the Western Territories (Hsi-yü 西域) encompassing the present Kan-su 甘肅 and Ching-hai 青海 provinces during the Han 漢 dynasty. After emigrating to China, they settled down and gradually expanded to other places, such as Shen-hsi 陝西 and Shan-hsi 山西 provinces. After the reunification of Chinese territory by T'ang T'ai-chung (唐太宗, A.D. 627-650), they finally settled in Lang-yeh 瑯琊, Shan-tung 山東 province and adopted Tzu as their common surname in memory of their country

of origin.

538. Tzu³ 訾

According to <u>Hsing yüan</u> 姓苑, the surname Tzu 訾 branched from the surname Chi 祭 which was regarded as an ominous surname in antiquity and due to this fact, the surname was changed to Tzu 訾.

See also Chi⁴ 祭.

539. Tzu³ 紫

According to <u>Hsing shih k'ao lüeh</u> 姓氏考略, the surname Tzu 紫 derived from the following two sources: 1. Tzu 紫 originally was a surname from the tribal group of Hsi-chiang 西姜. It was later adopted as a common surname after the Hsi-chiangs emigrated and settled in Han 漢 territories. 2. The surname Tzu 紫 derived from a change of surname from the surname Tzu 姐.

See also Tzu³ 姐.

540. Tzu³ 姐

The surname Tzu 姐 was scantily mentioned in <u>Hsing shih k'ao lüeh</u> 姓氏考略 as follows: Tzu 姐 was a rare surname and it was later changed into the surname Tzu 紫 which was adopted more widely than the surname Tzu 姐.

See also Tzu³ 紫.

541. Wan⁴ 萬

In <u>Wan hsing t'ung p'u</u> 萬姓統譜, the origin the surname Wan 萬 was stated as follows: The surname Wan originated from Jei Po-wan 芮伯萬 who was a Marquise of Chou 周 and was enfeoffed at the vassal state Jei ch'eng 芮城, located in the present Ch'ao-i hsien 朝邑縣, Shen-hsi 陝西 province. His descendants adopted his social name Wan as their common surname and settled in Fu-fung 扶風, Ho-nan 河南 province.

542.  Wang[1] 汪

According to <u>Yüan ho hsing tsuan</u> 元何姓纂, <u>Wan hsing t'ung p'u</u> 萬姓統譜, and <u>Ku chin hsing shih shu pien cheng</u> 古今姓氏書辨證, the surname Wang 汪 derived from the ancestral line of Wang-mang shih 汪芒氏 from the State of Lu (Lu kuo 魯國) and the original settlement of the family was Hsin-an 新安, Shen-hsi 陝西 province.

543.  Wang[2] 王

The surname Wang (king 王) came from a prestigious background and branched from several surnames that were adopted by the descendants of royal families or kings. According to <u>T'ung chih Shih tsu lüeh</u> 通志氏族略, the surname branched mainly from the ancestral line of Chou Wen-wang 周文王 and Wang Tao 王導, who was the consort to Chin Yüan-ti (晉元帝, A.D. 317-323), was the most famous descendant of the family. This branch of the family settled primarily in Shan-tung 山東 province. Except from Chou Wen-wang 周文王, the surname also came from the lineage of Yü Ti-shun 虞帝舜 or Pi-kan 比干 in the Shang 商 dynasty. The descendants of the Wang family spread all over the country and the largest settlements are in the following places (in descending order): Lang-yeh 瑯琊 (Shan-tung 山東), T'ai-yüan 太原 (Shan-hsi 山西), Ch'en-liu 陳留 (Ho-nan 河南), Kao-p'ing 高平, Ching-chao 京兆, T'ien-shui 天水 (Kan-su 甘肅), Chung-shan 中山, Chang-wu 章武 (Ho-pei 河北), Chin-ch'eng 金城 (Chiang-su 江蘇), and Ch'ang-sha 長沙 (Hu-nan 湖南) provinces.

544.  Wang[2]-Sun[1] 王孫

According to <u>T'ung chih Shih tsu lüeh</u> 通志氏族略, the surname Wang-sun 王孫 can be traced to the following two sources: 1. "Wang-sun 王孫", meaning "the king's grandson", was adopted as a common surname by the grandsons of a Chou 周 king. 2. The founder of the surname was Wang-sun Man 王孫滿 who was a grand master (ta-fu 大夫) of the Chou dynasty.

545. Wei² 韋

The surnames Wei 韋 and Peng 彭 both came from the lineage of Peng Tsu 彭祖. According to <u>Yüan ho hsing tsuan</u> 元何姓纂, Yüan-che 元哲, the grandson of Peng Tsu, was the founder of the Wei family name. The surname Wei originated from the name of the feudal territory, Shih-wei 豕韋, bestowed on Yüan-che, and adopted as a common surname by his descendants. The family initially settled in T'ung-shan hsien 銅山縣, Chiang-su 江蘇 province where the feudal territory was located.

See also Peng² 彭.

546. Wei² 微

According to <u>Ch'ien fu lun</u> 潛夫論, the surname Wei 微 derived from the ancestral line of the Shang 商 king Ch'eng-t'ang 成湯 and its founder was Wei Tzu 微子 in the Chou 周 dynasty.

547. Wei² 危

According to <u>Ch'ien fu lun</u> 潛夫論, the surname Wei 危 is an aboriginal surname which derived from the Tribe of Miao 苗, one of the ethnic minorities living in China since the Han 漢 and T'ang 唐 dynasties. They initially settled in Chiang-hsi 江西 and later pervaded Ssu-ch'uan 四川, Yün-nan 雲南, Kuei-chou 貴州, and Kuang-hsi 廣西 provinces.

548. Wei³ 隗

The surname Wei 隗 derived from two sources. 1. According to <u>Hsing shih k'ao lüeh</u> 姓氏考略, the surname Wei originated from Ta Wei shih 大隗氏 during the Legendary Period. 2. <u>Ming hsien shih tsu yen hsing lei kao</u> 名賢氏族言行類稿 says that the surname was initially adopted by the descendants from the State of Chai (Chai kuo 翟國) in the Spring and Autumn (Ch'un ch'iu 春秋) Period.

549. Wei⁴ 衛

According to <u>Yüan ho hsing tsuan</u> 元何姓纂, the founder of the surname Wei 衛 was K'ang Shu 康叔, who was a son of Chou Wen-wang 周文王. He was commonly known as Wei K'ang-shu 衛康叔 because he was initially enfeoffed at the feudal territory of K'ang 康 and later re-enfeoffed at the State of Wei (Wei kuo 衛國). His descendants adopted Wei as the common surname and settled in Ho-nan 河南 province.

See also K'ou⁴ 寇.

550. Wei⁴ 蔚

According to <u>Hsing shih k'ao lüeh</u> 姓氏考略, the surname Wei 蔚 originated from the place name, Wei hsien 蔚縣, in Ho-pei 河北 province. It was adopted as the common surname by the residents of Wei hsien in the Chou 周 dynasty. The simplified character of the name, Wei 尉, was subsequently adopted by the descendants of the Wei 蔚 family. Both Wei families settled primarily in Lang-yeh 瑯琊, Shan-tung 山東 province. Wei 蔚 and Yü 鬱 were homonyms in ancient usage. Some of the descendants of the Wei 蔚 family adopted Yü 鬱 as a common surname during the Warring States (Chan kuo 戰國) Period.

See also Yü⁴ 鬱, Wei⁴ 尉.

551. Wei⁴ 尉

According to <u>Hsing shih k'ao lüeh</u> 姓氏考略, the surname Wei 尉 branched from the surname Wei 蔚 of Wei hsien 蔚縣, Ho-pei 河北 province.

See also Wei⁴ 蔚, Yü⁴ 鬱.

552. Wei⁴ 魏

<u>Yüan ho hsing tsuan</u> 元何姓纂 describes the origin of the surname Wei 魏 as follows: The surname Wei belongs to the lineage of Chou Wen-

wang 周文王 and originated from the name of a feudal territory, the State of Wei (Wei kuo 魏國), bestowed on a descendant of his fifteenth son, Pi Kung-kao 畢公高 during the Warring States (Ch'an kuo 戰國) Period. Wei was adopted as a common surname by the descendants of Pi Kung-kao and they initially settled in Ho-pei 河北 and Shan-hsi 山西 provinces where the State of Wei was located.

553. Wei$^2$-sheng$^1$ 微生

According to Lu shih 路史, the surname Wei-sheng 微生 branched from the surname Chi 姬 of the lineage of Chou Wen-wang 周文王 and derived from Wei-sheng shih 微生氏 who was a high-ranking officer in the State of Ch'i (Ch'i kuo 齊國). Settled originally in Shan-tung 山東 province at the location of the State of Ch'i, the Wei-sheng family later expanded to Shan-hsi 山西 and adopted the ancestral hall name (t'ang ming 堂名) of Chin Commandery (Chin chün 晉郡) in memory of their ancestors.

554. Wen$^1$ 溫

The surname Wen 溫 derived from two sources. 1. According to Kuang yün 廣韻 and Yüan ho hsing tsuan 元何姓纂, the surname originated from the name of the feudal territory Wen 溫 bestowed on a descendant of T'ang Shu-yü 唐叔虞 during the reign of Chou K'ang-wang 周康王. Wen was adopted as a common surname and the family settled in T'ai-yüan 太原, Shan-hsi 山西 province. 2. Wan hsing t'ung p'u 萬姓統譜 states that the surname originated from the name of a vassal state, the District of Wen (Wen i 溫邑), bestowed on Ch'üeh Chih 卻至 and he subsequently adopted the social name of Wen-chi 溫季. Wen was adopted as a common surname by his descendants and the family initially settled in T'ai-yüan 太原, Shan-hsi 山西 and later pervaded Ch'ing-ho 清河, Ho-pei 河北 provinces.

555. Wen$^2$ 文

According to Feng shu t'ung 風俗通, the surname

Wen 文 originally came from the ancestral line of Huang-ti 黃帝 and was adopted posthumously by the descendants of Chou Wen-wang 周文王.

556.  Wen² 聞

Feng shu t'ung 風俗通 and T'ung chih Shih tsu lüeh 通志氏族略 trace the origin of the surname Wen 聞 as follows: Wen originated from the social name (hao 號), Wen-jen 聞人, of Shao Cheng-mau 少正卯, who came from the State of Lu (Lu kuo 魯國) in the Spring and Autumn (Ch'un ch'iu 春秋) Period. Wen-jen was adopted as the common surname by his descendants. According to Ming hsien shih tsu yen hsing lei kao 名賢氏族言行類稿, the surname Wen 聞 branched from the surname Wen-jen 聞人 and was adopted in the Sung 宋 period. The family settled primarily in Che-chiang 浙江 province.

See also Wen²-jen² 聞人.

557.  Wen²-jen² 聞人

The multiple surname Wen-jen 聞人 follows the ancestral line of Duke Ch'i Huan (Ch'i Huan kung 齊桓公) from the State of Lu (Lu kuo 魯國) and the founder of the surname was Shao Cheng-mau 少正卯. He was a celebrity (wen-jen 聞人) in the State of Lu and was commonly known by his social name Wen-jen 聞人; his descendants later adopted Wen-jen as their common surname.

See also Wen² 聞.

558.  Weng¹ 翁

Yüan ho hsing tsuan 元何姓纂 and Hsing shih k'ao lüeh 姓氏考略 cite the origin of the surname Weng 翁 as follows: The surname Weng belongs to the lineage of Chou Wen-wang 周文王 and originated from the name of a vassal state, the District of Weng (Weng i 翁邑), bestowed on a son of Chou Chao-wang (周昭王, 1052-1001 B.C.). A mountain in that area was also named after the surname Weng as the Mountain of Weng (Weng shan 翁山). The native place of the family was located in Chien-t'ang 錢塘, Che-chiang 浙江 province.

**559. Wo⁴ 沃**

The surname Wo 沃 derived from two sources. 1. <u>Feng shu t'ung</u> 風俗通 and <u>Ming hsien shih tsu yen hsing lei kao</u> 名賢氏族言行類稿 trace the origin of the surname as follows: The surname Wo was adopted posthumously from the Shang 商 king Wo-ting (沃丁, 1720-1691 B.C.). 2. According to <u>Hsing shih k'ao lüeh</u> 姓氏考略, Wo also derived from the name of a mountain, the Mountain of Wo-chou (Wo-chou shan 沃州山), located in Hsin-ch'ang hsien 新昌縣, Che-chiang 浙江 province. The Wo family initially settled in Che-chiang 浙江 and later prospered in Wu-hsing 吳興, Che-chiang 浙江 province.

**560. Wu¹ 鄔**

The surname Wu 鄔 originated from two different sources. 1. According to <u>Ming hsien shih tsu yen hsing lei kao</u> 名賢氏族言行類稿, the surname Wu follows the ancestral line of Ssu-ma Mi-mou 司馬彌牟 who was the Grand Master (ta-fu 大夫) of the Wu Commandery (Wu chün 鄔郡) during the Spring and Autumn (Ch'un ch'iu 春秋) Period. 2. <u>T'ung chih Shih tsu lüeh</u> 通志氏族略 says: Wu derived from the name of a vassal state, the District of Wu (Wu i 鄔邑), bestowed on the Grand Master (ta-fu 大夫) Wu Tsang 鄔臧 of the State of Chin (Chin kuo 晉國) in the Spring and Autumn (Ch'un ch'iu 春秋) Period. <u>Hsing shih k'ao lüeh</u> 姓氏考略 traces the initial settlement of the family to several places in Chiang-hsi 江西 province: Nan-ch'ang 南昌, Fu-chou 撫州, and Ch'ung-jen 崇仁.

**561. Wu¹ 巫**

<u>Hsing shih k'ao lüeh</u> 姓氏考略 describes the origin the surname Wu 巫 as follows: The surname Wu follows the ancestral line of Wu P'eng 巫彭 who was the Imperial Doctor of Huang-ti 黃帝. Wu was adopted as the common surname by Wu P'eng's descendants and the family settled in Chou hsien

鄒縣, Shan-tung 山東 province.

**562. Wu¹ 烏**

Hsing shih k'ao lüeh 姓氏考略 describes the origin the surname Wu 烏 as follows: The surname Wu follows the ancestral line of Shao Hao 少昊 and originated from the name of the official title, wu-t'ai 烏臺, blackbird pavilion. From Han 漢 on, Wu-t'ai was an unofficial reference to the Censor-in-Chief (yü-shih ta-fu 御史大夫), because in Han times the Censorate's (Yü-shih t'ai 御史臺) quarters were distinguished by a large cedar tree frequented by large numbers of birds. The founder of the family name was Wu-niao shih 烏鳥氏 and the family initially settled in Ying-ch'uan 潁川, Ho-nan 河南 province.

**563. Wu² 毌**

Hsing shih k'ao lüeh 姓氏考略 traces the origin of the surname Wu 毌 as follows: Wu Kou 毌句, the maker of musical stones (ch'ing 磬) to T'ang Ti-yao 唐帝堯, was the founder of the surname Wu. The Wu family settled primarily in P'eng-chou 蓬州, Ssu-ch'uan 四川 province.

**564. Wu² 吳**

In the Spring and Autumn (Ch'un ch'iu 春秋) Period, Chiang-nan 江南, south of the Yangtze River, belongs to the territory of the State of Wu (Wu kuo 吳國). According to T'ung chih Shih tsu lüeh 通志氏族略, the surname Wu 吳 was adopted by the descendants from the State of Wu and the family initially settled in Wu-hsi 無錫, Chiang-su 江蘇 province where the State of Wu was located and later expanded to Che-chiang 浙江 and Shan-tung 山東 provinces.

**565. Wu³ 伍**

Hsing shih k'ao lüeh 姓氏考略 traces the origin of the surname Wu 伍 as follows: The surname Wu follows the ancestral line of Wu Hsü 伍胥 who was the Grand Minister (ta-ch'en 大臣) to Huang-ti 黃帝. The family initially settled in An-ting 安定 and Wu-ling 武陵 of Ho-pei 河北 province.

566. Wu³ 武

The surname Wu 武 derives from two sources. 1. According to Yüan ho hsing tsuan 元何姓纂, the surname Wu branched from the surname Chi 姬 and the founder of the family name was Chi Wu 姬武 who was a son of Chou P'ing-wang (周平王, 770-719 B.C.). 2. Feng shu t'ung 風俗通 describes the origin of the surname as follows: The surname Wu follows the ancestral line of the Duke Sung Wu (Sung Wu kung 宋武公) in the Spring and Autumn (Ch'un ch'iu 春秋) Period and it was adopted posthumously by his descendants. Hsing shih k'ao lüeh 姓氏考略 further indicates that the Wu family settled primarily in T'ai-yüan 太原, Shan-hsi 山西 and Hsiao hsien 蕭縣, Chiang-su 江蘇 provinces.

567. Wu¹-ma² 巫馬

This surname Wu-ma 巫馬 derived from the title of the official post, wu-ma 巫馬, the Sorcerer for Horses, in the Chou 周 dynasty. Wu-ma was a member of the Ministry of War (hsia-kuan 夏官) who can diagnose and cure sick horses that belong to the Chou's imperial court. According to T'ung chih Shih tsu lüeh 通志氏族略, the surname initially appeared in the State of Lu (Lu kuo 魯國). A member of the family was Wu-ma Shih 巫馬施 who was a disciple of Confucius in the State of Lu.

568. Wu¹-shih²-lan² 烏石蘭

See Shih² 石.

569. Yang² 楊

Yüan ho hsing tsuan 元何姓纂 describes the origin of the surname Yang 楊 as follows: The surname Yang branched from the surname Chi 姬 of the ancestral line of Chou Wu-wang 周武王 and its founder was Wu-wang's grandson Po Ch'iao 伯僑 from the State of Chin (Chin kuo 晉國). Po Ch'iao was bestowed as the Marquise of Yang (Yang hou 楊侯) and Yang was subsequently adopted as the common surname by his descendants. The family initially settled in Shan-hsi 山西 where the State of Chin was located.

See also Yün⁴ 惲.

570. Yang² 羊

According to <u>Ming hsien shih tsu yen hsing lei kao</u> 名賢氏族言行類稿 and <u>Yüan ho hsing tsuan</u> 元何姓纂, the surname Yang 羊 branched from the surname Yang-she 羊舌 and was initially adopted as a common surname during the Spring and Autumn (Ch'un ch'iu 春秋) Period. The family originally settled in Shan-hsi 山西 and later relocated to T'ai-shan 泰山, Shan-tung 山東 province during the Warring States (Ch'an kuo 戰國) Period.

See also Yang²-she² 羊舌.

571. Yang² 陽

Yang 陽 was the name of a state in the Chou 周 dynasty, located in I-shui hsien 沂水縣, Shan-tung 山東 province. According to <u>Hsing shih k'ao lüeh</u> 姓氏考略 and <u>T'ung chih Shih tsu lüeh</u> 通志氏族略, the State of Yang (Yang kuo 陽國) was taken over by its neighboring State of Ch'i 齊 during the reign of Chou Hui-wang (周惠王, 676-651 B.C.), the descendants of the State of Yang adopted Yang as their common surname and settled in Shan-tung 山東 province.

572. Yang³ 仰

<u>Hsing shih k'ao lüeh</u> 姓氏考略 describes the origin the surname Yang 仰 as follows: The founder of the surname Yang was Yang Yen 仰延 who was an imperial musician during the reign of Yü Ti-shun 虞帝舜. The family initially settled in Ch'ien-t'ang 錢塘, Che-chiang 浙江 province.

573. Yang³ 養

According to <u>Hsing shih k'ao lüeh</u> 姓氏考略, the surname Yang 養 originated from the name of a vassal state, the District of Yang (Yang i 養邑), in the State of Ch'u (Ch'u kuo 楚國) during the Spring and Authum (Ch'un ch'iu 春秋) Period. The family initially settled in Shen-ch'iu hsien 沈丘縣, Ho-nan 河南 province.

574. Yang²-chiao³ 羊角

According to <u>Hsü T'ung chih Shih tsu lüeh</u> 續通志氏族略, the surname Yang-chiao 羊角 derived from the name of a vassal state, the Yang-chiao District (Yang-chiao i 羊角邑), bestowed on a grand master (ta-fu 大夫) of the State of Wei (Wei kuo 衛國) during the Spring and Autumn (Ch'un ch'iu 春秋) Period and it was later adopted as the common surname by his descendants.

575. Yang²-she² 羊舌

<u>T'ung chih Shih tsu lüeh</u> 通志氏族略 describes the origin of the surname Yang-she 羊舌 as follows: The surname Yang-she branched from the surname Ch'i 祈 and its founder was Ch'in Ch'i-ying 秦祈盈 who was the Grand Master (ta-fu 大夫) of the State of Chin (Chin kuo 晉國) during the Spring and Autumn (Ch'un ch'iu 春秋) Period. Yang-she was adopted as a common surname from the name of a vassal state, the Yang-she District (Yang-she i 羊舌邑), bestowed on Ch'in ch'i-ying.

See also Ch'i² 祈, Yang² 羊.

576. Yao² 姚

According to <u>T'ung chih Shih tsu lüeh</u> 通志氏族略, Yü Ti-shun 虞帝舜 was born in Yao-hsü 姚墟, so he adopted Yao 姚 as his surname. The Yao family settled primarily in Wu-hsieng 吳興, Chiang-su 江蘇 province.

See also Ch'en² 陳, Hu² 胡, Man³ 滿, T'ien² 田.

577. Yeh⁴ 葉

According to <u>Tso chuan</u> 左傳, the surname Yeh 葉 originated from the name of the vassale state in She hsien 葉縣, bestowed on the Grand Master (ta-fu 大夫) Shen I-wu 沈伊戌 of the State of Ch'u 楚 (Ch'u kuo 楚國) in the Spring and Authum (Ch'un ch'iu 春秋) Period. Yeh was later adopted as a common surname by his descendants and the family initially settled in Nan-yang hsien 南陽縣, Ho-nan 河南 province where She hsien 葉縣 was located.

See also Shen³ 沈.

578. Yen¹ 鄢

The surname Yen 鄢 derived from the name of the feudal territary, the State of Yen (Yen kuo 鄢國), in the Chou 周 dynasty. The family initially settled in Yen-ling hsien 鄢陵縣, Ho-nan 河南 province where the State of Yen was located.

579. Yen¹ 燕

Yen 燕 symbolizes the Ho-pei 河北 province. It is called by this name because of the majestic ranges of the Yen Mountain (Yen shan 燕山) which is the symbol of Ho-pei 河北 province. The State of Yen (Yen kuo 燕國) was made up of two separate regions during the Warring States (Ch'an kuo 戰國) Period. The surname was traced to the following sources: 1. <u>Ming hsien shih tsu yen hsing lei kao</u> 名賢氏族言行類稿 says: Chao-kung Shih 召公奭 was bestowed with the feudal territory of the State of North Yen (Pei Yen kuo 北燕國) which was located in the present Ho-Pei 河北 province. 2. According to <u>T'ung chih Shih tsu lüeh</u> 通志氏族略, a desdendant of Huang-ti 黃帝 was bestowed with the feudal territy of the State of South Yen (Nan Yen kuo 南燕國) which was located in the present Ho-nan 河南 province. Yen was later adopted as the common surname by both branches of the Yen families. 3. The surname can also be traced to the nomadic group of the Hu 胡 people. According to Hsing shih k'ao lüeh 姓氏考略, Mu-jung shih 慕容氏 of the Group of Hsien-pei 鮮卑 had claimed frontier in Han 漢 territories, which was divided into five regional States of Yen during the Southern and Northern Dynasties (Nan-pei ch'ao 南北朝). They were the Front Yen (Chien Yen 前燕), Back Yen (Hou Yen 後燕), Hsi Yen (Western Yen 西燕), Nan Yen (Southern Yen 南燕), and Pei Yen (Northern Yen 北燕). The States residents later adopted Yen as their common surname and settled in northern China.

580. Yen² 言

The surname Yen 言 derived from the surname Chi 姬 of the ancestral line of Chou Wen-wang 周文王. According to Yüan ho hsing tsuan 元何姓纂, the founder of the surname was Yen Yen 言偃 who was commonly known by his social name Tzu-yu 子游. He was a prominent disciple of Confucius in the Spring and Autumn (Ch'un ch'iu 春秋) Period. Ch'ien fu lun 潛夫論 points out another source of the name's origin as follows: During the Warring States (Chan kuo 戰國) Period, some members of the Han 韓 family, originally from the State of Han (Han kuo 韓國) adopted Yen 言 as their common surname. The Yen family settled primarily in Chiang-nan 江南 including Chiang-su 江蘇 and Che-chiang 浙江 provinces.

See also Han² 韓.

581. Yen² 顏

The surname Yen 顏 derived from the following two sources: 1. According to Yüan ho hsing tsuan 元何姓纂, the surname originated from I-fu 夷父 who was a great grandson of Lu-chung 陸終 from the ancestral line of Huang-ti 黃帝. 2. T'ung chih Shih tsu lüeh 通志氏族略 says: The founder of the surname was Po-ch'in 伯禽 who was a son of the Duke of Chou (Chou kung 周公) from the State of Lu (Lu kuo 魯國). Yen originated from the name of a vassal state, the District of

Yen (Yen i 顏邑), bestowed on Po-ch'in and was later adopted as the common surname by his descendants. The Yen families initially settled in Shan-tung 山東 province.

See also Liao[4] 廖.

582. Yen[2] 閻

The surname Yen 閻 generated from two different sources. 1. According to <u>T'ang shu tsai hsiang shih hsi piao</u> 唐書宰相世系表, Chou Wu-wang 周武王 bestowed the Village of Yen (Yen hsiang 閻鄉) on his descendant Chung-i 仲奕 and Yen was subsequently adopted as the common surname by the family. 2. <u>Ming hsien shih tsu yen hsing lei kao</u> 名賢氏族言行類稿 describes the origin of the surname Yen as follows: The surname Yen follows the ancestral line of T'ang Shu-yü 唐叔虞 who was bestowed with the feudal territory of the State of Chin (Chin kuo 晉國) by his brother Chou Ch'eng-wang 周成王. Yen originated from the name of a vassal state, the District of Yen (Yen i 閻邑), bestowed on a descendant of T'ang Shu-yü and was later adopted as a common surname. The family initially settled in T'ien-shui 天水, Ho-nan 河南 and later pervaded Shan-hsi 山西, Hu-pei 湖北, and Ho-nan 河南 provinces.

583. Yen[2] 嚴

The surname Yen 嚴 branched from the surname Chuang 莊 of the ancestral line of Chuang-wang (莊王, 696-681 B.C.) in the State of Ch'u (Ch'u kuo 楚國) of the Spring and Autumn (Ch'un ch'iu 春秋) Period. According to <u>Yüan ho hsing tsuan</u> 元何姓纂, Chuang was adopted posthumously by the descendants of Chuang-wang. <u>Hsing shih k'ao lüeh</u> 姓氏考略 cites that Chuang Kuang 莊光 changed his name to Yen Kuang 嚴光 during the regin of Han Ming-ti (漢明帝, A.D. 58-76) to aviod using the same as that of the king. The Yen family initially settled in Che-chiang 浙江 province.

See also Chuang[1] 莊, Nein[2] 年.

584. Yen³ 偃

T'ung chih Shih tsu lüeh 通志氏族略 traces the origin of the surname Yen 偃 as follows: The surname Yen 偃 derived from the lineage of Kao T'ao 皋陶 who was the chieftain of the tribal group of Tung-i 東夷 and was born in Ch'ü-fu 曲阜, Shan-tung 山東 where he was given the honorary surname Yen 偃 by a Chou 周 king. Yen was later adopted as a common ssurname by his descendants and the family initialy settled in Shan-tung 山東 province.

See also Ying¹ 英.

585. Yen⁴ 晏

Hsing shih k'ao lüeh 姓氏考略 describes the origin of the surname Yen 晏 as follows: The surname Yen belongs to the lineage of Chuan Hsü 顓頊 and its founder was Yen An 晏安 from the State of Ch'i (Ch'i kuo 齊國) during the Spring and Authum (Ch'un ch'iu 春秋) Period. The Yen family prospered in Shan-tung 山東 province where the State of Ch'i was located.

586. Yin¹ 陰

According to Yüan ho hsing tsuan 元何姓纂, the founder of the surname Yin 陰 was Kuan Hsiu 管修, he was the Grand master (ta-fu 大夫) of the State of Ch'u (Ch'u kuo 楚國) during the Spring and Authum (Ch'un ch'iu 春秋) Period. The surname Yin came from his social name Yin ta-fu 陰大夫 and was adopted as the common surname by his descendants. The family settled primarily in Nan-yang 南陽, Ho-nan 河南 province which became the center of prosperity for the Yin families.

587. Yin³ 尹

Wan hsing t'ung p'u 萬姓統譜 and T'ung chih Shih tsu lüeh 通志氏族略 trace the origin of the surname Yin 尹 to the place name called Yin ch'eng 尹城. It was bestowed on a son of Shao

Hao 少昊 in the Legendary Period and was later adopted as a common surname by his descendants. The family settled primarily in Ho-chien 河間, Ho-pei 河北 province.

588. Yin⁴ 印

According to both <u>Kuang yün</u> 廣韻 and <u>Yüan ho hsing tsuan</u> 元何姓纂, the surname Yin 印 belongs to the lineage of Chou Wen-wang 周文王 and its founder was Yin Tuan 印段 who was the Grand Master (ta-fu 大夫) of the State of Cheng (Cheng kuo 鄭國) in the Spring and Autumn (Ch'un ch'iu 春秋) Period. Yin was adopted as a common surname by his descendants and the family originally settled in Ho-nan 河南 province where the State of Cheng was located and later prospered in Feng-i 馮翊, Shen-hsi 陝西 province.

589. Ying¹ 英

The surname Ying 英 derived from two sources. 1. According to <u>Hsisng p'u</u> 姓譜, the surname Ying branched from the surname Yen 偃 of the lineage of Kao T'ao 皋陶 who was the chieftain of the tribal group of Tung-i 東夷 and was enfeoffed at Ying 英. After the feudal territory Ying was defeated by Ch'eng-wang 成王 of the State of Ch'u (Ch'u kuo 楚國), his descendants adopted Ying as their common surname and settled in Shan-tung 山東 province. 2. <u>Chung-kuo hsing shih chi</u> 中國姓氏集 traces the origin of the surname Ying to Ying Pu 英布 in the Han 漢 dynasty. He was demoted by the Han 漢 Emperor Kao-tsu 高祖 (Liu Pang 劉邦), his face was tattooed (ch'ing mien 黥面) and name was changed into Ch'ing Pu 黥布.

See also Yen³ 偃, Ch'ing² 黥.

590. Ying¹ 殷

<u>Yüan ho hsing tsuan</u> 元何姓纂 traces the origin the surname Yin 殷 as follows: The surname Ying originated from the name of a dynastic title adopted by the Shang 商 King Ch'eng-t'ang (成湯,

1766-1753 B.C.). After Chou 周 conquered the Shang 商 territory, the descendants of Ch'eng-t'ang adopted his title as a common surname in his memory. The original settlement of the family located in the present Ho-pei 河北 and Ho-nan 河南 provinces.

591. Ying[2] 嬴

Two versions of the Ying 嬴 surname's origin are listed as follows: 1. According to Hsing shih k'ao lüeh 姓氏考略, the founder of the surname Ying 嬴 was Po I 伯益. He was a descendant of Chuan Hsü 顓頊 and was graciously given the surname Ying 嬴 by Yü Ti-shun 虞帝舜 because of his contribution in training birds and taming animals for the Hsia 夏 Emperor, the Great Yü (Ta Yü 大禹). Ying was later adopted as a common surname by the descendants of Po I. 2. Shuo wen chieh tzu 說文解字 traces the name's origin as follows: Po I 伯益 was a wise and virtuous man during the reign of Yü Ti-shun 虞帝舜. He assisted the Great Yü 大禹 in preventing and managing floods and was graciously given the surname Ying 嬴 and later appointed to the administrative post of Yü-kuan 虞官, Supervisor of Forestry and Hunting, by Yü Ti-shun 虞帝舜. Some of his descendants adopted Ying 嬴 and others adopted I 益 as the common surname.

See also Ku[3] 谷, I[4] 益.

592. Ying[4] 應

Both Kuang yün 廣韻 and Hsing shih k'ao lüeh 姓氏考略 trace the origin of the surname Ying 應 as follows: The surname Ying originated from the name of a feudal territory bestowed on the Duke of Ying (Ying hou 應侯) who was the fourth son of Chou Wu-wang 周武王. Ying was later adopted as a common surname by the descendants of the Duke of Ying and the family settled initially in Ho-nan 河南 province and later concentrated primarily in Ju-nan 汝南 and Ying-ch'uan 穎川 during the Han 漢 period.

593.  Yu² 尤

Yüan ho hsing tsuan 元何姓纂 traces the genealogy of the surname Yu 尤 as follows: The surname Yu 尤 branched from the surname Shen 沈 and derived from the name of a feudal territory bestowed on Pu Chi 哺季 who was the tenth son of Chou Wen-wang 周文王. The surname Shen 沈 was simplified and changed into Yu 尤 to avoid its phonetic conflict with Wang Shen-chih 王審知 who was the Emperor of Min 閩王 during the epoch of the Five Dynasties (Wu-tai 五代, A.D. 907-59). The Yu 尤 family initially settled in Fu-chien 福建 and later expanded to Chiang-su 江蘇 provinces. At present, these two places contain the largest concentration of the Yu families.

See also Shen³ 沈.

594.  Yu² 游

According to Yüan ho hsing tsuan 元何姓纂, the surname Yu 游 derived from the social name Tzu-yu 子游 of the Prince Yen 偃 who was a son of the Duke Cheng Mu (Cheng Mu kung 鄭穆公) in the Spring and Autumn (Ch'un ch'iu 春秋) Period. Yu was adopted as a common surname by the descendants of Prince Yen and the family initially settled in Ho-nan 河南 province where the State of Cheng (Cheng kuo 鄭國) was located.

595.  Yu³ 有

According to Lu shih 路史, the surname Yu 有 came from the legendary Chinese ruler, Yu-ch'ao shih 有巢氏, who taught the people to build tree houses for protection against wild beasts. Yu was a common name some two thousand years ago but has nearly disappeared in the past six hundred years due to the change of name to Yü 宥, which was recorded in Ming shih 明史.

See also Yü⁴ 宥.

596.  Yu³ 酉

The surname Yu 酉 derived from the place name Yu-yang 酉陽 in Ssu-ch'uan 四川 province where a descendant of Shao Hao 少昊 named Tseng 曾 was bestowed. Yu was later adopted as a common surname and the family settled primarily in Ssu-ch'uan 四川 province.

597. Yü² 俞

According to <u>Hsing shih k'ao lüeh</u> 姓氏考略 and <u>Shih chi</u> 史記, the founder of the family name Yü 俞 was Yü Fu 俞柎 who was an imperial doctor to Huang-ti 黃帝. Yü was adopted as a common surname by the descendants of Yü Fu and the family settled initially in Chiang-ling 江陵, Hu-pei 湖北 province.

See also Yü⁴ 喻.

598. Yü² 于

<u>Yüan ho hsing tsuan</u> 元何姓纂 and <u>T'ung chih Shih tsu lüeh</u> 通志氏族略 trace the genealogy of the surname Yü 于 as follows: The surname Yü originated from the name of a feudal territory bestowed on Yü Shu 邘叔 who was the second son of Chou Wu-wang 周武王. Some of his desendants adopted Yü 邘 and others adopted its simplified version of Yü 于 as their common surname. The family's initial settlement was Yü-ch'ang 邘城, Ho-nan 河南 province where the feudal territory was located.

599. Yü² 虞

The surname Yü 虞 belongs to the ancestral line of Huang-ti 黃帝 and two versions of the name's origin was listed in <u>Yüan ho hsing tsuan</u> 元何姓纂 as follows: 1. The surname Yü originated from the name of the feudal territory, the State of Yü (Yü kuo 虞國), bestowed on a son of Yü Ti-shun 虞帝舜. Yü was adopted as a common surname the family and they settled in Yü-ch'eng hsien 虞城縣, Ho-nan 河南 province where the State of Yü was located. 2. The surname Yü derived from the name of the feudal territory, the State of Yü (Yü kuo 虞國), which was bestowed on Chung-yüng 仲雍 who was an uncle of Chou Wu-wang 周武王. Yü was later adopted as a common surname by his descendants and the family settled in P'ing-lu hsien 平陸縣, Shan-hsi 山西 province.

600. Yü² 於

Shih pen 世本 describes the origin of the surname Yü 於 as follows: The founder of the family name was Yü Tse 於則 who was an imperial shoemaker to Huang-ti 黃帝. The surname Yü originally derived from the place name, Yu-yü ts'un 友於村, located in Nei hsiang 內鄉, Chiang-su 江蘇 province, where Yü Tse 於則 was enfeoffed by Huang-ti. Yü was later adopted as a common surname by the descendants of Yü Tse and the family initially settled in Kuang-lin 廣陵, located in the present Chiang-tu hsien 江都縣, Chiang-su 江蘇 province.

601. Yü² 魚

The surname Yü 魚 branched from the surname Chi 姬 of the ancestral line of Huang-ti 黃帝 and later followed by the lineage of the Shang 商 king Ch'eng-t'ang 成湯. Hsing shih k'ao lüeh 姓氏考略 and T'ung chih Shih tsu lüeh 通志氏族略 trace the origin of the surname to the feudal prince of the State of Sung (Sung kuo 宋國) who was a son of the Duke Sung Huan (Sung Huan kung 宋桓公) in the Spring and Autumn (Ch'un ch'iu 春秋) Period and was commonly known by his social name Tzu-yü 子魚. Yü was adopted as a common surname by his descendants and the family initially settled in Feng-i 馮翊, Shan-hsi 山西 province.

602. Yü² 漁

Hsing shih hsün yüan 姓氏尋源 traces the origin of the surname Yü 漁 to the following two sources: 1. The surname derived from the name of a feudal territory, Yü-yang 漁陽, located in the present Mi-yün hsien 密雲縣, Peking 北京 city of

the Hu-pei 湖北 province and it was bestowed on
a grand master (ta-fu 大夫) of the State of Yen
(Yen kuo 燕國) in the Warring States (Chan kuo
戰國) Period. 2. The surname Yü also derived
from the occupational name of Yü-fu 漁夫,
fisherman, and was later adopted as a common
surname by the family whose members were
fishermen.

603. Yü² 余

Yü 余 and She 佘 are two different surnames of
the same origin. According to Yüan ho hsing
tsuan 元何姓纂, the founder of the surname Yü 余
was Yu Yü 由余 who was a minister in the Ch'in
秦 dynasty. The surname She 佘 came about
because of a writing mistake of Yü 余 which took
place in the T'ang 唐 dynasty. Both families
settled primarily in She hsien 歙縣, An-hui 安徽
province.

See also She¹ 佘.

604. Yü³ 禹

According to T'ung chih Shih tsu lüeh
通志氏族略, the surname Yü 禹 derived from two
sources. 1. The surname originated from the
name of an ancient state, the State of Yü (Yü
kuo 鄑). Its simplified form was adopted as a
common surname and the family initially settled
in Lang-yeh 琅琊, Shan-tung 山東 province. 2.
The surname derived from the ancestral line of
the Great Yü (Ta Yü 大禹) from the Hsia 夏
dynasty and was later adopted as a common
surname by his descendants.

605. Yü³ 庾

According to Shuo wen chieh tzu 說文解字, "yü
庾" means granary. Yüan ho hsing tsuan 元何姓纂
traces the surname Yü 庾 to the title of the
granary official, chang-yü ta-fu 掌庾大夫,
established during the reign of T'ang Ti-yao
唐帝堯. Yü was later adopted as a common
surname by the descendants of a granary offical

and the family originally settled in Yen-shih hsien 偃師縣 and later prospered in Yen-ling 鄢陵 and Hsin-yeh 新野 of the Ho-nan 河南 province.

606.  Yü⁴ 喻

Hsing shih k'ao lüeh 姓氏考略 describes the origin of the surname Yü 喻 as follows: The surname Yü 喻 branched from the surname Yü 俞 and its founder was Yü Fu 俞柎.  In the Sung 宋 dynasty, a Yü 俞 family member was given the honorary surname Yü 喻 by a king. The Yü 喻 family initially settled in Chien-te 建德, Che-chinag 浙江 province.

See also Yü² 俞.

607.  Yü⁴ 郁

Hsing shih k'ao lüeh 姓氏考略 describes the origin of the surname Yü 郁 as follows: The surname originated from the name of an ancient vassal state, the District of Yü (Yü i 郁邑), bestowed on a grand master (ta-fu 大夫) of the State of Wu (Wu kuo 吳國) in the Chou 周 dynasty.  Yü 郁 was later adopted as a common surname and the family settled in the area of the present Chiang-su 江蘇 and Che-chiang 浙江 provinces where the District of Yü was located.

608.  Yü⁴ 鬱

The surname Yü 鬱 brnached from the surname Wei 蔚 in the Chou 周 dynasty.  According to Hsing shih k'ao lüeh 姓氏考略, the surname Wei 蔚 originated from the place name, Wei hsien 蔚縣, located in Ho-pei 河北 province. Because Wei 蔚 and Yü 鬱 were homonyms in ancient times, Yü 鬱 was later adopted as a common surname by descendants from the Wei 蔚 family during the Warring States (Chan kuo 戰國) Period.  The Yü 鬱 family initially settled in T'ai-yüan 太原, Shan-hsi 山西 province.

See also Wei⁴ 蔚, Wei⁴ 尉.

609. Yü⁴ 宥

According to <u>Ming shih</u> 明史, the surname Yü 宥 branched from the surname Yu 有 as the result of a change of surname. The founder of the surname was Yu Jih-hsing 有日興. He changed his surname into Yü 宥 because it was an honorary name given to him by the Ming 明 Emperor T'ai-tsu 太祖 for his achievements and contributions to the Ming 明 dynasty. Yü 宥 was subsequently adopted as a common surname by his descendants.

See also Yu³ 有.

610. Yü⁴-ch'ih² 尉遲

<u>T'ung chih Shih tsu lüeh</u> 通志氏族略 traces the origin of the surname Yü-ch'ih 尉遲 as follows: During the Southern and Northern Dynasties (Nan-pei ch'ao 南北朝, A.D. 420-581), Yü-ch'ih was a tribal name of the Hsien-pei 鮮卑 Group which pervaded northern China. After successive battles which strenghtened Hsien-pei's power and status in China, the leader of the Tribe was bestowed with the status of Marquise (hou 侯) during the Northern Wei (Pei Wei 北魏) Period and subsequently Yü-ch'ih was adopted as a common surname during the reign of Hsiao Wen-ti (孝文帝, 471-500 A.D.) and members of the Tribe permanently settled in Han 漢 territories.

611. Yü³-wen² 宇文

<u>T'ung chih Shih tsu lüeh</u> 通志氏族略 details the origin of the surname Yü-wen 宇文 as follows: During the Southern and Northern Dynasties (Nan-pei ch'ao 南北朝), many nomadic groups sought aggressively for the chance to invading China. An unearthed imperial seal belonging to the Hsien-pei 鮮卑 Group was believed to contain a message from God (Yü 宇, in tribal language) to authorize its leader to be the ruler (wen 文, in tribal language) of China. Thus, the leader of the Hsien-pei 鮮卑 Group changed his title of reign to Yü-wen 宇文. Coincidentally, the Group successfully established the Northern Chou (Pei

Chou 北周, 557-581 A.D.) Dynasty and Yü-wen was subsequently adopted as a common surname. The original settlement of the Yü-wen family was located in Wu-ch'uan 武川, Sui-yüan 綏遠 province.

## 612. Yüan² 元

The surname Yüan 元 derives from three sources. 1. According to Hsing shih wu shu 姓氏五書, the founder of the family name was Yüan Hsien 元銑 who was a senior historian and minister to the Shang 商 king Ti-i (帝乙, 1191-1154 B.C.). 2. Feng shu t'ung 風俗通 describes the origin of the surname as follows: The surname Yüan belongs to the lineage of Chou Wen-wang 周文王 and its founder was Pi Wan 畢萬 who was a descendant from the fifteenth son of Chou Wen-wang. Pi Wan was bestowed in Yüan-shih hsien 元氏縣 of the State of Wei (Wei kuo 魏國) and Yüan was later adopted as a common surname by his descendants. The family originally settled in Ho-pei 河北 province where the State of Wei was located. 3. Wei shu Kao-tsu chi 魏書高祖紀 cites the orgin of the surname as follows: The surname Yüan came from a Hsien-pei 鮮卑, To-pa shih 拓跋氏 who belongs to the collective nomadic group of the Hu 胡. To-pa shih 拓跋氏 changed his surname to Yüan 元 after the family was assimilated into the Chinese culture during the reign of Hsiao-wen ti (孝文帝, A.D. 471-500) in the Northern Wei (Pei Wei 北魏) dynasty. This branch of the the Yüan family initially settled in Ho-nan 河南 province.

See also T'o⁴-pa² 拓跋.

## 613. Yüan² 袁

According to T'ang shu tsai hsiang shih hsi piao 唐書宰相世系表 and T'ung chih Shih tsu lüeh 通志氏族略, the founder of the surname Yüan 袁 was T'ao T'u 濤塗 who was a grandson of Hu Kung-man 胡公滿 and was commonly known by his social name Chuang-yüan 莊爰. Since Yüan 爰 and Yüan 袁 were homonyms, T'ao T'u's descendants adopted

Yüan 袁 as their common surname and they settled in Huai-yang hsien 淮陽縣, Ho-nan 河南 province.

### 614. Yüeh⁴ 岳

According to <u>Hsing shih k'ao lüeh</u> 姓氏考略, the surname Yüeh 岳 derived from the name of the official post, ssu-yüeh 四岳, Heads of Four Dignitaries or Mountains, established during the reign of T'ang Ti-yao 唐帝堯. Ssu-yüeh was a collective reference to the heads of units of territorial administration, streching geographically among four (ssu 四) dignitaries from province (sheng 省) level down to districts (hsien 縣). Yüeh was later adopted as a common surname and the family initially settled in Shan-yang 山陽, Shan-tung 山東 province. Shan-yang was also adopted as the ancestral hall name (t'ang ming 堂名) by the family.

### 615. Yüeh⁴ 越

<u>Hsing shih k'ao lüeh</u> 姓氏考略 traces the ancestral line of the surname Yüeh 越 to the Great Yü (Ta Yü 大禹). Shao-kang 少康, the fifth accession of the Hsia 夏 throne following the Great Yü, bestowed his son on Kuei-chi 會稽, Che-chiang 浙江 province. The young prince adopted the appelatic title of Yüeh and the State of Yüeh (Yüeh kuo 越國) was established. Yüeh was subsequently adopted as the common surname by the descendants of Shao-kang and the State of Yüeh prospered for over two thousand years until it was defeated by the State of Ch'u 楚 in the Spring and Autumn (Ch'un ch'iu 春秋) Period. The family settled primarily in Kuei-chi 會稽, Che-chiang 浙江 province.

### 616. Yüeh⁴ 樂

See Yüeh⁴-cheng⁴ 樂正.

### 617. Yüeh⁴-cheng⁴ 樂正

According to <u>Shang yu lu</u> 尙友錄 and <u>Yüan ho hsing tsuan</u> 元何姓纂, the multiple surname Yüeh-cheng 樂正 derived from the name of the official post yüeh-cheng 樂正, also called yüeh-shih 樂師, in the Chou 周 dynasty. Yüeh-chengs were the music masters and members of the Ministry of Rites (ch'un-kuan 春官) who conducted music during state rituals and instructed children of court officials in various musical instruments and dancing. The title was initially adopted as a common surname but the single character surname Yüeh 樂 became more popular and brought about the decline in the population of the Yüeh-chengs.

618. Yün² 雲

According to <u>Hsing shih k'ao lüeh</u> 姓氏考略, the surname Yün 雲 originated from the title of the offical post called chin-yün 縉雲. Under the reign of Huang-ti 黃帝, chin-yün was the official of summer (hsia-kuan 夏官), traditionally considered the season for war; and was responsible for advising the ruler in all military matters. Yün was later adopted as the common surname and the family initially settled in Lang-yeh 瑯琊, Ho-nan 河南 province.

619. Yün³ 允

The surname Yün 允 derived from two origins. 1. The surname follows the ancestral line of Shao Hao 少昊 and its founder was his grandson Yün Ko 允格. 2. The surname originally used by the ancient tribal group of Jung 戎 and was later adopted as a surname by the Han 漢 People after the group settled in Han territories.

620. Yün⁴ 惲

The surname Yün 惲 originated from two sources. 1. According to <u>Hsing shih k'ao lüeh</u> 姓氏考略, the surname Yün branched from the surname Mi 芈 of the ancestral line of Ch'eng-wang 成王 whose first name was Yün 惲; he came from the State of Ch'u (Ch'u kuo 楚國) in the Spring and Autumn (Ch'un ch'iu 春秋) Period. Yün 惲 was later adopted as a common surname by his descendants.

2. The surname Yün 惲 branched from the surname Yang 楊 and its founder was Yang Yün 楊惲. He was bestowed as the Marquise Yen-t'ung (Yen-t'ung hou 嚴通侯) in the Western Han (Hsi Han 西漢) dynasty. He was accussed of disloyalty to the emperor and was sentenced to death. After his death, his son escaped from his homeland and subsequently changed his family name into Yün 惲.

See also Mi[3] 芈, Yang[2] 楊.

### 621. Yün[4] 員

Hsing chieh 姓解 traces the origin of the surname 員 as follows: 1. The furname came from the ancestral line of Chuan Hsü 顓頊 and its founder was the Grand Master (ta-fu 大夫) Wu Yüan 伍員 from the State of Ch'u (Ch'u kuo 楚國) in the Chou 周 dynasty. 2. During the Spring and Autumn (Ch'un ch'iu 春秋) Period, Liu Ning-chih 劉凝之 of the State of Sung (Sung kuo 宋國) fled to the State of Wei (Wei kuo 魏國), he admired the patriotism and loyalty of Wu Yüan 伍員 to his country and changed his surname to Yün 員.

See also Liu[2] 劉.

### 622. Yüng[1] 雍

T'ung chih Shih tsu lüeh 通志氏族略 and Ming hsien shih tsu yen hsing lei kao 名賢氏族言行類稿 describe the origin of the surname Yüng 雍 as follows: The surname belongs to the ancestral line of Chou Wen-wang 周文王 and its founder was Wen-wang's thirteenth son, the Earl of Yüng (Yüng-po 雍伯). He was bestowed with the feudal territory of the State of Yüng (Yüng kuo 雍國) and his descendants later adopted Yüng as their common surname. The family originally settled in Ch'in-yang hsien 沁陽縣 and Hsiu-wu hsien 修武縣, Ho-nan 河南 province where the State of Yüng was located.

Sources:

1. Catalogues of the Harvard-Yenching Library: Chinese catalogue. 39 vols. v.1-28: Author/title index; v.29-38: Subject index; v.39: Serial records.

2. Chang, Chiu-ling 張九齡. (T'ang 唐 dynasty). Hsing yüan yün p'u 姓源韻譜. 1 chüan.

3. Chang, Po 張勃. (Chin 晉 dynasty). "Wu lu 吳錄." In Shuo fu: 100 chüan; shu fu hsü: 46 chüan 說郛: 一百卷; 說郛序: 四十六卷. [s.l.]: Wan wei shan t'ang, [1646], vol. 2.

4. Chang, Shu 張澍, 1732-1847. (Ch'ing 清 dynasty). Hsing shih hsün yüan 姓氏尋源. 45 chüan. Hu-nan: Yüeh lu shu she, 1992.

5. Chang, Shu 張澍, 1732-1847. (Ch'ing 清 dynasty). Hsing shih wu shu 姓氏五書.

6. Chang, Ting 張定. (Sung 宋 dynasty). "Ming hsien shih tsu yen hsing lei kao 名賢氏族言行類稿", 60 chüan. In Ssu k'u ch'üan shu 四庫全書, issue no. 1, vol. 211-234.

7. Chang, Tzu-lieh 張自烈, fl. 1627. (Ch'ing 清 dynasty). Cheng tzu t'ung: shih erh chüan 正字通: 十二卷. [China]: Hung wen shu yüan, [1671].

8. Ch'en, I 陳毅. (Ch'ing 清 dynasty). Wei shu kuan shih chih: shu cheng 魏書官氏志: 疏証.

9. Ch'en, Ming-yüan 陳明遠 and Wang Tsung-hu 汪宗虎. Chung-kuo hsing shih ta chüan 中國姓氏大全. Pei-ching: Pei-ching ch'u pan she, 1987.

10. Ch'en, Shou 陳壽, 233-297. (Chin 晉 dynasty). San kuo chih 三國志. 20 vols. Shang-hai: Chung-hua hsüeh i she, 1931.

11. Ch'en, Shou 陳壽, 233-297. (Chin 晉 dynasty). San kuo chih Hsien-pei chuan 三國志鮮卑傳.

12. Ch'en, Shou 陳壽, 233-297. (Chin 晉 dynasty). "San kuo chih Wu chih Chu-ko Chin chuan 三國志吳志諸葛瑾傳." In San kuo chih Wu chih 三國志吳志, v. 16-20. Shang-hai: Chung-hua hsüeh i she, 1931.

13. Ch'en, T'ing-wei 陳廷煒. (Ch'ing 清 dynasty). <u>Hsing shih k'ao lüeh</u> 姓氏考略. Pei-ching: Chung-hua shu chü, 1985.

14. Cheng, Ch'iao 鄭樵, 1104-1162. (Sung 宋 dynasty). <u>T'ung chih</u> 通志. 200 chüan. 1,500 vols. T'ai-pei: Shang wu yin shu kuan, 1983.

15. Cheng, Ch'iao 鄭樵, 1104-1162. (Sung 宋 dynasty). "<u>T'ung chih Shih tsu lüeh</u> 通志氏族略." In <u>T'ung chih lüeh</u> 通志略, 52 chüan. Shang-hai: Shang wu yin shu kuan, 1934.

16. Cheng, Hsüan 鄭玄, 127-220. (Eastern Han 東漢). <u>Chou li; 12 chüan.</u> 周禮: 十二卷. 6 vols. on double leaves. [s.l.]: Hu-pei kuan shu chü, [1886].

17. Cheng, Wen-pao 鄭文寶. (Sung 宋 dynasty). <u>Chiang piao chih</u> 江表志. Pei-ching: Chung-hua shu chü, 1991.

18. Chiang, Wei 江微. (Chin 晉 dynasty). "<u>Ch'en Liu Feng su chuan</u> 陳留風俗傳." In <u>Shuo fu: 100 chüan; shu fu hsü: 46 chüan</u> 說郛: 一百卷; 說郛序: 四十六卷. [s.l.]: Wan wei shan t'ang, [1646], vol. 64.

19. Ch'ing, Sheng-tsu 清聖祖, Emperor of China, 1654-1722. <u>Yü chih Pai chia hsing</u> 御製百家姓.

20. Ch'üan, Tsu-wang 全祖望, 1705-1755. (Ch'ing 清 dynasty). <u>Chieh ch'i t'ing chi</u> 鮚琦亭集. 24 vols. Yao-chiang: Chieh shu shan fang, [1804?].

21. <u>Chung-kuo pai chia hsing chieh shuo tz'u tien</u> 中國百家姓解說辭典. T'ai-pei: Hsin wen feng chu pan kung ssu, 1985.

22. Fan, Yeh 范曄, 398-445. (Ming 明 dynasty). <u>Hou Han shu</u> 後漢書. 12 vols. in 6 cases. Pei-ching: Chung-hua shu chü, 1965 (1995 printing).

23. Fang, Ch'iao 房喬, 578-648. (Chou 周 dynasty). <u>Chin shu: 130 chüan</u> 晉書: 一百三十卷. 10 vols. Pei-ching: Chung-hua shu chü, 1974.

24. Fang, Ch'iao 房喬, 578-648. (Chou 周 dynasty). <u>Chin shu Ho-lien Po-po tsai chi</u> 晉書赫連勃勃載記.

25. Ho, Ch'eng-t'ien 何承天. (Nan ch'ao 南朝). <u>Hsing yüan</u> 姓苑. 10 chüan.

26. Hook, Brian, ed. <u>The Cambridge encyclopedia of China.</u> Cambridge, London; New York: Cambridge University Press, 1982.

27. Hsü, Shen 許慎, d. 120? (Han 漢 dynasty). Annotated by Tuan, Yü-ts'ai 段玉裁. <u>Shuo wen chieh tzu</u> 說文解字. 15 chüan. 4 vols., double leaves in case. Shang-hai: Shang wu yin shu kuan, 1914.

28. Hsüeh, Yüan 學元. <u>Pai hsing tsu tsung t'u tien</u> 百姓祖宗圖典. Shen-chün, China: Hai tien chu pan she, 1993.

29. Huang, T'ing-chien 黃庭堅, 1045-1105. (Sung 宋 dynasty). <u>Shan ku chi</u> 山谷集. 39 chüan. <u>Shih i</u> 拾遺, 5 chüan.

30. Hucker, Charles O. <u>A dictionary of official titles in imperial China.</u> Stanford, CA: Stanford University Press, 1985.

31. Kao, Yu 高誘. (Eastern Han 東漢). <u>Chan kuo ts'e</u> 戰國策. 6 vols. Hu-pei: Ch'ung wen shu chü, 1912.

32. Kung-yang, Kao 公羊高. <u>Kung-yang chuan</u> 公羊傳. 28 chüan. 4 vols. on double leaves. [s.l.]: Hu-pei kuan shu chü, [1886].

33. K'ung, An-kuo 孔安國. (Han 漢 dynasty). <u>Shu ching</u> 書經. T'ai-pei: National Central Library, 1973.

34. Le, Shih 樂史. (Sung 宋 dynasty). <u>T'ai p'ing huan yü chi</u> 太平寰宇記. 200 chüan. [China]: Chin ling shu chü, 1882.

35. Li, Yen-shou 李延壽, ca. 600-680. (T'ang 唐 dynasty). <u>Pei shih</u> 北史. 100 chüan. 10 vols. Pei-ching: Chung-hua shu chü, 1974.

36. Liang, Shih-ch'iu 梁實秋. <u>A new practical Chinese-English dictionary</u>. T'ai-pei: Yüan tung t'u shu chu pan kung ssu, 1973.

37. Liao, Yüng-hsien 廖用賢. (Ming 明 dynasty). <u>Shang yu lu: erh shih erh chüan</u> 尚友錄: 二十二卷. [Fu-chien: s.n., 1621-1627?].

38. Ling, Pao 林寶. (T'ang 唐 dynasty). <u>Yüan ho hsing tsuan</u> 元何姓纂. 4 vols. T'ai-pei: Shang wu yin shu kuan, 1975.

39. Ling, Ti-chih 凌迪知. (Ming 明 dynasty). Wang hsing t'ung p'u 萬姓統譜. 140 chüan. 40 vols. T'ai-pei: Hsin hsing shu chü, 1579, 1971.

40. Lo, Chen-yü 羅振玉, 1866-1910? (Ch'ing 清 dynasty). T'ang shu tsai hsiang shih hsi piao 唐書宰相世系表. Pei-ching: Chung-hua shu chü, 1934.

41. Lo, Pi 羅泌, ca. 1176. (Sung 宋 dynasty). Lu shih 路史. 8 vols. in 2. Shang-hai: Chung-hua shu chü, [1936?].

42. Lu, Fa-yen 陸法言. (Sui 隋 dynasty). Revised and enlarged by Ch'en, Peng-nien 陳彭年, 961-1017, et al. (Sung 宋 dynasty). Kuang yün 廣韻, or, Ch'ieh yün 切韻. 4 vols. in 1. T'ai-pei shih: T'ai-wan shang wu yin shu kuan, [1968].

43. Lü, Pu-wei 呂不韋, 290-235 B.C. (Ch'in 秦 dynasty). Lü shih ch'un ch'iu 呂氏春秋. 26 chüan. 4 vols. in 1. Shang-hai: Chung-hua shu chü, [1936?].

44. Ma, Tuan-lin 馬端臨. (Yüan 元 dynasty). Wen hsien t'ung k'ao 文獻通考. 1,500 vols. T'ai-pei: T'ai-wan Shang wu yin shu kuan, 1983-

45. Mayers, William Frederick. The Chinese reader's manual: a handbook of biographical, historical, mythological, and general literary reference. Detroit: Gale Research Co., 1910.

46. Ou-yang, Hsiu 歐陽修, 1007-1072. (Sung 宋 dynasty). T'ang shu 唐書, or, Hsin T'ang shu 新唐書. 225 chüan. Shang-hai: Shang wu yin pen, 1937.

47. Pan, Ku 班固, A.D. 32-92. (Eastern Han 東漢). Han shu: 100 chüan 漢書: 一百卷. 3 vols. T'ai-pei: Ch'i ming shu chü, [1961].

48. P'eng, Ta-i 彭大翼, fl. 1573-1565. (Ming 明 dynasty). Shan t'ang ssu k'ao 山堂肆考. 64 vols. [China] : Chang Yü-hsüeh pu hsiu, [1595, 1619].

49. The Pinyin Chinese-English dictionary. Beijing; Hong Kong: The Commercial Press, 1979.

50. Shao, Ssu 邵思. (Sung 宋 dynasty). <u>Hsing chieh</u> 姓解. Pei-ching: Chung-hua shu chü, 1985.

51. Shu, Hsin-ch'eng 舒新城. <u>Tz'u hai</u> 辭海. 3 vols. Shang-hai: Chung-hua shu chü, 1937,1948.

52. Ssu-ma, Chen 司馬貞. (T'ang 唐 dynasty). <u>Shih chi so yin</u> 史記索引. 30 chüan. 1,500 vols. T'ai-pei: Kuo li ku kung po wu yüan, [19--].

53. Ssu-ma, Ch'ien 司馬遷, ca. 145-86 B.C. (Han 漢 dynasty). <u>Shih chi</u> 史記. 20 vols. T'ai-pei shih: T'ai-wan shang wu yin shu kuan, [1965].

54. Ssu-ma, Ch'ien 司馬遷, ca. 145-86 B.C. (Han 漢 dynasty). <u>Shih chi Ch'u shih chia</u> 史記楚世家.

55. Ssu-ma, Ch'ien 司馬遷, ca. 145-86 B.C. (Han 漢 dynasty). <u>Shih chi Chung-ni ti tzu lieh chuan</u> 史記仲尼弟子列傳.

56. Ssu-ma, Ch'ien 司馬遷, ca. 145-86 B.C. <u>Shih chi K'ung-tze shih chia</u> 史記孔子世家.

57. Sung, Chung 宋衷, annotator. (Han 漢 dynasty). <u>Shih pen</u> 世本. Pei-ching: Chung-hua shu chü, 1985.

58. T'ao, Tsung-i 陶宗儀. (Yüan 元 dynasty). <u>Shuo fu: 100 chüan; shu fu hsü: 46 chüan</u> 說郛: 一百卷; 說郛序: 四十六卷. 170 vols. [s.l.]: Wan wei shan t'ang, [1646].

59. Teng, Hsien-ching 鄧獻鯨. <u>Chung-kuo hsing shih chi</u> 中國姓氏集. T'ai-pei shih: Chih ta t'u shu wen chü chiao yü yüng p'in ku fen yu hsien kung ssu, 1971.

60. Teng, Ming-shih 鄧明世, fl. 1133. (Sung 宋 dynasty). <u>Ku chin hsing shih shu pien cheng: fu chiao kan chi</u> 古今姓氏書辯證: 附校勘記. 8 vols. Pei-ching: Chung-hua shu chü, 1985.

61. Ting, Ch'ien 丁謙, 1843-1919. (Ch'ing 清 dynasty). <u>Han shu Hsiung-nu chuan</u> 漢書匈奴傳. 2 vols. China: Che-chiang Library, ts'ung-shu, [19--].

62. Tso-ch'iu, Ming 左丘明. (Chou 周 dynasty). <u>Tso chuan</u> 左傳. 12 chüan. [s.l.: s.n.. 1582?].

63. Tso-ch'iu, Ming 左丘明. (Chou 周 dynasty). <u>Kuo yü</u> 國語. 6 vols. in 1. Shang-hai: Chung-hua shu chü, [1936?].

64. Wang, Ch'i 王圻, chin shih 1565. (Ming 明 dynasty). <u>Hsü Wen hsien t'ung k'ao</u> 續文獻通考. 64 vols. [s.l.: s.n., 1603?].

65. Wang, Chia 王嘉, 4th cent. (Chin 晉 dynasty). <u>Shih i chi</u> 拾遺記. Pei-ching: Chung-hua shu chü, 1981.

66. Wang, Chien 王儉. (Nan Ch'i 南齊). <u>Hsing p'u: 216 chüan</u> 姓譜: 二一六卷. [s.l. : s.n., 19--?].

67. Wang, Fu 王符. (Eastern Han 東漢). <u>Ch'ien fu lun</u> 潛夫論. 3 vols. Shang-hai: Ku chi ch'u pan she, 1978.

68. Wang, Ying-lin 王應麟, 1223-1296. (Sung 宋 dynasty). <u>Hsing shih chi chiu p'ien: 2 chüan</u> 姓氏急就篇: 二卷.

69. Wei, Shou 魏收, 506-572. (Pei Ch'i 北齊). <u>Wei shu</u> 魏書. 114 chüan. Pei-ching: Chung-hua shu chü, 1739, 1974.

70. Wilkinson, Endymion. <u>The history of imperial China: a research guide.</u> Cambridge, MA: Harvard University Press, 1973.

71. Yang, Shih-ch'i 楊士奇, 1365-1444. (Ming 明 dynasty). <u>Tung li wen chi</u> 東里文集. 20 vols. T'ai-pei: Shang wu yin shu kuan, 1977.

72. Yang, Ta-ch'u 楊達初. <u>Ch'ien chia hsing</u> 千家姓. Hon-kong: San jung hsing hao, 1923.

73. Yao, Ssu-lien 姚思廉, d. 637. (T'ang 唐 dynasty). <u>Liang shu</u> 梁書. 56 chüan. 3 vols. Pei-ching: Chung-hua shu chü, 1973.

74. Ying, Shao 應劭, fl. 189-194. (Eastern Han 東漢). <u>Feng shu t'ung hsing shih pien</u> 風俗通姓氏篇. Pei-ching: Chung-hua shu chü, 1985.

75. Yüan, Chiung 袁褧. (Sung 宋 dynasty). <u>Feng ch'uang hsiao tu</u> 楓窗小牘. Pei-ching: Chung-hua shu chü, 1985.

76. Yüan, Yü-liu 袁玉騮. <u>Chung-kuo hsing ming hsüeh</u> 中國姓名學. Pei-hing: Kuang ming jih pao chu pan she, 1994.

Chapter 3

# BIBLIOGRAPHY OF CHINESE SURNAMES

1. Chang, Meng-lun 張孟隆. Han Wei jen ming k'ao 漢魏人名考.
   Kan-shu: Yang-chou ta hsüeh ch'u pan she, 1988.

   Analysis of personal names originating in the Han and Wei
   dynasties. Primary emphasis is on the explanation of
   factors which attribute to the naming pattern in these
   dynasties. The book also includes genealogical tables of
   the emperors of Han and Wei dynasties. For general and
   scholarly use.

2. Chang, Pi-te 昌彼得. T'ai-wan kung ts'ang tsu p'u chieh ti
   臺灣公藏族譜解題. [s.l.: s.n., 1990].

   Catalog of genealogical collections in public libraries in
   Taiwan.

3. Chang, Po 張勃. (Chin 晉 dynasty). "Wu lu 吳錄." In Shuo fu:
   100 chüan; shu fu hsü: 46 chüan 說郛: 一百卷; 說郛序:
   四十六卷. [s.l.]: Wan wei shan t'ang, [1646], vol. 2.

4. Chang, Shu 張澍, 1732-1847. (Ch'ing 清 dynasty). Hsing shih
   hsün yüan 姓氏尋源. 45 chüan. Hu-nan: Yüeh lu shu she,
   1992.

   Tracing the origin of surnames. The book contains forty-
   five chapters (chüan 卷). Surnames start with the same
   phonetic sound are grouped in one chüan and subdivided by
   stroke order. Each surname listed contains the description
   of its origin and the title of the work which the name was
   originally cited. For both general and scholarly use.

5. Chang, Shu-p'ing 張書平. Erh nü ming ming hui tien
   兒女命名彙典. T'ai-nan: Hsin hung ch'u pan she, 1984.

   This book shows you how to choose an auspicious Chinese
   name for your children according to the name's number of
   strokes, its meaning and origin, Chinese yin 陰 (female)
   and yang 陽 (male), wu hsing 五行 (five activities), pa tzu
   八字 (eight characters), rhyme, and shape. A list of
   suggested names is provided and analyzed by the criteria
   given. For general use.

6. Chang, T'ai-ku 張泰谷. Pi ming yin te 筆名引得. T'ai-pei
   shih: Wen hai ch'u pan she, 1971.

226

Index to pseudonyms. The book is arranged by the character stroke order and contains two parts: a personal name index and a pseudonym index. For general reference on modern Chinese authors.

7.  Chang, Ting 張定. (Sung 宋 dynasty). "Ming hsien shih tsu yen hsing lei kao 名賢氏族言行類稿", 60 chüan. In Ssu k'u ch'üan shu 四庫全書, issue no. 1, vol. 211-234.

8.  Chang, Tzu-lieh 張自烈, fl. 1627. (Ch'ing 清 dynasty). Cheng tzu t'ung: shih erh chüan 正字通: 十二卷. [China]: Hung wen shu yüan, [1671].

Dictionary of etymology. The characters in the dictionary are grouped under their radicals and sub-arranged in the order of the the number of character strokes. Under each character, variant forms and their meaning are given followed by quotations and references. The volume contains twelve chapters (chüan 卷) and traces more than 5,000 names and phrases. For reference.

9.  Chang, Wei-hsiang 張惟驤. Li tai hui tzu p'u 歷代諱字譜. [s.l.: s.n.], 1932.

Lists of taboo names (hui ming 諱名) which were forbidden during a particular dynasty. The book contains a compilation of characters arranged by the rhymes of Chinese sounds, of limited or restricted use. Reasons for their restricted use include: conflict on sound, rhyme, place name, official rank, or total number of strokes with the names of the Chinese emperors and government officials.

10.  Chang shih chih p'u 張氏支譜. [s.l.: s.n., 1988].

A branch genealogy of the Chang family.

11.  Chao, Kung-i 趙功義. Chung-kuo hsing shih chien ming tz'u tien 中國姓氏簡明辭典. Pei-ching: Ch'ang-ch'eng ch'u pan she, 1988.

A compact dictionary of Chinese surnames. The volume contains a collection of 3,660 names arranged by Hanyu pinyin. For general reference.

12.  Chao shih tsu p'u 趙氏族譜. T'ai-pei: Hsing sheng ch'u pan she, 1973.

The genealogical history of the Chao family. Traces historical lineage of contemporary Chao families in Taiwan and includes a collection of photographs of Chao family members.

13. Ch'en, Cheng-chih 陳澄之. <u>A biographical & bibliographical dictionary of Chinese authors =</u> <u>Chung-kuo chu tso chia tz'u tien</u> 中國著作家辭典. 2 vols. New York, NY: Oriental Society, 1976.

This dictionary contains over 4,000 names of Chinese authors compiled by Mr. Chen from international works published prior to 1970. Arranged alphabetically by Chinese surname in romanized form, the dictionary contains biographical records of authors with their Chinese names, birth and death dates, and the authors' works listed in their original titles. A contribution of western scholarship on China. For both advanced scholars and students of Oriental studies.

14. Ch'en, Chieh-hsien 陳捷先. <u>Chung-kuo ti tsu p'u</u> 中國的族譜. T'ai-pei: Hsing cheng yüan wen hua chien she wei yüan hui, 1984.

Introduction to Chinese genealogy including history, origin, and a step-by-step guide to tracing your own family history. For general use.

15. Ch'en, Han-chen 陳翰珍. <u>Shih chieh Ch'en shih tsung ch'in ta tsu p'u</u> 世界陳氏宗親大族譜. T'ai-pei: Hua mao ch'u pan she, 1983.

A comprehensive multilineage genealogy of the Ch'en family. The family ranks as the largest of families in the population of Taiwan.

16. Ch'en, I-wen 陳逸紋. <u>Pai chia hsing</u> 百家姓. T'ai-pei: Shih feng ch'u pan she, 1991.

More than 400 commonly used Chinese surnames are introduced in this book. For general use.

17. Ch'en, Kuo-wei 陳國緯. <u>Chiang-chou I-men Ch'en shih tsung p'u</u> 江州義門陳氏宗譜. Singapore: Manyang Khek Community Chen Shih Association, 1983.

The genealogy of the I-men Ch'en clan from Chiang-chou, China. Traces the genealogical history of the Ch'en family from the founder, Yü Ti-shun 虞帝舜 to the ninety-first generation of his descendants in the Ming 明 dynasty.

18. Ch'en, Mei-kuei 陳美桂. <u>T'ai-wan ch'ü tsu p'u mu lu</u> 臺灣區族譜目錄. T'ai-wan : T'ai-wan sheng ko hsing li shih yüan yüan fa chan yen chiu hsüeh hui, 1987.

   Catalog of Chinese genealogies in Taiwan. The volume contains 10,613 items on genealogical subjects. It covers records collected in Taiwan between 1975 and 1985 as the result of the Genealogical Society of Utah's "Taiwan Project." Comprehensive. For scholarly research and general use.

19. Ch'en, Ming-yüan 陳明遠 and Wang Tsung-hu 汪宗虎. <u>Chung-kuo hsing shih ta chüan</u> 中國姓氏大全. Pei-ching: Pei-ching ch'u pan she, 1987.

   A dictionary of Chinese surnames. The authors have collected more than 5,600 ancient and modern Chinese names including single and compound surnames. The book is arranged alphabetically according to Hanyu Pinyin. For general use.

20. Ch'en, Nai-ch'ien 陳乃乾. <u>Li tai jen wu shih ming pieh hao t'ung chien</u> 歷代人物室名別號通檢. Hsiang-kang: T'ai-p'ing shu chü, 1964.

   This book is a joint publication of the author's two works: <u>Pieh hao so yin</u> 別號索引. and <u>Shih ming so ying</u>. 室名索引. Suitable for consultation by historians, librarians, genealogists, and scholars. The coverage of this book is from the Legendary Period to the Ming 明 dynasty.

21. Ch'en, Nai-ch'ien 陳乃乾. <u>Pieh hao so yin</u> 別號索引. Shang-hai: K'ai ming shu tien, 1943.

   Index to anonyms, pseudonyms, and nicknames of ancient Chinese politicians, soldiers, poets, emperors, government officials, and so on. Arranged according to character stroke order, each pseudonym, or hao 號 refers to the person's real name by which he is identified in literature and includes the dynasty the person belongs to and the province where the person was born. For reference use.

22. Ch'en, Nai-ch'ien 陳乃乾. <u>Shih ming so yin</u> 室名索引. Shang-hai: K'ai ming shu tien, 1934.

Index to the house name (shih ming 室名), or ancestral name of ancient Chinese politicians, soldiers, poets, emperors, and government officials. More than 5,000 personal names were indexed in this book. For reference use.

23.  Ch'en, Shou 陳壽, 233-297. (Chin 晉 dynasty). San kuo chih 三國志. 20 vols. Shang-hai: Chung-hua hsüeh i she, 1931.

The history of the Three Kingdoms. It includes biographical histories of the Wei 魏, Shu 蜀 and Wu 吳 Kingdoms. This twenty volume set covers the years A.D. 220-280 and is a compilation of three representative works from the above mentioned Kingdoms: History of the Wei (Wei chih 魏志, 30 chüan, v. 1-12), History of the Shu (Shu chih 蜀志, 15 chüan, v. 13-15) and History of the Wu (Wu chih 吳志, 20 chüan, v. 16-20).

24. Ch'en, Shao-hsing 陳紹馨 and Morton H. Fried. The distribution of family names in Taiwan. T'ai-pei: Department of Sociology, College of Law, National Taiwan University; New York: Department of Anthropology, Columbia University, East Asian Institute , 1968.

This book presents raw data compiled from records of the 1956 Taiwanese census. It covers the distribution of surnames in Taiwan by townships and prefectures. Suitable for population statistics and surname distribution analysis in Taiwan.

25.  Ch'en, Shih-yüan 陳士元. Hsing hsi: fu lu, cha chi 姓觿: 附錄劄記. 3 vols. Pei-ching: Chung-hua shu chü, 1985.

This three volume set contains a collection of 3,625 names including 2,179 single syllable and 1,446 multisyllable surnames. The set is divided into ten chapters and arranged by the pronunciation of the names and character stroke order. The contents of the set is quite comprehensive. Each name includes the description of its origin, references which trace the derivation of the name, and historical persons with that name. For general and scholarly use.

26.  Ch'en, Te-yün 陳得芸. Ku chin jen wu pieh ming so yin 古今人物別名索引. T'ai-pei: I wen yin shu kuan, 1969.

Index of nicknames, pen names, tzu 字 and hao 號 of ancient

and modern Chinese literary authors. The book indexes over 70,000 pen names from the T'ang 唐 dynasty to the Republican eras. For scholars of Chinese literary studies.

27. Ch'en, T'ing-wei 陳廷煒. (Ch'ing 清 dynasty). Hsing shih k'ao lüeh 姓氏考略. Pei-ching: Chung-hua shu chü, 1985.

Research analysis on surnames. Published in one volume with Feng shu t'ung hsing shih pien 風俗通姓氏篇 written by the Han 漢 scholar Ying Shao 應劭, the present work is a major resource for researching the genealogy of Chinese surnames. For reference and scholarly use.

28. Ch'en, Yü-t'ang 陳玉堂. Chung kung tang shih jen wu pieh ming lu 中共黨史人物別名錄. Shang-hai: Hung-ch'i ch'u pan she, 1987.

Directory of party and government officials of Communist China. A collection of 192 persons is included in this directory. The volume contains not only indexes to pen names, assumed names, tzu hao 字號, anonyms, and pseudonyms of these persons but also detailed descriptions of their political histories. For general reference.

29. Ch'en, Yü-t'ang 陳玉堂. Chung-kuo chin hsien tai jen wu ming hao ta tz'u tien 中國近現代人物名號大辭典. Hang-chou, China: Che-chiang ku chi ch'u pan she, 1993.

A concise biographical dictionary of Chinese nicknames. The volume covers the period from 1840 to 1949 which includes persons from the fields of politics, education, science, the military, medicine, journalism, literature, and religion as well as government officials and emperors of the Ch'ing 清 dynasty. It contains a total of 10,112 biographical descriptions. The book is arranged according to character stroke order by personal name. For research use by scholars and historians of Chinese studies.

30. Ch'en shih chih p'u erh chüan 陳氏支譜二卷. [T'ai-pei]: s.n., 1985.

Genealogical history of the Ch'en family who relocated from several villages in An-hui 安徽, Ho-fei hsien 合肥縣 to Taiwan. A total number of thirty-four generations are traced in this book.

31. Cheng, Ch'iao 鄭樵, 1104-1162. (Sung 宋 dynasty). T'ung chih 通志. 200 chüan. 1,500 vols. T'ai-pei: Shang wu yin shu kuan, 1983.

Comprehensive history of institutions. This 1,500 volumes set is a reprint of the original work published in 1149. The work is divided into four major sections: chi 紀 (annals), p'u 譜 (chronological tables), lüeh 略 (monographic studies), and chuan 傳 (biographies). It traces a collection of more than 2,000 surnames and covers the period extends from earliest historical times to the end of the Sui 隋 dynasty in the lüeh and p'u sections. For reference and scholarly use.

32. Cheng, Ch'iao 鄭樵, 1104-1162. (Sung 宋 dynasty). "T'ung chih Shih tsu lüeh 通志氏族略." In T'ung chih lüeh 通志略, 52 chüan. Shang-hai: Shang wu yin shu kuan, 1934.

A study of clan and royal family genealogies. The work contains a collection of more than 2,000 surnames and their origins. The names are arranged according to their rhyme and the work covers genealogy from the earliest times to the end of the Sui 隋 dynasty. For reference and scholarly use.

33. Cheng, Hsüan 鄭玄, 127-220. (Eastern Han 東漢). Chou li: 12 chüan. 周禮: 十二卷. 6 vols. on double leaves. [s.l.]: Hu-pei kuan shu chü, [1886].

The ritual of Chou dynasty. A comprehensive resource for surnames generated from the name of official titles in the Chou dynasty. For reference and scholarly use.

34. Cheng, Wen-pao 鄭文寶. (Sung 宋 dynasty). Chiang piao chih 江表志. Pei-ching: Chung-hua shu chü, 1991.

Biographical history of the Southern T'ang 南唐 kingdom. The book covers the years A.D. 937-975. For reference and scholarly use.

35. Chi-yang K'o Ts'ai shih ta tsu p'u 濟陽柯蔡氏大族譜. Kao-hsiung: K'o Ts'ai tsung ch'in ta tsu p'u pien chi pu, 1974.

Covers the genealogical history of the K'o and Ts'ai families living in Taiwan.

36. Chia, I-chün 賈逸君. <u>Chung-hua ming-kuo ming jen chuan</u> 中華名國名人傳. 2 vols. Pei-ching, China: Peiping weh hua hsüeh she, 1932-1933.

A "Who's who" of more than three hundred Chinese who have been prominent since the 1911 revolution. The work is divided according to professions into twelve sections, and in each section the names are arranged according to the number of strokes. It is a current biography for prominent Chinese in the twentieth century. For reference use.

37. Chiang, Lan 江藍. <u>Hung shih (Tun-huang) tsu p'u</u> 洪氏(敦煌)族譜. [s.l.: s.n., 1985].

Traces the author's own genealogical origins from the first to the tenth generations. This book is the result of the author's forty years of research on the origins of his family.

38. <u>Chiang-su sheng Fu-ning hsien Ch'eng shih tsung p'u</u> 江蘇省阜寧縣程氏宗譜. T'ai-pei: Fu-ning Ch'eng shih tsung ch'in hui, 1985.

Includes multilineage genealogies of the Ch'eng family who moved to Taiwan from Fu-ning hsien in Chiang-su province in China.

39. Chiang, Wei 江微. (Chin 晉 dynasty). "<u>Ch'en Liu Feng su chuan</u> 陳留風俗傳." In <u>Shuo fu: 100 chüan; shu fu hsü: 46 chüan</u> 說郛: 一百卷; 說郛序: 四十六卷. [s.l.]: Wan wei shan t'ang, [1646], vol. 64.

40. <u>Chiao shih tsung tsu yüan liu</u> 焦氏宗族源流. T'ai-pei: Chiao shih tsung ch'in hui, 1979.

Traces the origin of the Chiao family. The book contains multilineage genealogies of the Chiao family now living in Taiwan.

41. <u>Chien shih ta tsu p'u</u> 簡氏大族譜. T'ai-pei: Chien shih ta tsu p'u pien chi pu, 1986.

Traces the descendants of the Chien families living in Taiwan.

42. <u>Chih-shan Chang shih tsu p'u</u> 赤山張氏族譜. T'ai-chung:

Chung-hua ming tsu p'u hsi yen chiu chung hsin, [19--].

Contains macro registers of the descendants of the Chang family living in Taiwan.

43. Chin, Harry, comp. <u>Chin shih tsu p'u</u> 陳氏族譜, or, <u>The Chin family tree</u>. Kuang-tung: [s.n.] ; [Printed in Vancouver, Canada], 1980.

This Chinese and English publication was compiled by the twenty-seventh generation descendant of the Chin clan from K'u-ch'ung 庫充 village of Chung-shan 中山 district of Kuang-tung 廣東 province in China. The volume traces the genealogies of this Chin family whose heritage goes back nearly 800 years.

44. <u>Chin-shui Huang shih tsu p'u</u> 金水黃氏族譜. Chin-men, T'ai-wan: Chin-shui Huang shih ta tsung pien yin, 1983.

Covers the complete genealogical history of the Huang family who originated in Chin-shui 金水, Chin-men hsien 金門縣 in Taiwan.

45. <u>Ch'ing-hsi Yü-tu Hsü shih chia p'u</u> 清溪虞都許氏家譜. 8 vols. [T'ai-wan: T'ai-wan wen hsien lei pien, 1993].

A comprehensive genealogical register that traces the Hsü family from its origin to the twenty-third generation.

46. <u>Ch'ing tai shu hua chia tzu hao yin te</u> 清代書畫家字號引得 = <u>Index to the fancy names of the calligraphers and painters of the Ch'ing dynasty</u>. T'ai-pei: [s.n.]; Distributed by Chinese materials and Research Aids Service Center, 1966.

An index to the names of 5,787 Chinese painters and calligraphers. This volume contains two parts. Part one is an index to personal names and part two is an index to pseudonyms. For general and scholarly use.

47. Ch'iu, Hsiu-chiang 丘秀強. <u>Ho-nan t'ang Ch'iu shih wen hsien</u> 河南堂丘氏文獻. 4 vols. T'ai-pei: Ch'iu shih wen hsien she, 1982.

Describes the clan history and genealogy of the Ch'iu family in Taiwan.

48. Chou, Ch'ing-i 周慶義 and Chou Chin 周瑾. <u>Hsüeh shih chia</u>

*tsu jen wu chih* 薛氏家族人物志. [Shan-hsi]: Shan-hsi jen ming ch'u pan she, 1990.

Describes the prominent figures of the descendants of the Hsüeh family in Chinese history. The book is arranged chronologically from the Legendary Period to the Ch'ing 清 dynasty.

49. Chou, Yen-mou 周燕謀. *Wan tsu ta hsing p'u* 萬族大姓譜. T'ai-pei: Han chen shu chü, 1984.

Multilineage genealogies of surnames. A total of 5,300 names is collected in this book, including 3,200 one-syllable, 2,000 two-syllable, 120 three-syllable, 6 four-syllable, and 2 five-syllable surnames. For both general and scholarly use.

50. Chu, Tse-k'uei 朱則奎. *Hsing shih chien chieh* 姓氏簡介. T'ai-pei: Shan ming shu chü, 1991.

An introduction to Chinese surnames, including a detailed description of the origin of each name arranged by the Four-corner system (ssu chiao hao ma 四角號碼, invented by Mr. Wang Yün-wu 王雲五). A useful bibliography for consultation and further research on the subject of Chinese names is included. One drawback of this book is the use of the Four-corner system, one not popularly in use. For scholarly use.

51. Ch'üan, Tsu-wang 全祖望, 1705-1755. (Ch'ing 清 dynasty). *Chieh ch'i t'ing chi* 鮚埼亭集. 24 vols. Yao-chiang: Chieh shu shan fang, [1804?].

52. *Chung-hua hsing shih yüan liu t'ang hao k'ao* 中華姓氏源流堂號考. T'ai-pei: Chung-kuo ming jen chuan chi chung hsin (Chinese Who's Who Publishing Center), 1985.

Presents the lineages of Chinese surnames. The volume traces the most frequently appearing 100 surnames in Taiwan. The most interesting part of this book is its guide to step-by-step tracing of your own family tree. It provides genealogical forms for personal use. For general readers.

53. *Chung-kuo hsing shih hui pien* 中國姓氏匯編. Pei-ching: Jen min yu tien ch'u pan she, 1984.

A compact dictionary of Chinese surnames in both Hanyu Pinyin and Mandarin pronunciation. This volume collects a total of 5,730 surnames including 3,470 one-syllable names, 2,085 two-syllable names, 163 three-syllable names, 9 four-syllable names, and 3 five-syllable names. For general reference.

54. <u>Chung-kuo jen hsing p'u</u> 中國人姓譜. 2 vols. Chung-ho, T'ai-pei: Shuang ho pien wei hui, 1984.

Chinese surname registers. Volume one covers the origin of the 290 most frequently used names. Volume two details less frequently used surnames. The description of each surname is quite comprehensive, including the name's historical background, its predominant use in Chinese provinces, and the name's usage as distributed in various areas in Taiwan. The major drawback of this book is its random arrangement which makes searching of a particular name quite difficult. For general reference.

55. <u>Chung-kuo jen ming ta tz'u tien</u> 中國人名大辭典. T'ai-pei: T'ai-wan shang wu ying shu kuan, 1990.

Chinese biographical dictionary. The volume collects over 40,000 names including people from the Legendary Period to the Ch'ing 清 dynasty. For general reference.

56. <u>Chung-kuo pai chia hsing chieh shuo tz'u tien</u> 中國百家姓解說辭典. T'ai-pei: Hsin wen feng chu pan kung ssu, 1985.

Dictionary of Chinese surnames from <u>Pai chia hsing</u> 百家姓. The book is arranged by the surname order in <u>Pai chia hsing.</u> It contains the origin of more than six hundred Chinese surnames and includes references which trace the derivation of these names. For general and reference use.

57. "The family names." In <u>Key to Wade-Giles romanization of Chinese characters.</u> (Washington, D.C. : U.S. Army, Corps of Engineers, 1944): 139-47.

Includes a list of nearly 2,200 Chinese surnames and correspondent transliterations in Wade-Giles. The list was compiled from two major books of authority on Chinese surnames: <u>Pai chia hsing</u> 百家姓 and <u>Ku chin tu shu chi ch'eng</u> 古今圖書集成.

58. <u>Fan shih tsung p'u</u> 樊氏宗譜. T'ai-pei: Fan shih tsung ch'in hui, 1981.

Describes the clan history and genealogy of the Fan family in Taiwan.

59. Fan, Yeh 范曄, 398-445. (Ming 明 dynasty). <u>Hou Han shu</u> 後漢書. 12 vols. in 6 cases. Pei-ching: Chung-hua shu chü, 1965 (1995 printing).

The history of the Later Han dynasty. This twelve volume set is a reprint of the original work published in the Ming dynasty. It covers the years A.D.25-220. For reference and scholarly use.

60. Fang, Ch'iao 房喬, 578-648. (Chou 周 dynasty). <u>Chin shu: 130 chüan</u> 晉書：一百三十卷. 10 vols. Pei-ching: Chung-hua shu chü, 1974.

The history of the Chin dynasty. The volume covers the years A.D. 265-419. For reference and scholarly use.

61. Fang, Hsüan-ch'en 方炫琛. <u>Chou t'ai hsing shih erh fen chi ch'i ch'i yüan shih t'an</u> 周代姓氏二分及其起源試探. T'ai-pei: Hsüeh hai ch'u pan she, 1988.

The Chou dynasty plays a major role in the origin of Chinese surnames. Its naming system is closely connected with its social structure and politics. This book analyzes the separation of hsing 姓 and shih 氏 in the Chou dynasty and traces the names originating from and commonly used in the dynasty. For general and scholarly use.

62. <u>Fei-lü-pin Chi-yang K'o Ts'ai tsung ch'in tsung hui liu-shih chou nien chi nien t'e kan</u> 菲律賓濟陽柯蔡宗親總會六十周年紀念特刊. Manila: Che Yong Cua & Chua Association, 1970.

The sixtieth anniversary publication of the Che Yong Cua & Chua Association. The association, established in Manila, in the early 1990s, was a center for connecting the K'o and Ts'ai families living in Philippines and Taiwan. This book contains a directory of the descendants of these two families and furnishes family group pictures taken of their social gatherings.

63. <u>Feng-ch'i Ho shih tsung chih</u> 峰崎何氏宗志. T'ai-pei : [Ho

Yü-chi pien], 1983.

Transcribes the genealogical history of the Ho family settled in Feng-ch'i, located in Hui-an hsien 惠安縣 in Fu-chien 福建 province. The compiler of this volume is the twenty-first generation of the family.

64. <u>Fu-chien Yüng-ch'un Lin shih lü T'ai tsu chih</u> 福建永春林氏旅台族志. T'ai-pei: Yüng-ch'un t'ung hsiang hui, 1977.

This book was compiled by the descendants of the Lin family who originated in Yüng-ch'un in Fu-chien province now living in Taiwan.

65. <u>Han, Ho, Lan shih tsu p'u</u> 韓, 何, 藍氏族譜. Chi-lung, T'ai-wan: Tung nan yin shu chü, 1964.

Traces the genealogical history of the Han, Ho, and Lan families.

66. Ho, Ch'eng-t'ien 何承天. (Nan ch'ao 南朝). <u>Hsing yüan</u> 姓苑. 10 chüan.

A collection of Chinese surnames and its origin. For general and scholarly use.

67. Ho, Kuang-yüeh 何光岳 and Nieh Hsin-sen 聶鑫森. <u>Chung hua hsing shih t'ung shu: Ch'en hsing</u> 中華姓氏通書：陳姓. Hu-nan: San huan ch'u pan she, 1991.

Traces the genealogical origins of the Ch'en family and includes descriptions of its prominent historical figures.

68. <u>Hou shih tsung p'u</u> 侯氏宗譜. T'ai-pei: Hou shih tsung ch'in hui, 1978.

Describes the genealogical origins of the Hou family and lists the descendants of the family now settled in Taipei, Taiwan.

69. <u>Hsi-ho Lin shih tsu chih</u> 西河林氏族志. Manila: Lü Fei Hsi-ho Lin shih tsung ch'in tsung hui, 1960.

Traces the genealogical origins of the Lin family and lists the names of its descendants who are members of the Genealogical Society of the Lin Family in Manila, the

Philippines.

70. <u>Hsi-hu Yang hsing Tun-su kung yen p'ai ta tsu p'u</u>
溪湖楊姓敦素公衍派大族譜. Chang-hua, T'ai-wan: Yang
Ch'un-mu, 1976.

A clan history of the Yang family living in Hsi-hu 溪湖,
Chang-hua hsien 彰化縣 in Taiwan.

71. Hsiao, I. 蕭繹, 508-554. (Northern Wei 北魏). <u>Ku chin t'ung
hsing ming lu</u>; <u>Chiu shih t'ung hsing ming lüeh: fu pu i</u>
古今同姓名錄; 九史同姓名略: 附補遺. 8 vols. Pei-ching:
Chung-hua shu chü, 1985.

This eight volume set is divided into two major parts. The
first part is a comprehensive directory of Chinese names.
The second part records the directory of names compiled
from the following nine historical works: <u>Old books of the
T'ang dynasty</u> (Chiu T'ang shu 舊唐書), <u>New books of the
T'ang dynasty</u> (Hsin T'ang shu 新唐書), <u>Old history of the
Five Dynasties</u> (Chiu Wu tai shih 舊五代史), <u>New history of
the Five Dynasties</u> (Hsin Wu tai shih 新五代史), <u>History of
the Sung dynasty</u> (Sung shih 宋史), <u>History of the Liao
dynasty</u> (Liao shih 遼史), <u>History of the Ch'in dynasty</u>
(Ch'in shih 秦史), <u>History of the Yüan dynasty</u> (Yüan shih
元史), and <u>History of the Ming dynasty</u> (Ming shih 明史).
For scholarly use.

72. Hsiao, Kuo-chien 蕭國建. <u>Hsiang-kang Hsin-chieh chia tsu fa
chan</u> 香港新界家族發展. Hsiang-kang: Hsien ch'ao shu shih,
1991.

The development of clans in the New Territories of Hong
Kong. The following families are described in this book:
Tang 鄧, Man 文, Liu 劉, Hau 侯, Pang 彭, T'ao 陶, Chan 陳
and Chang 鄭 in Tsuen Wan 荃灣 and Tsang 曾 in Shatin 沙田.

73. Hsiao, Kuo-chün 蕭國鈞 and Hsiao Kuo-chien 蕭國建. <u>Tsu p'u
yü Hsiang-kang ti fang shih yen chiu</u> 族譜與香港地方史研究.
Hsiang-kang: Hsien chao shu shih, 1982.

This book describes genealogical history and its
development in Hong Kong. It lists the recent acquisition
of genealogical resources from the New Territories arranged
by the names of family and village, charts the entry of
Hakka clans into Hong Kong area in Ming 明 and Ch'ing 清
periods, and indicates the major holdings of local

genealogies in the Hong Kong libraries and institutions. Useful for researchers on the genealogical study of Hong Kong.

74. Hsiao, Yao-t'ien 蕭遙天. <u>Chung-kuo jen ming ti yen chiu</u> 中國人名的研究. T'ai-pei: T'ai ching ch'u pan she, 1979.

Research on Chinese surnames. The book contains three major parts: 1. research on surnames in ancient China including the origin, historical background, and naming patterns of the names of Chinese emperors; 2. the social significance of the variation of Chinese names including generation names, occupation names, religious names, and assumed names, as well as the relationship of these names with Chinese calenders and Chinese ink; and 3. a discussion on how to avoid choosing bad names, use of pen names in the literary field, and the reasons for nameless persons in ancient China.

75. <u>Hsieh shih wen hsien chia pien</u> 謝氏文獻甲編. 4 vols. T'ai-pei: Hsieh shih tsung ch'in hui, 1970.

This four volume set traces the genealogical origins of the Hsieh family from the reign of Ming Shen-tsung 明神宗 (A.D. 1573-1620), to the present time in Taipei, Taiwan.

76. <u>Hsing shih jen ming yüng tzu fen hsi t'ung chi</u> 姓氏人名用字分析統計. Pei-ching: Yü wen ch'u pan she, 1991.

A statistical analysis of Chinese names. The book contains a statistical listing of Chinese surnames arranged by the following provinces or areas in China: Pei-ching 北京, Shang-hai 上海, Shan-hsi 山西, Liao-ning 遼寧, Ssu-ch'uan 四川, Kuang-tung 廣東, and Fu-chien 福建. For general and scholarly use on census population statistics and surname distribution and naming in China.

77. Hsü, Chün-yüan 徐俊元, Chang Chan-chün 張占軍 and Shih Yü-hsin 石玉新. <u>Kuei hsing ho lai?</u> 貴姓何來? Ho-Pei: Ho-pei ko hsüeh chi shu ch'u pan she, 1986.

The book entitled: Where's your name come from? contains three major parts: 1. discussions of the creation, formation, and development of Chinese names, the relationship of names to the Chinese feudal system, and the names origins and meanings; 2. traces the most commonly used 1,048 surnames in China; and 3. broad descriptions of ancient and modern Chinese surnames arranged by Hanyu Pinyin. 5,093 common and uncommon names are introduced in this third part. A comprehensive reference tool for researchers as well as general readers.

78. Hsü, Hsüeh-chi 許雪姬. <u>Lung-ching Lin chia ti li shih</u> 龍井林家的歷史. T'ai-pei : Institute of Modern History, Academic Sinica, 1990.

Traces the genealogical history of the Lin family living in Lung-ching, Taiwan.

79. Hsü, Kuang-p'u 徐光溥, fl. 1247. (Sung 宋 dynasty). <u>Tzu hao lu</u> 自號錄. Pei-ching: Chung-hua shu chü, 1985.

Index of Chinese anonyms and pseudonyms. For general use.

80. Hsü, Nai-hsiang 徐迺翔 and Chin Hung 欽鴻. <u>Chung-kuo hsien tai wen hsüeh tso che pi ming lu</u> 中國現代文學作者筆名錄. Hu-nan: Hu-nan wen yi ch'u pan she, 1988.

A directory of pseudonyms of modern Chinese literary authors. All the Chinese authors who published between 1917 and 1949 are included in this directory. There are three parts to this volume. Part one contains a list of personal names with indexes to their pseudonyms, pen names, chih 字 and hao 號. Part two is an index of pseudonyms. Part three comprises an index in Hanyu Pinyin of personal names. For reference on modern Chinese literary authors and their works.

81. Hsü, Shen 許慎, d. 120? (Han 漢 dynasty). Annotated by Tuan, Yü-ts'ai 段玉裁. <u>Shuo wen chieh tzu</u> 說文解字. 15 chüan. 4 vols., double leaves in case. Shang-hai: Shang wu yin shu kuan, 1914.

The earlist Chinese dictionary on etymology. There are 9,431 different characters and 1,279 variant forms in this dictionary arranged under 540 radicals. For each character, a brief description of its structure and meaning is given and references quoted from other sources are included. For ready reference and scholarly use.

82. <u>Hsü shih ta tsung p'u</u> 徐氏大宗譜. T'ai-pei: Hsü shih ta tsung p'u pien ying kuan, 1984.

A comprehensive genealogical history of the Hsü family. It

traces the family's origins from the Hsia 夏 dynasty during the reign of the Great Yü (Ta Yü 大禹) and describes the prominent figures in Chinese history from the Shang 商 to the Ch'ing 清 dynasties. The book also contains the modern generations of the Republican era as well as listing their descendants now living in Taiwan.

83. <u>Hsü shih tsung ch'in hui hui k'an</u> 許氏宗親會會刊. T'ai-pei: Hsü shih tsung ch'in hui, 1982-

A magazine of the Genealogical Society of the Hsü family. Each volume includes the family's genealogy, branches, descendants, activites, and reports of the meetings of the Society.

84. Hsü, Wei-min 徐爲民. <u>Chung-kuo chin hsien tai jen wu pieh ming tz'u tien</u> 中國近現代人物別名辭典. Shen-yang: Shen-yang ch'u pan she, 1993.

A comprehensive dictionary of Chinese names. The volume covers all notable contemporary Chinese who were born from 1840 to the present. An index of more than 40,000 assumed names, including nicknames, pen names, house names, religious names, and other forms of names as well as a collection of 14,000 names of the persons who adopted those names, are covered in this dictionary. For reference use.

85. Hsüeh, Yüan 學元. <u>Pai hsing tsu tsung t'u tien</u> 百姓祖宗圖典. Shen-chün, China: Hai tien chu pan she, 1993.

A graphical dictionary of surnames from <u>Pai chia hsing</u> 百家姓. The book contains the derivation of surnames, pictures of historical persons with that name, an index of surnames according to the name order in <u>Pai chia hsing</u> 百家姓 and a stroke number index. For general readers and ready references.

86. <u>Hsün-hai Shih shih ta tsung p'u</u> 潯海施氏大宗譜. T'ai-pei: Lung wen ch'u pan she, 1993.

Shih Lang 施琅 was a minister in the navy of the Fu-chien 福建 province in the Ch'ing 清 dynasty. This book traces the genealogical origins of his family and includes a complete list of his descendants.

87. <u>Hu shih ta tsu p'u</u> 胡氏大族譜. T'ai-pei: Hu shih tsu p'u pien chi wei yüan hui, 1976.

Traces the genealogical origins of the Hu family and its development to the present time and lists the descendants of the family now settled in Taiwan.

88. Hu shih tsu p'u 胡氏族譜. [T'ai-wan: s.n., 1982].

This book is a genealogical register of the Hu family. It includes genealogical charts of the family from the first to the twenty-first generation and a description of the family ancestors including their personal names and birth and death dates.

89. Huan ch'iu Kuo shih tsung p'u 環球郭氏宗譜. T'ai-pei: Kuo shih tsung ch'in hui, 1981.

This volume contains four chapters. Chapter one describes the prominent historical figures of the family. Chapter two traces the genealogical origins of the family. Chapter three details the family genealogical registers as documented in Chinese history. Chapter four includes a description of various branches of the Kuo family settled in Fu-chien 福建, Kuang-tung 廣東 and Taiwan provinces.

90. Huang, I-te 黃譯德. Hsing ming hsüeh hsin chieh 姓名學新解. T'ai-nan shih: Hsi pei ch'u pan she, 1985.

An analysis of Chinese names explaining the significance of the number of strokes, meaning, sound, and shapes of the characters used for naming. This book is a typical guide to fortunetelling by names. For general use.

91. Huang shih ta tsu p'u 黃氏大族譜. T'ai-pei: Huang shih tsung ch'in hsiu p'u wei yüan hui, [1982].

A revised and updated edition published in 1977. Except for materials originally covered in the previous edition, this book provides the most recent membership list of the Genealogical Society of the Huang family living in Taiwan.

92. Huang shih ta tsung p'u 黃氏大宗譜. T'ai-pei: Huang shih tsung ch'in hui, 1977.

Traces the Huang family from Chiang-hsia 江夏 in Hu-nan 湖南 province. The volume includes a list of its descendants now settled in Taiwan.

93. Hung shih tsung p'u 洪氏宗譜. Hang-chou, Che-chiang:

Che-chiang jen min ch'u pan she, 1982.

Traces from the first to the twenty-first generation of the Hung family. Each entry includes a brief description of the descendant's name and his birth and death dates.

94. I, Ni 伊妮. Ch'ien ch'iu kuo chia meng: Kuang-chou Kao-ti chieh Hsü shih chia tsu 千秋國家夢: 廣州高第街許氏家族. 2 vols. Kuang-tung : Kuang-tung jen ming ch'u pan she, 1994.

Arranged chronologically, the book identifies and describes the contributions of the Hsü family descendants to the Chinese history. For general use.

95. I, Pen-lang 易本琅, d. 1863 or 1864? (Ch'ing 清 dynasty). Hsing hsi kan wu: fu cha chi 姓觿刊誤: 附劄記. Pei-ching: Chung-hua shu chü, 1985.

Supplement of printing corrections for the book entitled: Hsing hsi: fu lu, cha chi. 姓觿: 附錄, 劄記 written by Ch'en, Shih-yüan 陳士元. The work is a comprehensive three volume set for researching the genealogy of Chinese surnames.

96. I-lan Chang shih tsu p'u 宜蘭張氏族譜. 3 vols. [T'ai-wan: s.n., 1980].

Records the history of the Chang family that originated in I-lan, Taiwan. The set covers several subject areas, including the origin and genealogical lineage of the Chang family, biographies, lists of descendants who have made significant contributions to Chinese society, clan policy and rules of order, honors awarded to family members, and a documentary history of collections relating to or written by Chang family members.

97. Ju-nan Chou shih ta tsu p'u 汝南周氏大族譜. Hsin-chu, T'ai-wan: Chou shih tsung ch'in hui, 1981.

Includes the clan history and genealogy of the Chou family living in Taiwan.

98. Ju-nan t'ang Lan shih tsu p'u 汝南堂藍氏族譜. T'ai-pei: Lan shih tsung ch'in hui, 1984.

Traces the origin of the Lan family and lists the members of its family who belong to the Lan shih Genealogical

Society.

99. <u>Jui-an Yao shih chia ch'eng</u> 瑞安姚氏家乘. T'ai-pei: Chüeh shih chai, 1964.

A clan history of the Yao family living in Jui-an, Taiwan.

100. K'ang-hsi 康熙, Emperor of China, 1654-1722. <u>Ch'ing pen pai chia hsing</u> 清本百家姓. Hsiang-kang: Chung shan t'u shu kung so, 1974.

The <u>Pai chia hsing</u> in the Ch'ing dynasty version. The book contains a selected list of 480 surnames most commonly used in the Ch'ing dynasty. For general use.

101. Kao, Chih-ping 高志彬. <u>Long-yü Chang shih tsu p'u</u> 龍嶼張氏族譜. 8 vols. T'ai-pei: Lung wen ch'u pan she, [19--].

A genealogical history of the Chang family living in Lung-yü, Taiwan. The family moved from Fu-chien 福建, China at the end of the Yüan 元 dynasty to Taiwan.

102. Kao, Wen-te 高文德 and Ts'ai Chih-ch'un 蔡志純. <u>Meng-ku shih hsi</u> 蒙古世系. Pei-ching: Chung-kuo she hui k'e hsüeh ch'u pan she, 1979.

This volume comprises three major parts: 1. a list of 48 genealogical charts which starts with Genghis Khan 成吉思漢 and ends in the Ch'ing 清 dynasty, coverning a period of 1,200 years; 2. endnotes of important historical figures and events as well as a supplement of genealogical significance to part one, and 3. a name index.

103. Kao, Yu 高誘. (Eastern Han 東漢). <u>Chan kuo ts'e</u> 戰國策. 6 vols. Hu-pei: Ch'ung wen shu chü, 1912.

History of the Warring States Period. The book covers the years 403-221 B.C.

104. <u>K'o shih tsu p'u</u> 柯氏族譜. T'ai-chung: K'o shih tsu p'u pien chi wei yüan hui, 1981.

Traces the origins of the K'o family and includes the names of the descendants who came from Hui-an hsien 惠安縣 in Fu-chien 福建 province.

105. Ku shih tsung p'u 古氏宗譜. [T'ai-pei: Ku shih tsung ch'in hui, 1961].

Includes the genealogical history of the Ku family and lists names of the descendants living in Taiwan.

106. K'ung, An-kuo 孔安國. (Han 漢 dynasty). Shu ching 書經. T'ai-pei: National Central Library, 1973.

Commomly called Shang shu 尚書, the work is one of the thirteen Confucian Classics with philosophical documents for teachings on the moral and political life in the Han period.

107. K'ung fu tang an hsüan pien 孔府檔案選編. Pei-ching: Chung hua shu chü, 1982.

This book compiles the documents preserved in the K'ung family's archives of the Society for the Cultural Preservation of Chü-fu, Shan-tung province (Shan-tung Chü-fu wen wu kuan li wei yüan hui 山東曲阜文物管理委員會). The archival materials have been preserved for more than three hundred years. It reflects the family's development in politics, economics, culture, and history.

108. Kung-yang, Kao 公羊高. Kung-yang chuan 公羊傳. 28 chüan. 4 vols. on double leaves. [s.l.]: Hu-pei kuan shu chü, [1886].

One of the three representative works in The Spring and Autumn Annals (Ch'un ch'iu 春秋). It was the court chronicle of the State of Lu 魯 and recorded historical events of the years 722-480 B.C. The volume contains three commentaries and one of them is the Commentary of Kung-yang (Kung-yang chuan 公羊傳). For scholarly use.

109. Kuo hsüeh wen hsien kuan hsien ts'ang Chung-kuo tsu p'u hsü lieh hsüan k'an 國學文獻館現藏中國族譜序列選刊. T'ai-pei: Kuo hsüeh wen hsien kuan, 1983.

The work is made up of the genealogical series that traces the following surnames: Ch'en 陳, Lin 林, Huang 黃, Wang 王, Chang 張, Li 李, Wu 吳, Liu 劉, Ts'ai 蔡, and Yang 楊. These commonly used names comprise over half of the population in Taiwan. For general use.

110. Kuo shih tsu p'u 郭氏族譜. Kee-lung, T'ai-wan: Kuo shih tsu

p'u pein chi wei yüan hui, 1966.

Traces the genealogical roots of the Kuo family and includes the names of the descendants living in Taiwan.

111.    Lai, Chih-chang 賴志彰. T'ai-wan Wu-feng Lin chia liu chen chi, 1897-1947 臺灣霧峰林家留真集. T'ai-pei: Tzu li pao hsi wen hua ch'u pan she, 1989.

Two albums of photographs to complement the genealogical history book written by Johanna Menzel Meskill entitled A Chinese pioneer family: the Lins of Wu-feng, Taiwan, 1729-1895. The first album contains 155 pictures showing the political, economic, educational, and public activities of the Lins who played prominent roles in the modern history of Taiwan. The second album consists of 351 photographs showing the Lins' home and social life during the first decade of this century.

112.    Lai shih ta tsung p'u 賴氏大宗譜. Chia-i, T'ai-wan: Lai shih tsung ch'in hui, 1982.

Traces the genealogical origins of the Lai family and includes the names of the descendants living in Taiwan.

113.    Le, Shih 樂史. (Sung 宋 dynasty). T'ai p'ing huan yü chi 太平寰宇記. 200 chüan. [China]: Chin ling shu chü, 1882.

114.    Li, Hun-ju 李鴻儒. Li shih li tai jen wu chih 李氏歷代人物誌. T'ai-pei: Wei hsing shu chü, 1990.

Traces the genealogical ancestry of the Li familiy.

115.    Li, Lin 李林. Man tsu chia p'u hsüan pien 滿族家譜選編. Liao-ning: Liao-ning ming tsu ch'u pan she, 1988.

Contains the genealogical history of Manchu clans. The book covers the commonly used single surnames such as Chang 張, Kao 高, Pai 白, Na 那, Kuan 關, Wang 王, Chao 趙 and Wu 吳 as well as a large number of compound surnames.

116.    Li, Shuang-kuei 李雙桂. Li shih tsu p'u 李氏族譜. Hsin-chu, T'ai-wan: [s.n.], 1972.

Traces the origins of the Li family and lists the names of its descendants living in Taiwan.

117. <u>Li tai jen wu pieh shu chü ch'u ming tung chien</u> 歷代人物別署居處名通檢. T'ai-pei: Shih chieh shu chü, 1962.

Index to house names (shih ming 室名) of the prominant figures in Chinese history. The book focuses mainly on people from the Sung 宋, Yüan 元, Ming 明 and Ch'ing 淸 dynasties. For reference use.

118. <u>Li tai t'ung hsing ming lu yin te</u> 歷代同姓名錄引得. T'ai-pei: Ch'eng wen Publishing Co. ; Distributed by Chinese Materials and Research Aids Services Center, 1966. (Photocopy of: Peiping: Harvard-Yenching Institute, 1931.)

An index to <u>Li t'ai t'ung hsing ming lu</u> 歷代同姓名錄. The book was written by Liu Chang-hua 劉昌華 and completed in 1871. It is in twenty-two chapters (chüan 卷) with a one chapter supplement. The book is considered to be one of the most comprehensive works in the field of Chinese surname research. For scholarly use.

119. Li, Yen-shou 李延壽, ca. 600-680. (T'ang 唐 dynasty). <u>Pei shih</u> 北史. 100 chüan. 10 vols. Pei-ching: Chung-hua shu chü, 1974.

The history of the Northern dynasties. This ten volume set contains one hundred chapters (chüan 卷) and covers biographical histories of the prominent historical figures for the years 368-618 A.D.

120. Liao, Fu-pen 廖福本. <u>T'ai-wan pai hsing yüan liu</u> 臺灣百姓源流. T'ai-pei: Tso wen ch'u pan she, 1990.

Traces the origins of the most commonly used one hundred Chinese surnames in Taiwan.

121. <u>Liao shih ta tsung p'u</u> 廖氏大宗譜. Yün-lin, T'ai-wan: Liao shih tsung ch'in hui, 1981.

Traces the genealogical history of the Liao family and lists the names of its descendants living in Taiwan.

122. Liao, Yüng-hsien 廖用賢. (Ming 明 dynasty). <u>Shang yu lu: erh shih erh chüan</u> 尚友錄: 二十二卷. [Fu-chien: s.n., 1621-1627?].

A collection of brief biographiies of important persons from the earliest times to the end of the Ming dynasty.

For ready reference use.

123. <u>Lin shih ta tsung p'u</u> 林氏大宗譜. T'ai-pei: Lin hsing tsung miao pien chi wei yüan hui, 1984.

Traces the genealogy of the Lin family and lists the names of its descendants living in Taiwan.

124. Ling, Pao 林寶. (T'ang 唐 dynasty). <u>Yüan ho hsing tsuan</u> 元何姓纂. 4 vols. T'ai-pei: Shang wu yin shu kuan, 1975.

The earliest study on the origin of Chinese surnames. The work is arranged according to the rhyme of the names and the major emphasis of the book is placed on the surnames which were most common during the T'ang 唐 dynasty. It is a study of particular importance for students and scholars of that period. For reference and sholarly use.

125. Ling, Ti-chih 凌迪知. (Ming 明 dynasty). <u>Wang hsing t'ung p'u</u> 萬姓統譜. 140 chüan. 40 vols. T'ai-pei: Hsin hsing shu chü, 1579, 1971.

A collection of brief biographies of important persons, from very early times to the Ming dynasty. Surnames are arranged by their rhyme and biographies are arranged chronologically under the surnames. It is a useful biographical material for ready reference and a valuable resource for researching the origin of Chinese surnames.

126. <u>Liu shih tsu p'u</u> 劉氏族譜. 2nd ed. T'ai-pei: Liu shih tsu p'u pien chi wei yüan hui, 1981.

Includes the genealogical history of the Liu family and lists the names of its descendants in Taiwan.

127. Lo, Chen-yü 羅振玉, 1866-1910? (Ch'ing 清 dynasty). <u>T'ang shu tsai hsiang shih hsi piao</u> 唐書宰相世系表. Pei-ching: Chung-hua shu chü, 1934.

Index to the genealogical tables of families of chief ministers in the Hsitory of the T'ang dynasty.

128. Lo, Pi 羅泌, ca. 1176. (Sung 宋 dynasty). <u>Lu shih</u> 路史. 8 vols. in 2. Shang-hai: Chung-hua shu chü, [1936?].

Traces the Chinese biographical and genealogical history from the early period to 1766 B.C.

129. <u>Lu-chiang Ho shih tsu p'u</u> 盧江何氏族譜. T'ai-pei: Ho shih tsung ch'in hui, 1982.

Includes the genealogical history of the Ho family from Lu-chiang, An-hui 安徽 province.

130. Lu, Fa-yen 陸法言. (Sui 隋 dynasty). Revised and enlarged by Ch'en, Peng-nien 陳彭年, 961-1017, et al. (Sung 宋 dynasty). <u>Kuang yün</u> 廣韻, or, <u>Ch'ieh yün</u> 切韻. 4 vols. in 1. T'ai-pei shih: T'ai-wan shang wu yin shu kuan, [1968].

Dictionary of phonology. Originally compiled in 601 A.D. by Lu Fa-yen under the title <u>Ch'ieh yün</u>, the present volume is a revised and enlarged edition under Imperial auspices in 1011 by Ch'en Peng-nein and others. It is the oldest rhyming dictionary still extant for tracing early changes in the proununciation of Chinese characters. A collection of 26,194 characters is included in this work. The volume serves as the most important source for tracing surnames with changes in phonetic sounds. For reference and scholarly use.

131. Lu, Kuei-meng 陸龜蒙, d. ca. 881. (T'ang 唐 dynasty). <u>Hsiao ming lu</u> 小名錄. Pei-ching: Chung-hua shu chü, 1985.

Dictionary of nicknames. The book covers nicknames of persons from the Ch'in 秦 dynasty to the Southern and Northern Dynasties (Nan-pei ch'ao 南北朝). For scholarly use.

132. Lü, Pu-wei 呂不韋, 290-235 B.C. (Ch'in 秦 dynasty). <u>Lü shih ch'un ch'iu</u> 呂氏春秋. 26 chüan. 4 vols. in 1. Shang-hai: Chung-hua shu chü, [1936?].

133. <u>Lu shih tsu p'u</u> 盧氏族譜. T'ai-chung: Lu shih tsu p'u pien chi wei yüan hui, 1972.

Includes the genealogical origins of the Lu family and lists the names of its descendants in Taiwan.

134. <u>Lü T'ai Chi shih tsung p'u</u> 旅台季氏宗譜. T'ai-pei: Chi shih tsung ch'in hui, 1985.

Traces the genealogical history of the Chi family living in Taiwan and includes a directory of the Chi's descendants with their photographs.

135. Lung, Chin-lung 龔錦隆. <u>Pai chia hsing ming tsu hsien</u>
百家姓名祖先. Yüng-ho, T'ai-pei: Ch'ang ch'un shu shu fang,
1983.

The ancestory of Chinese surnames. This book introduces
the origins of 144 commonly used surnames. Each surname
contains a description of its origin, records the time when
the name was used during different dynasties, and describes
the prominent figures in Chinese history who are under the
same surname. The appendix contains an interesting
collection of names with contradictory meanings, a list of
rarely used surnames, various types of names with their
most significant meanings, such as place, country,
occupation, official position, and community group, etc.,
and a collection of the most widely used compound names.
For general use.

136. Ma, Tuan-lin 馬端臨. (Yüan 元 dynasty). <u>Wen hsien t'ung k'ao</u>
文獻通考. 1,500 vols. T'ai-pei: T'ai-wan Shang wu yin shu
kuan, 1983-

General history of institutions and critical examination of
documents and studies. This comprehensive 1,500 volume set
is a reprint of the original work published in 1224. It
traces a collection of 3,736 surnames. For reference and
scholarly use.

137. <u>Man ming ch'en chuan</u> 滿明臣傳. 6 vols. T'ai-pei: Ming wen
shu chü, 1985.

A comprehensive biographical dictionary of statesmen in the
Manchu 滿州 dynasty giving their titles of honor and
nobility. For scholarly research on historical and
biographical studies in the Manchu dynasty.

138. Miao, Shih-hsin 苗士心. <u>Chung-kuo hsien tai tso chia pi ming
so yin</u> 中國現代作家筆名索引. Chi-nan, Shan-tung: Shan-tung
ta hsüeh ch'u pan che, 1986.

An index of over 9,000 pen names and pseudonyms of the
2,000 contemporary Chinese literary authors. For general
reference.

139. <u>Mo-chuang Liu shih chih ch'uang shih yü fan yen</u>
墨莊劉氏之創始與蕃衍. 2 vols. T'ai-wan: T'ai-wan sheng
Shang wu ying shu kuan, 1988.

_Liu shih Mo Chuang chi_ 劉氏墨莊記 was written by Chu Hsi 朱熹, a great scholar in the Sung 宋 dynasty. This volume was based on the documented genealogical history excerpted from the book. It traces the origins of the Liu family and lists its prominent descendants from the Sung 宋 to the Ch'ing 清 dynasty.

140.   Mu, Liu-shen 穆柳森. _Pai chia hsing tz'u tien_ 百家姓辭典. Hsiang-kang: I wen yin shu kuan, 1977.

A dictionary of clan names. Contains surnames from _Pai chia hsing_ 百家姓, the derivation of these surnames, an index in character stroke order, and a general history of Chinese names. It is a comprehensive reference tool for both upper-division students and scholars.

141.   Niu, Ju-chen 牛汝辰 and Wei Yen-yün 魏燕云. _Yüan yü ti ming ti Chung-kuo hsing shih_ 源於地名的中國姓氏. Pei-ching: T'ien tzu kung yeh ch'u pan she, 1988.

Introduces Chinese names which originated from place names. Arranged by Hanyu Pinyin, 477 names are included in this book. For general readers.

142.   Ou, Ch'ang-hsin 歐昌欣. _Hsing ming hsüeh chih kuan nien yü she chi_ 姓名學之觀念與設計. T'ai-pei: Hsi t'ai ch'u pan kung ssu, 1980.

The principles and design of name giving. The book includes the following major subjects: humorous stories associated with analogous names, name structure, the importance of naming in Chinese history, the typical classification or types of names, notes on how to choose an auspicious name, the importance of strokes associated with naming, and fortunetelling by names. For general use.

143.   Ou-yang, Hsiu 歐陽修, 1007-1072. (Sung 宋 dynasty). _T'ang shu_ 唐書, or, _Hsin T'ang shu_ 新唐書. 225 chüan. Shang-hai: Shang wu yin pen, 1937.

The new history of the T'ang dynasty. The book contains 225 chapters (chüan 卷) and covers biographical history of the prominent historical figures for the years 618-906.

144.   _Pa ch'i Man-chou shih tsu t'ung p'u_ 八旗滿州氏族通譜. Liao-ning: Liao shen shu she, 1989.

Compiled in the Ch'ing 清 dynasty, this book contains
multilineage genealogies of the Manchu clans of the Eight
Banners (pa ch'i 八旗). The volume covers 1,114 surnames
from A.D. 1735 (during the reign of Emperor Yüng-cheng
雍正) to 1744 (during the reign of Emperor Ch'ien-lung
乾隆). It traces military Manchu clans that belong to the
Eight Banners but excludes members of the loyal family,
Ai-hsin Chüeh-lo 愛新覺羅.

145. Pan, Ku 班固, A.D. 32-92. (Eastern Han 東漢). Han shu 漢書,
or, Ch'ien Han shu 前漢書. 100 chüan 卷. 3 vols. T'ai-pei:
Ch'i ming shu chü, [1961].

The history of the Former Han dynasty. The book contains
one hundred chapters (chüan 卷) and covers biographical
history of the prominent historical figures between the
years 209 B.C. and A.D. 25.

146. Pan, Ying 潘英. T'ai-wan jen ti chu chi yü hsing shih fen pu
臺灣人的祖籍與姓氏分佈. T'ai-pei: T'ai yüan ch'u pan she,
1991.

Analysis of the origins of the Taiwanese people and the
distribution of surnames in Taiwan. This book contains two
parts. The first part introduces the most popular and the
least popular names used in Taiwan and the second part
includes the origin and distribution of the most popularly
used names in Taiwanese cities and counties. For research
in genealogical history and statistical analysis of
surnames in Taiwan as well as study of Chinese local
history and anthropology.

147. P'eng-ch'eng Liu shih ta tsu p'u 彭城劉氏大族譜. [s.l.]:
T'ai-wan sheng ko hsing li shih yüan yüan fa chan yen chiu
hsüeh hui, 1983.

Traces the origins of the Liu family and includes a list of
its descendants in Taiwan.

148. P'eng, Kuei-fang 彭桂芳. T'ai-wan hsing shih chih yen chiu
臺灣姓氏之研究. Hsin-chu, T'ai-wan: T'ai-wan sheng li
Hsin-chu she hui chiao yü kuan, 1981.

Research analysis on Taiwanese surnames. The book covers
the most commonly used surnames in Taiwan. Each entry
gives the origin and historical background of the name, and

the census population and distribution of the name in Taiwan. For general reference.

149. P'eng, Kuei-fang 彭桂芳. <u>T'ai-wan pai chia hsing kao</u> 臺灣百家姓考. T'ai-pei: Li ming wen hua shih yeh kung ssu, 1988.

Analysis of the most commonly used one hundred Chinese surnames in Taiwan. For general use.

150. P'eng, Ta-i 彭大翼, fl. 1573-1565. (Ming 明 dynasty). <u>Shan t'ang ssu k'ao</u> 山堂肆考. 64 vols. [China] : Chang Yü-hsüeh pu hsiu, [1595, 1619].

An encyclopedia on Chinese names. For reference and scholarly use.

151. <u>P'ing-hsiang Ch'i-pao Chung shih tsu p'u hsi chien p'u</u> 萍鄉七保鍾氏族譜系簡譜. T'ai-pei: Lung-hung yin shua ch'ang, 1976.

According to the research findings in this book, the descendants of the Chung family living in Taiwan came primarily from Chiang-hsi 江西, Fu-chien 福建 and Kuang-tung 廣東 provinces. This volume covers the genealogy of the Chung family from P'ing-hsiang hsien 萍鄉縣, Nan-hsi hsiang 南溪鄉, Ch'i-pao village 七保村 in Chiang-hsi 江西 province.

152. <u>Po-ku Yüng-k'eng Huang shih tsu p'u</u> 檗谷永坑黃氏族譜. T'ai-chung: Hsin yüan tung ch'u pan che, 1976.

Traces the origins, branches, and descendants of the Huang family in Taiwan and includes genealogical charts of the Huang family tree.

153. Shao, Ssu 邵思. (Sung 宋 dynasty). <u>Hsing chieh</u> 姓解. Pei-ching: Chung-hua shu chü, 1985.

An explanation of surnames. This book of surnames covers the history and origin of surnames and includes historical persons who adopted these surnames. For general use.

154. Shen, Ch'i-hsin 沈其新. <u>Chung-hua hsing shih t'ung shu: Chao hsing</u> 中華姓氏通書: 趙姓. Hu-nan: Shan huan ch'u pan she, 1991.

Traces the genealogical history of the Chao family. Chao is the first surname listed in the book, <u>Pai chia hsing</u> 百家姓. For general use.

155. Sheng, Ch'ing-i 盛清沂. <u>Chung-kuo tsu p'u pien tsuan chien shuo</u> 中國族譜編纂簡說. T'ai-pei: Lien ho pao, 1987.

Introductory explanation of how to compile your own genealogy. For general use.

156. <u>Shih chieh Li shih tsung ch'in lien ho tsung hui hui k'an</u> 世界李氏宗親聯合總會會刊. 4 vols. T'ai-pei shih : Ssu chieh Li shih tsung ch'in tsung hui, [1972-1975].

A directory of the descendants of the Li family who belong to the World-wide Li Family Joint Clansmen General Association.

157. <u>Shih chieh Ou-yang, Ou, Ou, Yang shih tsung p'u</u> 世界歐陽, 歐, 區, 陽氏宗譜. T'ai-pei: Shih chieh Ou-yang, Ou, Ou, Yan shih tsung p'u tsuan hsiu wei yüan hui, 1983.

Ou-yang, Ou, Ou, and Yang are four names of the same genealogical origin. This book includes the description of the names origins as well as chronological lists of the genealogical significance of its descendants from ancient times to the contemporary era.

158. Shih, Kuo-ch'iang 史國強. <u>Chung-kuo hsing shih ch'i yüan</u> 中國姓氏起源. Shang-tung: Shang-tung ta hsüeh ch'u pan she, 1990.

The origins of Chinese names. Four-hundred and forty-nine Chinese surnames are introduced in this volume. An index of the names in character stroke order is provided for easy reference to these names. For general readers.

159. <u>Shih-shan Feng-p'o Liang shih tsung p'u</u> 詩山鳳坡梁氏宗譜. 7 vols. T'ai-pei: Lung wen ch'u pan she, 1993.

Shih-shan Feng-p'o is located in the south of Fu-chien 福建 province. This branch of the Liang family immigrated to Fu-chien at the end of the Yüan 元 dynasty. The book contains the genealogical history of the family as well as charts of its descendants.

160. Shu, Austin C. W. <u>Modern Chinese authors: a list of</u>

pseudonyms. 2nd rev. and enl. ed.  East Lansing, MI: Asian Studies Center, Michigan State University, 1969.

Indexes of Chinese pseudonyms and personal names of modern authors. For general reference.

161.   Shu, Hsin-ch'eng 舒新城. Tz'u hai 辭海. 3 vols.  Shang-hai: Chung-hua shu chü, 1937,1948.

One of the earliest Chinese dictionary of phrases.  The characters are arranged according to their radicals and sub-arranged by the character strokes.  Varied meaning of phrases are explained and these are often illustrated by quotations.  Besides ordinary phrases, the work also includes the titles of books, modern technical terms, and Chinese and foreign personal and place names.  It is a valuable source for searching the meaning of names and their origins.  For general, scholarly and ready references.

162.   Shun i Yao shih p'ai shih yüan liu k'ao 舜裔姚氏百世源流考. T'ai-pei: Yao shih tsung ch'in hui, 1981.

Traces the genealogical history of the Yao family from its founder, the Emperor Shun 舜 to its one-hundredth generation.

163.   Ssu-ma, Ch'ang-an 司馬長安. Chung-kuo hsing ming hsüeh 中國姓名學. Hsiang-kang: Li wen ch'u pan she, 1985.

The study of Chinese family pedigrees.  The book explains the factors which affect the choice of Chinese personal names and shows how the decision should be made in order to pick the best possible name for yourself and your children. The various factors which affect the choice of a name include: Chinese yin 陰 (female) and yang 陽 (male), wu hsing 五行 (five forces), shih-erh sheng hsiao 中Q二生肖 (the twelve animal symbols), and character stroke order. These name choices, being associated with their meanings of good luck or of evil spirits, play important roles in the Chinese naming tradition. For general use.

164.   Ssu-ma, Chen 司馬貞. (T'ang 唐 dynasty). Shih chi so yin 史記索引. 30 chüan.  Reprint. 1,500 vols.  T'ai-pei: Kuo li ku kung po wu yüan, [19--].

Index to Shih chi 史記. For reference and scholarly use.

165. Ssu-ma, Ch'ien 司馬遷, ca. 145-86 B.C. (Han 漢 dynasty).
<u>Shih chi</u> 史記. 20 vols. T'ai-pei shih: T'ai-wan shang wu
yin shu kuan, [1965].

The records of the grand historian. It is a work of the
history of China from the earliest times to the Han
dynasty. The volume contains two main categories, the
monographs (shu 書 or chih 志) and the collected
biographies (lieh chuan 列傳), which are biographical
profiles of both famous and less famous people of each age.
For reference and scholarly use.

166. Sung, Chung 宋衷, annotator. (Han 漢 dynasty). <u>Shih pen</u>
世本. Pei-ching: Chung-hua shu chü, 1985.

History of China from the earliest times to 221 B.C. The
book traces the genealogy of Chinese nobility including
ancient Chinese kings and rulers. For general and
scholarly use.

167. <u>T'ai-wan Hsü shih tsung p'u</u> 臺灣許氏宗譜. [T'ai-wan]: Hsü
shih tsung ch'in hui, 1977.

Genealogical registor of the descendants of the Hsü family
who settled in Taiwan from the twelfth to the twentieth
generations.

168. Tai, Ying-hsin 戴應新. <u>Che shih chia tsu shih lüeh</u>
折氏家族史略. Hsi-an, Shen-hsi: Shan ch'in ch'u pan she,
1989.

Traces the genealogy of the Che family. The book includes
a directory of the family descendants and contains the
historical findings of genealogical documents and
tombstones in China.

169. T'ao, Tsung-i 陶宗儀. (Yüan 元 dynasty). <u>Shuo fu: 100 chüan;</u>
<u>Shu fu hsü: 46 chüan</u> 說郛: 一百卷; 說郛序: 四十六卷. 170
vols. [s.l.]: Wan wei shan t'ang, [1646].

170. Telford, Ted A., Melvin P. Thatcher, and Basil P. N. Yang,
comp. <u>Chinese genealogies at the Genealogical Society of</u>
<u>Utah: an annotated bibliography.</u> T'ai-pei: Cheng Wen
Publishing Co., 1983.

An annotated bibliography of Chinese clan and lineage

genealogies and other genealogical works from the post-T'ang and Republican eras. Over 4,300 genealogical titles are now located in the Chinese collection of the Genealogical Society of Utah. It is a unique resource center in United States for genealogical research on Chinese family names and history.

171.    Teng, Hsien-ching 鄧獻鯨. <u>Chung-kuo hsing shih chi</u> 中國姓氏集. T'ai-pei shih: Chih ta t'u shu wen chü chiao yü yüng p'in ku fen yu hsien kung ssu, 1971.

A dictionary of Chinese names. The book contains a collection of 5,662 names which includes 3,484 single, 2,032 double, and 146 triple-character surnames. For general reference.

172.    Teng, Hung-p'o 鄧洪波. <u>Chung-hua hsing shih t'ung shu: Chang hsing</u> 中華姓氏通書: 張姓. Hu-nan: Hai-nan ch'u pan she, 1993.

The surname Chang is one of the most popular surnames in both China and Taiwan. According to <u>The distribution of family names in Taiwan</u>, over 7.1 percent of the population in Taiwan and more than 10 percent of the people in China today adopted the surname Chang.

173.    Teng, Ming-shih 鄧明世, fl. 1133. (Sung 宋 dynasty). <u>Ku chin hsing shih shu pien cheng</u> 古今姓氏書辯證. Pei-ching: Chung-hua shu chü, [1134, 1985?].

The study of the origin of surnames. The name entries are arranged according to their rhyme. Besides the historical and explanatory materials quoted under each surname, there are critical notes written by the compiler. Comprehensive. For general reference and scholarly use.

174.    Teng, Ming-shih 鄧明世, fl. 1133. (Sung 宋 dynasty). <u>Ku chin hsing shih shu pien cheng: fu chiao kan chi</u> 古今姓氏書辯證: 附校勘記. 8 vols. Pei-ching: Chung-hua shu chü, 1985.

This work includes both the main volume of <u>Ku chin hsing shih shu pien cheng</u> and its supplement for the study of the origin of Chinese names. It is of particular use for students interested in Chinese customs, the feudal system, and the introduction of different foreign names into China during periods of alien domination. For general and scholarly use.

175. Ting, Ch'ien 丁謙, 1843-1919. (Ch'ing 淸 dynasty). <u>Han shu Hsiung-nu chuan</u> 漢書匈奴傳. 2 vols. China: Che-chiang Library, [19--?].

The biographies of Hsiung-nu recorded in <u>Han shu.</u>

176. Tso-ch'iu, Ming 左丘明. (Chou 周 dynasty). <u>Tso chuan</u> 左傳. 12 chüan. [s.l.: s.n.. 1582?].

One of the three representative works in <u>The Spring and Autumn Annals</u> (Ch'un ch'iu 春秋). It was the court chronicle of the State of Lu 魯 and recorded historical events of the years 722-480 B.C. The volume contains three commentaries and one of them is the <u>Commentary of Tso</u> (Tso chuan 左傳). For scholarly use.

177. Tso-ch'iu, Ming 左丘明. (Chou 周 dynasty). <u>Kuo yü</u> 國語. 6 vols. in 1. Shang-hai: Chung-hua shu chü, [1936?].

The study of history and its people during the Spring and Authumn (Ch'un ch'iu 春秋) period, 722-481 B.C. Biographical profiles of people in that period are traced in this volume. For reference and scholarly use.

178. Wang, Ch'i 王圻, chin shih 1565. (Ming 明 dynasty). <u>Hsü Wen hsien t'ung k'ao</u> 續文獻通考. 64 vols. [s.l.: s.n., 1603?].

Supplement to <u>General history of institutions and critical examination of documents and studies</u> (Wen hsien t'ung k'ao 文獻通考). The volume traces a collection 4,657 surnames. For general and scholarly use.

179. Wang, Chia 王嘉, 4th cent. (Chin 晉 dynasty). <u>Shih i chi</u> 拾遺記. Pei-ching: Chung-hua shu chü, 1981.

180. Wang, Chien 王儉. (Nan Ch'i 南齊). <u>Hsing p'u: 216 chüan</u> 姓譜: 二一六卷. [s.l.: s.n., 19--?].

Genealogy of Chinese surnames. For reference and scholarly use.

181. Wang, Chien-hua 王建華. <u>Wen hua ti ching hsiang: jen ming</u> 文化的鏡象: 人名. Ch'ang-ch'un: Chi-lin chiao yü ch'u pan she , 1990.

The reflection of Chinese culture on names. The volume discusses the historical development of names and the status and importance of names in Chinese culture, religion, and society.

182. Wang, Ch'üan-ken 王泉根. <u>Hua-hsia ch'ü ming i shu</u> 華夏取名藝術. T'ai-pei: Yün lung ch'u pan she, 1993.

The art of giving a Chinese name. There are three parts in this book: 1. the psychological, cultural, and philosophical representation of Chinese names; 2. analysis from ancient times to the present of the Chinese naming patterns and their relationship to the surrounding cultural environment and to contemporary society; and 3. introduction to the various types of Chinese names including chih 字, hao 號, house name, pen name, flower name, religious name, posthumous name, and other pseudonyms.

183. Wang, Ch'üan-ken 王泉根. <u>Hua-hsia hsing ming mien mien kuan</u> 華夏姓名面面觀. Nan-ning, Kuang-hsi: Kuang-hsi jen min ch'u pan she, 1988.

Various views on Chinese names. This book includes the following chapters: 1. details the historical background of Chinese names including the explanation of hsing 姓 and shih 氏; 2. points out several factors which affect the choice of a Chinese name, such as: the naming pattern of ancient people, place, local custom, nickname, generation name, and the mythology; 3. discusses assumed names, chih 字, hao 號, and others; 4. analyzes names of nobility, year name, or nien hao 年號 of a dead emperor; 5. discusses names of minorities, religious names, and names affected by local culture; and 6. compares the naming pattern of eastern versus western names, names associated with poems, riddles, places, and luck. The list of names from the book <u>Pai chia hsing</u> 百家姓 in Hanyü Pinyin and English pronunciation is included in the Appendix. For both general and scholarly use.

184. Wang, Ch'üan-ken 王泉根. <u>Hua-hsia hsing shih chih mi</u> 華夏姓氏之謎. T'ai-pei: Chih shu fang ch'u pan she, 1992.

Traces the mystery of Chinese surnames from ancient times to the contemporary era. There are seven chapters in this book: 1. from totem to Chinese names; 2. the ancestral system in the Western Chou 西周 dynasty and the difference between two types of early Chinese names, hsing 姓 and shih 氏; 3. the nobel system in the Wei 魏 and Chin 晋 dynasties and the use of social names during that period; 4. the combination of names used by the minorities in China; 5. changing society as reflected in the change in surnames; 6. tracing your family roots and ancestors; and 7. the Chinese cultural tradition and genealogical studies. For general use.

185. Wang, Fang-pang 王方邦. <u>Hsing shih tz'u tien</u> 姓氏辭典. Ho-nan sheng: Ho-nan jen ming ch'u pan che, 1991.

A dictionary of Chinese surnames arranged by Hanyu Pinyin. For general reference.

186. Wang, Fu 王符. (Eastern Han 東漢). <u>Ch'ien fu lun</u> 潛夫論. 3 vols. Shang-hai: Ku chi ch'u pan she, 1978.

A study of ancient Chinese history and biography from the earliest times to the Han 漢 dynasty. For scholarly use.

187. Wang, Hui-tsu 汪輝祖, 1731-1807. (Ch'ing 清 dynasty). <u>San shih t'ung ming lu</u> 三史同名錄. 4 vols. Pei-ching: Chung-hua shu chü, 1985.

An index to the biographies in the <u>Liao shih</u> 遼史, <u>Chin shih</u> 金史 and <u>Yüan shih</u> 元史 of all non-Chinese whose surnames were the same for two or more persons. The names in this work are arranged by the rhyme of the first character of the name commonly recorded. For reference and scholarly use.

188. Wang, Kuei 王貴. <u>Tsang tsu jen ming yen chiu</u> 藏族人民研究. Pei-ching: Min tsu ch'u pan she, 1991.

An analysis of Tibetan names. The book traces the origins of Tibetan names and provides a list of 543 Chinese names adopted by the Tibetan people with transliterations in Chinese characters and in Hanyu Pinyin. For reference use.

189. <u>Wang shih k'ai tsung pai shih lu</u> 王氏開宗百世錄. Singapore: Singapore Hokkien Ong Clansmen General Association, 1971.

Traces the genealogical origins of the Wang family and lists the names of its descendants in Singapore.

190. Wang, Su-ts'un 王素存. <u>Chung-hua hsing fu</u> 中華姓府. T'ai-

pei: Chung-hua ch'ung shu pien shen wei yüan hui, 1969.

A dictionary of Chinese surnames. This book contains a collection of 7,720 surnames and each surname comprises a detailed description of its history and origin.

191. Wang, Te-i 王德毅. Ch'ing jen pieh ming tzu hao so yin: fu i ming piao 清人別名字號索引: 附異名表. T'ai-pei: Hsin wen feng ch'u pan kung ssu, 1985.

An index of anonyms and pseudonyms of Chinese names from the Ch'ing dynasty. Based on biographies published in the Ch'ing period, the author consulted more than thirty-three historical documents and books, plus numerous clan histories and other genealogical resources. The book is arranged by character stroke order with a personal name index arranged by Wade-Giles romanization for easy access. An excellent resource for scholars doing extensive research on biographies in the Ch'ing dynasty.

192. Wang, Ying-lin 王應麟, 1223-1296. (Sung 宋 dynasty). Hsing shih chi chiu p'ien: 2 chüan 姓氏急就篇: 二卷. [s.l.: s.n., 19--?].

A study on the origin of surnames from the earliest times to the Sung dynasty. For general and scholarly use.

193. Wei, Shou 魏收, 506-572. (Pei Ch'i 北齊). Wei shu 魏書. 114 chüan. Pei-ching: Chung-hua shu chü, 1739, 1974.

The history of the Wei dynasty. The volume covers biographical history of the prominent historical figures for the years 386-550 A.D.

194. Wu, K'un-lun 吳昆倫 and Lin Yu-mu 林猷穆. T'ai-wan hsing shih yüan liu 臺灣姓氏源流. T'ai-pei: T'ai-wan sheng cheng fu hsin wen ch'u, 1971.

Traces the most frequently used sixty surnames and provides a directory of genealogical societies in Taiwan. For general use.

195. Wu shih tsung ch'in hui chi nien t'e chi 武氏宗親會紀念特輯. T'ai-pei: Wu shih tsung ch'in hui, 1973.

Traces the history and genealogy of the Wu family and includes a list of the descendants in Taiwan.

196. Yang, Hsü-hsien 楊緒賢. <u>T'ai-wan ch'ü hsing shih t'ang hao k'ao</u> 臺灣區姓氏堂號考. T'ai-pei: T'ai-wan hsin sheng pao she, 1980.

A survey of surnames and genealogical societites in Taiwan. According to the author, the recorded number of 1,694 surnames are currently used in Taiwan. This book traces the early Taiwanese immigrants from China, analyzes the distribution of Taiwanese surnames, and describes the historical background of the most frequently used one hundred surnames. A directory of genealogical societies in Taiwan is provided in the appendix. For general use.

197. Yang, Shih-ch'i 楊士奇, 1365-1444. (Ming 明 dynasty). <u>Tung li wen chi</u> 東里文集. 20 vols. T'ai-pei: Shang wu yin shu kuan, 1977.

198. <u>Yang shih p'u hui</u> 楊氏譜匯. T'ai-chung: T'ai-wan sheng ko hsing li shih yüan yüan fa chan yen chiu hsüeh hui, 1984.

A genealogical history of the Yang family in Taiwan.

199. <u>Yang shih ta tsu p'u</u> 楊氏大族譜. Hsin-chu, T'ai-wan: Hsin-chu hsien Yang hsing tsung ch'in hui, 1982.

Traces the history and genealogy of the Yang family and includes the list of its descendants in Taiwan.

200. Yang, Ta-ch'u 楊達初. <u>Ch'ien chia hsing</u> 千家姓. Hon-kong: San jung hsing hao, 1923.

Genealogical history of a thousand families. For general and reference use.

201. Yang, T'ing-fu 楊廷福 and Yang T'ung-fu 楊同甫. <u>Ch'ing ien shih ming pieh ch'eng tzu hao so yin</u> 清人室名別稱字號索引. Shang-hai: Shang-hai ku chi ch'u pan she, 1988.

An index of pseudonyms in the Ch'ing dynasty. In ancient China, it was considered impolite to call out someone or addresses by name directly, especially if the person was senior to the caller in generational rank. Rather, the nickname (hao 號) would be adopted to serve the purpose. The utilization of house name (shih ming 室名) and other pseudonyms prospered in the Ming 明 dynasty and it was widely used during the Ch'ing dynasty. This index covers all the prominent figures who were famous or important in politics, economics, science, medicine, literature, and music in the Ch'ing dynasty. More than 36,000 persons and as many as 103,000 pseudonyms are covered in this volume. For upper-division students and scholars on reference and research use.

202. Yao, Ssu-lien 姚思廉, d. 637. (T'ang 唐 dynasty). <u>Liang shu</u> 梁書. 56 chüan. 3 vols. Pei-ching: Chung-hua shu chü, 1973.

The history of the Liang dynasty. The volume covers biographicial history of the prominent historical figures for years 502-556 A.D.

203. <u>Yeh shih chia p'u</u> 葉氏家譜. Chi-lung, T'ai-wan: Chen kung ch'u pan she, 1965.

A genealogical history of the Yeh family in Taiwan.

204. <u>Yeh shih tsu p'u</u> 葉氏族譜. Chang-hua, T'ai-wan: Shang kuang wen hua ch'u pan she, 1979.

A clan history and genealogy of the Yeh family living in Taiwan.

205. <u>Yen shih tsu p'u</u> 顏氏族譜. Chang-hua, T'ai-wan: Yen shih tsu p'u pein chi pu, 1981.

Traces the genealogical history of the Yen family in Taiwan.

206. Ying, Shao 應劭, fl. 189-194. (Eastern Han 東漢). <u>Feng shu t'ung hsing shih pien</u> 風俗通姓氏篇. Pei-ching: Chung-hua shu chü, 1985.

The study of the origin of surnames and its relation with Chinese social customs. Published in one volume with <u>Hsing shih k'ao lüeh</u> 姓氏考略 written by Ch'en T'ing Wei 陳廷煒, this book contains three parts: 1. an introduction to popular surnames and their origns; 2. the research on rare names; and 3. biographical descriptions of the famous and important persons in the Northern Wei 北魏 dynasty. For general use.

207. <u>Yüan ch'ao chen ming lu</u> 元朝真名錄 = <u>Repertory of proper names in Yüan literary sources</u>. 3 vols. T'ai-pei: Nan tien

ch'u pan yu hsien kung ssu, 1988.

A comprehensive index of surnames of Chinese literary authors in the Yüan dynasty. For reference and research use.

208. Yüan, Chiung 袁裒. (Sung 宋 dynasty). <u>Feng ch'uang hsiao tu</u> 楓窗小牘. Pei-ching: Chung-hua shu chü, 1985.

A historical and biographical study of the prominent historical figures from the earliest times to the Sung dynasty. For general and scholarly use.

209. Yüan, Yü-liu 袁玉騮. <u>Chung-kuo hsing ming hsüeh</u> 中國姓名學. Pei-ching: Kuang ming jih pao chu pan she, 1994.

The study of Chinese surnames. The volume traces a total of 5,000 surnames including both single and multisyllable surnames. It is divided into ten chapters and the names are arranged by Hanyu Pinyin. For general and scholarly use.

210. Yüan, Yüng-chin 袁湧進. <u>Hsien tai Chung-kuo tso chia pi ming lu</u> 現代中國作家筆名錄 = <u>A list of pseudonyms of modern Chinese authors.</u> Pei-ping: The Library Association of China, 1936.

A pseudonym index to more than 550 modern Chinese authors arranged by character stroke order of their personal names. This volume is used as a dictionary on contemporary Chinese authors. For reference use.

1. Akhtar, Nasreen. "Indexing Asian names." The Indexer: Journal of the Society of Indexers. 16.3 (April 1989): 156-158.

   Western names always start with the given name and end with the surname. In Asian countries, the components of a person's name may be chosen and put together in very different ways. This article analyzes the basic structure and usage of Asian names including Chinese, Indian, and Arabic names.

2. Anderson, C. Frederick and Henriette Liu Levy. "A guide to Chinese names." FBI Law Enforcement Bulletin. 61 (March 1992): 10-15.

   This article discusses Chinese characters and dialects, the romanization systems commonly used for transliteration of Chinese names, and the decision-making on recording Chinese proper names. A practical guide for general readers and professionals who are experiencing difficulties in identifying individuals with Chinese names.

3. Ball, J. Dyer. "Names." In Things Chinese, or Notes connected with China. Detroit, MI: Tower Books, 1971, p. 413-418.

   Introduces the different names that a Chinese has, including the milk name (ju ming 乳名), book name (shu ming 書名), hao 號, official name (kuan ming 官名), posthumous name (shih ming 謚名), flowery name (hua ming 花名), clan or hall name (tang ming 堂名), and house name (shih ming 室名), and describes the various of names that a Chinese emperor has used. For general use.

4. Basler, Barbara. "In British Hong Kong, memorable monikers." New York Times. (October 28, 1993): International section, p. 15, col. 1.

   In Hong Kong, tens of thousands of young Chinese take English names each year. The practice took root about fifteen to twenty years ago. It began as a way of identifying with the ruling class, or being identified by it. Now it has become a Chinese custom with the people used to facilitate communicating with westerners. For general use.

5. Berlitz, Charles F. "Hwang it all -- which Wong are you?" Horizon. XIV.3 (June 1972): 120.

   Describes the phonetic difference between Chinese idiographic names that sound the same but can be written differently and have different meanings. The article includes examples of how American names such as Reagan, Nixon, and Kennedy can be translated into Chinese. For general use.

6. Bin, Zhu and Celia Millward. "Personal names in Chinese." Names. 35.1 (March 1987): 8-21.

   This paper includes the analysis of surnames, generation names, given names, and the description of other names used by the Chinese people including courtesy names, assumed names, childhood names, and epithet names. The authors compare the similarities and differences between English and Chinese surnames, trace the origin of the most commonly used Chinese surnames, provide the meanings of generation names with examples, and analyze the semantic fields represented by most given names. An excellent article on the basics of Chinese personal names.

7. Bostwick, Arthur E. "Modern Chinese personal names." Library Journal. 57 (October 15, 1932): 868.

   Suggests a uniform method of writing Chinese names in order to avoid the ambiguity and mistakes made in cataloging and processing of modern Chinese personal names.

8. Chait, Ralph Milton. A chronological arrangement of the names of all the Chinese emperors and the dates of their reign together with lists of Chinese seal, character and symbolic marks. New York: [Privately printed], 1928.

   This book was compiled by a Chinese art dealer who found the necessity of obtaining the precise information concerning the date and reign of an early emperor in order to process the many voluminous works written on China and its arts. A handy reference for students and collectors of Chinese art work. For general use.

9. Chen, Cheng-chih. A librarian's handbook for use in Chinese-Japanese collections. New York, NY: Oriental Society, 1971.

With nearly 800 pages, this volume contains lists of romanized Chinese and Japanese surnames, surnames in character stroke order, and Library of Congress classification schedules applied to the vernacular collections. For American and European librarians with limited capability in the Chinese and Japanese languages.

10. Ching, Frank. <u>Ancestors: 900 years in the life of a Chinese family</u> = <u>Ch'ing shih ch'ien tse shih</u> 秦氏千載史. New York, NY: William Morrow and Company, Inc., 1988.

Describes the author's research on the Qin 秦 clan of Wuxi 無錫. He journeyed during the past fifteen years throughout China, Hong Kong, and Taiwan. There were thirty-three generations from Qin Quan, a prominent poet of the Sung 宋 dynasty, going back in time 900 years. The book is divided into twenty eight chapters, each one introducing one male member of the Qin family. Genealogical diagrams of the Qin clan and its descendants are also included. For general readers as well as scholars in Asian history, genealogy, and archaeological studies.

11. Cohen, Myron L. "Lineage organization in North China." <u>Journal of Asian Studies</u>. 49.3 (August 1990): 509-534.

The characteristics of lineage, including social structure, symbolism, and arrangement of ritual in Yangmansa, a village of about 3,500 people and 650 families located in Xincheng County, Hebei 河北 province, are analyzed in this article. Pages 515-19 reproduce the ancestral tablets and ancestral scrolls furnished by Yangmansa villagers in providing evidence of the fixed genealogical mode of kinship presented in ritual and in social representation. For scholars interested in modern anthropological research of Chinese patrilineal kinship.

12. Dillon, Michael. <u>Dictionary of Chinese history</u>. London, England: Frank Cass, 1979.

This dictionary provides an easy reference to the names and terms relating to Chinese civilization, historical events, and personalities. Entries range from pre-history to the end of 1977. They cover the classical pre-imperial period, the whole of the empire from 221 B.C. until its collapse in 1911, the Republic, and the first twenty-eight years of the People's Republic. Important personalities, dynasties and events, historical trends, social and economic history, and technology are included in this volume. For general readers, historians, genealogists, and scholars.

13. "Exploring Chinese immigration." <u>American Teacher</u>. 79.3 (November 1994): 19.

Detailing Professor Betty Lee Sung's four-year project of sifting, reviewing, indexing and computer data entry of 581 boxes of Immigration and Naturalization Service documents at the New York Regional Archives of Chinese people who came to the United States. Information includes pictures, letters and extensive family histories of early Chinese immigrants who arrived in this country between 1882 and 1946. For general readers and scholars interested in researching Chinese immigration history.

14. Gates, Mary Jean. <u>Chinese-Korean readings of selected Chinese family names from Giles Chinese-English dictionary in McCune-Reischauer romanization</u>. [s.l.: s.n., 1919].

Lists the Chinese family names in Wade-Giles romanization with their Chinese equivalents followed by the McCune-Reischauer romanization. For reference use.

15. Giles, Herbert A. <u>A Chinese biographical dictionary</u> = <u>Chung-kuo jen ming ta tzu tien</u> 中國人民大字典. Taipei: Literature House, 1964.

Contains a collection of 2,579 biographical descriptions of Chinese statesmen, generals, writers, poets, and others. For general and academic audiences who are interested in the language, literature, and politics of modern China.

16. Harrison, Scott Edward. "Chinese names in English." <u>Cataloging & Classification Quarterly</u>. 15.2 (1992): 3-14.

Discusses the basic structure of Chinese names in the context of "standard Chinese" (Mandarin) and analyzes the variant forms of the names of ethnic Chinese from Malaysia, Singapore, and Hong Kong. For librarians and publishers who do not know Chinese but need to deal with the problem of identifying the variant forms of Chinese personal names appearing in English-language publications.

17. Hays, Constance L. "Archive yields rich details of era when Chinese were barred." <u>New York Times</u>. (July 17, 1994): Metro section, p. 25.

Includes the description of Ms. Betty Lee Sung's project, involving the organization of thousands of the early Chinese immigration documents within the period 1882 to 1943, for entry into a computer database known as "Chinese Immigration Records." For general readers and scholars researching Chinese immigration history.

18. Honey, David B. "Lineage as legitimation in the rise of Liu Yüan 劉淵 and Shih Le 石勒" <u>Journal of the American Oriental Society</u>. 110 (October 1990): 616-621.

Analyzes two prominent leaders in the nomadic conquest of the Western Chin 西晉. The article examines how Liu Yüan (ca. 250-310) linked the genealogical traditions associated with his surname to both royal Han 漢 dynasty and Hsiung-nu 匈奴 lines and reviews the reasons that induced Shih Le (ca. 280-332) to adopt both his surname of "Stone" (Shih 石) and personal name of "Inscription" (Le 勒) to take advantage of contemporary prophetic lore. For scholars tracing the history of the nomadic usage of Chinese surnames.

19. Hook, J. N. "The Chinese and the Indo-Chinese." In <u>Family names: how our surnames came to America</u>. New York, N.Y.: MacMillan Publishing Co., 1982, p. 302-310.

This chapter provides a brief overview of Chinese immigration history, discusses the origins of Chinese surnames, and explains the meaning of some common and representative Chinese names as usually spelled in America. For general readers.

20. Hu, Qianli. "How to distinguish and catalog Chinese personal names." <u>Cataloging & Classification Quarterly</u>. 19.1 (1994): 29-60.

This paper provides the following details: the distinction between Chinese last and first names, the derivation of Chinese names, the introduction of singular and compound names, different forms of Chinese names, and suggestions for Anglo American Cataloging Rules, 2nd edition, on the cataloging of Chinese names. Chinese popular names are listed in pinyin and Wade-Giles romanizations. For American librarians to distinguish and catalog Chinese personal names and for scholars interested in researching and identifying Chinese names.

21. Jones, Russell. Chinese names: notes on the use of surnames & personal names by the Chinese in Malaysia and Singapore. Selangor, Malaysia: Pelanduk Publications, 1984.

This book is based on a compilation of notes collected by the author. It discusses and analyzes the variant forms and sources of Chinese surnames and personal names commonly used by the Chinese in Malaysia and Singapore. A comprehensive handbook for both general readers and specialists in Chinese names.

22. Kang, Tai S. "Name and group identification." The Journal of Social Psychology. 86 (1972): 159-160.

In a study which examined the correlation between name change and social behavior of a group of Chinese students at the University of Minnesota in 1967, it was discovered that name changers showed better socialization, economic adjustment, and social control than non-changers. For use in social and psychological studies on Chinese names and the changing patterns of these names.

23. Kang, Tai S. "Name change and acculturation." Pacific Social Review. 14 (1971): 403-412.

Studies a group of Chinese students at the University of Minnesota concerning the phenomenon of name changes. Among the students being surveyed, those who have anglicized their first names showed better socialization, economic adjustment, and social control than those who did not. For use in social and psychological reviews of Chinese names, particularly in adopting western names.

24. Kiang, K'ang Hu 江亢虎. "Chinese family system." In On Chinese studies. Shanghai: The Commercial Press, Limited, 1934, p. [415]-457.

Presents a comprehensive analysis of the Chinese family system, including its origin, evolution in matrimonial custom, large family and polygamy, paternal power and filial piety, legacy and inheritance, clan organization, constitution of clan government and its functions, the ancestral hall, clan history, and the system of personal names. Upper-division undergraduate and scholars in Asian studies.

25. Kiang, K'ang Hu 江亢虎. "Genealogy and family name origins of the Chinese." In On Chinese studies. Shanghai, China: The Commercial Press, Limited, 1934, p. [126]-144.

This article traces the development of Chinese surnames, including single and compound names, from the Emperor Fu-hsi 伏羲 to the present, and describes the influence of foreign inhabitants on Chinese surnames and the derivation of these names from eighteen different sources. Other subjects include the system of family associations, the "hall for worship of ancestors (tz'u tang 祠堂) where the individual family's genealogical record is preserved, the family name poem which is composed of twenty unique characters in which all characters must be balanced in class and different in tones, the use of generation names in representing twenty generations from the same family, and the hereditary titles originating in the ancient feudal system. For researchers in Asian history, genealogy, and anthropological studies.

26. Kiang, K'ang Hu 江亢虎. On Chinese studies = Chung-kuo hsüeh shu yen chiu 中國學術研究. Shanghai, China: The Commercial Press, Limited, 1934.

This book covers the basics in understanding Chinese culture and its people. It includes chapters on the introduction of Chinese language, the analysis of ancient Chinese texts Four Books (Ssu shu 四書) and Five Canons (Wu ching 五經), the description of Chinese genealogy and family systems, women and education in China, Chinese examination system, poetry, art, printing, foreign trade, and political relations with foreign countries in the early 1990s. For general readers and researchers in Asian studies.

27. Kitano, Harry H. L., Yeung Wai-tsang, Chai Lynn, et. al. "Asian-American interracial marriage." Journal of Marriage and the Family. 46 (February 1984): 179-190.

Chinese surnames were used to measure the frequency of in and out marriages, as was also the surnames of Koreans and Japanese in Los Angeles and Hawaii. In Los Angeles, the Japanese rate of out marriages was the highest, followed by the Chinese. The second position was also taken by the Chinese in Hawaii.

28. Kroger, Rolf O., Ken Cheng, and Isabel Leong. "Are the rules of address universal? a test of Chinese usage." Journal of

Cross-Cultural Psychology. 10.4 (December 1979): 395-414.

Contains a questionnaire survey using Chinese names to formulate the Chinese forms of address as part of the cross cultural research on invariant norm of address.

29. Lau, Shuk-fong, and Vicky Wang. "Chinese personal names and titles: problems in cataloging and retrieval." Cataloging & Classification Quarterly. 13.2 (1991): 45-65.

Introduces the nature of Chinese characters, discusses the complications of cataloging and retrieval of Chinese names and titles, and proposes solutions to improve access to Chinese-language materials. The article analyzes Chinese surnames by distinguishing between the last and the first name, the choice between different names used by the same author, and the use of variant romanization schemes to transliterate the author's name and title. An excellent resource for librarians, publishers, and researchers.

30. Lawson, Edwin D. Personal names and naming: an annotated bibliography. Westport, CT: Greenwood Press, 1987.

Includes over 1,200 annotated entries of forty-eight subject categories ranging from art and psychology to zoology with cultural, ethnic, and geographical variations. Books and articles on the subject of Chinese names are covered in this bibliography. For general and academic audiences.

31. Li, David Leiwei. "The naming of a Chinese American "I": cross-cultural sign/ifications in The woman warrior." Criticism. XXX.4 (September 1988): 497-515.

Discusses the character names in Maxine Hong Kingston's work of fiction. Of the six main female characters in the book, two are referred to by their full names, two are addressed by their first names, and another two are not given proper names. The analysis of the Chinese naming system as it applies to the character names in the book and the connection of these names with the identity, gender, and person in Chinese society are reviewed. For scholars and writers interested in literary and social analyses of Chinese names.

32. Lin, Joseph C. "Chinese names containing a non-Chinese given name." Catalogings & Classification Quarterly. 9.1 (1988): 69-81.

Using actual examples, the author demonstrates the difficulties of identifying Chinese names containing a non-Chinese given name and suggests various entry elements for these names based on his analysis of Anglo-American Cataloging Rules, 1st and 2nd editions, concerning Chinese names.

33. Lin, Shan. <u>Name your baby in Chinese</u>. Union City, CA: Heian International, 1988.

The origin of Chinese surnames, Chinese surnames in Hanyu pinyin, commonly used Chinese given names, and English personal names with Chinese equivalents are discussed in this book. A perfect guide to assist parents in naming their children and to assist westerners in choosing a Chinese name.

34. Lin, Shan. <u>What's in a Chinese name</u>. Singapore: Federal Publications, 1986.

Includes chapters on the origin of Chinese surnames, the surnames list in Hanyu pinyin, commonly used Chinese given names, a name and its relation to the animal sign, and the Chinese equivalents of commonly used English personal names. The book contains over 900 examples of personal names in simplified characters and in Hanyu pinyin and is arranged alphabetically to help Chinese parents make the perfect choice in naming their children and to assist westerners in choosing a Chinese name knowing its meaning.

35. Lin, Yütang. "Certain Chinese names." In <u>The importance of living</u>. New York, NY: John Day Company, 1937, 427-429.

Contains an introduction and a sample list of Chinese literary scholars, including their literary names or tze 字 and fancy names or hao 號 given by the authors themselves or by others. For general use on names of Chinese literary scholars.

36. Lin, Yütang. "On Chinese names." In <u>The pleasures of a nonconformist</u>. New York: World Publishing Company, 1962, p. 225-227.

Contains comments on Chinese name styles and the usage of this practice. For general use.

37. Lip, Evelyn. <u>Choosing auspicious Chinese names</u>. Singapore: Times Books International, 1988.

Guides the reader in choosing an appropriate and auspicious Chinese name through the analysis of yin yang 陰陽 (female and male), wu hsing 五行 (the five elements), the total number of strokes in the full name, the Chinese horoscope, and pa tzu 八字 (the eight characters which refers to a person's year, month, day and time of birth). This volume is the first book written in English on the subject of analyzing Chinese names. For general readers of all levels

as well as scholars interested in researching Chinese names.

38. Mayers, William Frederick. "Index of proper names." In The Chinese reader's manual. Detroit, MI: Gale Research Company, 1968, p. 1-312.

Contains chiefly biographical information of the ancient Chinese scholars, emperors, military officials, and literary authors. Arranged alphabetically, the text collects a total number of 974 Chinese proper names. For general reference.

39. Meskill, Johanna Menzel. A Chinese pioneer family: the Lins of Wu-feng, Taiwan, 1729-1895. Princeton, N.J.: Princeton University Press, 1979.

The book takes the Lin family as the framework for social research on the Taiwanese local history. It describes not only the individuals of the Lin family but also locates them in Taiwan during the centuries of its rapid sinicization, especially from 1683 to 1895. The book is divided into three parts: 1. pioneers on a Chinese frontier; 2. the Lins and the crisis of the Chinese state; and 3. the making of a Taiwanese gentry family. It also contains maps and figures. For general readers as well as scholars of social and genealogical research on Taiwanese local history.

40. Mossman, Jennifer, ed. Pseudonyms and nicknames dictionary. 2 vols. Detroit, Michigan: Gale Research Company, 1987.

Identifies the original names behind the pseudonyms, stage names, nicknames, and other types of assumed names selected by individuals throughout the world. The dictionary contains more than 55,000 original names and 80,000 assumed names of authors, entertainers, athletes, politicians, criminals, military leaders, monarchs, and business executives, among others. Examples of prominent Chinese historical figures such as Confucius are covered. For reference use.

41. Reference aid: handbook for Pinyin romanization of Chinese proper names. Arlington, VA: Joint Publications Research Service, 1978.

This pamphlet discusses the adoption of the Chinese pinyin system by the State Council of People's Republic of China on January 1, 1979 to be used for the romanization of PRC names and places and includes Wade-Giles to Pinyin conversion charts, a list of major PRC political and military leaders' names, Chinese place names, and a PRC map in pinyin. For both general and scholarly use. Recommended for librarians, publishers, and book indexers who handle the transliteration or conversion of Chinese names from Wade-Giles to pinyin or vice versa.

42. Shanghai Evening News. "New findings in surname research." Beijing Review. 30.22 (June 1, 1987): 28-29.

Reports the findings in Chinese surname research by Du Ruofu and Yüan Yida at the Institute of Genetics of the Chinese Academy of Sciences. Based on the census statistical data collected in China and Taiwan, they found 1,066 surnames among the Han 漢 people. Further research will be achieved through the analysis of the blood relationship among the people carrying these names and their rate of migration in different regions. For general readers and scholars interested in researching Chinese surnames.

43. Smith, Arthur H. "Village nomenclature." In Village life in China. Boston, MA: Little, Brown and Company, 1970, p. 16-19.

Describes the attachment of Chinese surnames to the designation of villages, family settlements, or temples. Examples of using surnames in village nomenclature are given. For general use.

44. Smith, Arthur H. "Village boys and men." In Village life in China. Boston, MA: Little, Brown and Company, 1970, p. 179-195.

Describes the status of males in the traditional Chinese village and introduces the names given to Chinese children.

45. Smith, Elsdon C. "Names in other countries: China." In The story of our names. Detroit: Gale Research Company, 1970, p. [124]-129.

    Describes the history of Chinese surnames, the variant forms of names, and the common usage of these names. For general use.

46. Smith, Elsdon C. Personal names: a bibliography. New York, NY: The New York Public Library, 1952.

    This volume contains over 3,400 references on names with complete citations, location of the work, and comments (rated good, fair, or poor) on books, articles, and book chapters. It covers all areas of names and naming from animals and the Bible to nicknames and psychology. Forty-five entries are listed under the subject of Chinese names for works published between 1920 and 1950. The New York Public Library is the major location of the works listed in this bibliography. For reference use.

47. Smith, Frederick Porter. A vocabulary of proper names in Chinese and English of places, persons, tribes, and sects, in China, Japan, Korea, Anna, Siam, Burma, the Straits and adjacent countries. Shanghai: Presbyterian Mission Press, 1870.

    Arranged alphabetically according to Mandarin pronunciation, this bilingual Chinese and English list contains matters of historical, classical, geographical, and commercial interest of proper names of persons, places, dynasties, tribes, and sects. Suitable for general readers, writers, and translators who have an interest in and a relation to Asians. For reference use.

48. "Spotlight on Chinese immigration." On Campus. 14.2 (October 1994): 17.

    Describes Dr. Betty Lee Sung's research project at the New York Regional Archives. It involves the investigation of nearly 600 boxes of INS documents for early Chinese immigrants who came to the United States between 1882 and 1946. These records are entered into a database and can be made available to the general public and to scholars interested in researching Chinese immigration history.

49. Tan, Chek-neng. "Chinese personal names." Library Association

<u>Record</u>. 88 (November 1986): 551.

Includes a brief history of Chinese names and provides the format and practice of Chinese personal names in English. Suggestions are made to improve the standardization of these names in conformity with library cataloging rules. For general readers and library catalogers.

50. <u>Variant transliterations of Chinese surnames</u>. [s.l.: s.n.], 1966.

Lists variant spellings of Chinese surnames as found in official documents by the compiler over the past ten years. It includes variant forms of the name in Wade-Giles transliteration and the possible country of origin as supported in the original source.

51. Watson, Rubie S. "The name and the nameless: gender and person in Chinese society." <u>American Ethnologist</u>. 13 (November 1986): 619-631.

Personal naming marks an important social transition in Chinese society for both men and women. The distinctive feature of Chinese personal names is analyzed using the case study of ethnographic evidence gathered in the village of Ha Tsuen, a single-lineage village located in the northwest corner of Hong Kong New Territories. For academic audiences.

Ma$^3$ 馬, 5, 8, 126

Mai$^4$ 麥, 126

Man$^3$ 滿, 127

Man$^4$ 曼, 127

Man$^4$ 蔓, 9, 127

Mang$^3$ 蟒, 7

Mao$^2$ 毛, 5, 127

Mao$^2$ 茅, 128

Mei$^2$ 梅, 128

Meng$^2$ 蒙, 128

Meng$^4$ 孟, 6, 128

Meng$^4$-sun$^1$ 孟孫, 129

Mi$^2$ 麋, 5, 129

Mi$^3$ 米, 129

Mi$^3$ 芈, 130

Mi$^4$ 密, 130

Mi$^4$-hsü$^1$ 密須, 130

Miao$^2$ 苗, 5, 131

Miao$^4$ 繆, 131

Min$^3$ 閔, 6, 131

Ming$^2$ 明, 131

Mo$^4$ 莫, 5, 9, 132

Mo$^4$ 墨, 132

Mo$^4$ 幕, 9, 133

Mo$^4$-ch'i$^2$ 万俟, 133

Mo$^4$-t'ai$^2$ 墨台, 133

Mou$^2$ 牟, 133

Mu$^4$ 牧, 134

Mu$^4$ 木, 8, 134

Mu$^4$ 沐, 8

Mu$^4$ 穆, 134

Mu$^4$ 慕, 135

Mu$^4$-jung$^2$ 慕容, 135

Na$^4$ 那, 135

Nai$^4$ 能, 136

Nan$^2$ 南, 136

Nan$^2$-kung$^1$ 南宮, 137

Nan$^2$-kuo$^1$ 南郭, 5, 137

Nan$^2$-men$^2$ 南門, 137

Ni$^2$ 倪, 138

Ni$^2$ 郳, 138

Nieh$^4$ 聶, 138

Nieh$^4$ 乜, 139

Nien$^2$ 年, 139

Ning$^2$ 甯, 139

Ning$^2$ 寧, 140

# Stroke Number index

**Five Strokes**

**Six Strokes**

## Seven Strokes

## Eleven Strokes

## Thirteen Strokes

## Fourteen Strokes

318